Slavery, Imperialism, and Freedom

Slavery, Imperialism, and Freedom:

Studies in English Radical Thought

Gordon K. Lewis

Monthly Review Press
New York and London

Library of Congress Cataloging in Publication Data
Lewis, Gordon K
  Slavery, imperialism, and freedom.
  Bibliography: p. 343
  1. Radicalism—Great   Britain—Addresses,   essays,
lectures.   2. Socialism in Great Britain—Addresses,
essays, lectures. 3. Socialism and society. 4. Slavery
—Addresses,   essays,   lectures.   5. Imperialism—Ad-
dresses, essays, lectures. I. Title.
HN400.R3L48   320.5   78-2826
ISBN 0-85345-447-7

Monthly Review Press
62 West 14th Street, New York, N.Y. 10011
47 Red Lion Street, London WC1R 4PF

Manufactured in the United States of America

10 9 8 7 6 5 4 3 2 1

For the twins
Kathryn and Diana

[Contents]

[Preface]

I have brought together in this volume a collection of various essays and articles published over the years in American, Canadian, and Caribbean academic journals. They have been considerably revised in order to constitute an integral and connected study of various aspects of English radical thought since the eighteenth century.

I have attempted to do three things in compiling the collection. In the first place, I have sought to draw attention to certain neglected aspects of the general topic that have been overlooked by the conventional accounts; the chapter on the influence of the Paris Commune of 1871 is a case in point. Second, special emphasis has been placed on the international ramifications of the English radical and socialist tradition, thus offsetting the spirit of parochial insularism so characteristic of English academic history and political science. So, to take examples only, it is impossible to understand the Victorian Christian Socialist movement unless the influence of the pre-Marxist French socialist systems is taken into account, or to understand the Victorian free-thought movement unless some attention is paid to the influence of the German higher criticism in biblical studies. Third—and this is really a corollary to the second point—I have sought to emphasize the importance of the movements of colonialist expansion, imperialism, and slavery, and their collective aftermath, as they have been related to particular chapters in the history of English radicalism. That is why the collection, both in its introductory and final chapters, deals extensively with that aspect.

That last point deserves a little further commentary. It is an astonishing feature, still, of English life that notwithstanding the fact that England has left its mark, ever since the sixteenth century, on the world as a whole, the English as a people remain obdurately insular. The universities have reflected that temper. I myself can remember, as a young undergraduate at the University of Wales, that everything I learned at that time about the race-color issue was not in the college classroom but the result of extracurricular visits to the Tiger Bay "colored quarters" of Cardiff. Similarly, as an undergraduate at Oxford, I learned nothing about American government and politics that I did not already know. Nor were the American universities much better; and as a graduate student later at Harvard I learned nothing about the American black world that I had not already learned through personal experience of the west-side section of Los Angeles and the Chicago South Side. Not to mention the fact, of course, that any systematic teaching in Marxism and other socialist systems was conspicious by its absence in both Oxford and Harvard. And, finally, it has been my prolonged residence in the Caribbean since the 1950s that has enabled me to understand more fully the real nature of North Atlantic colonialism and imperialism from the viewpoint of the colonial victim. It is in this sense that this book may be seen as a bringing together of my early interest in European radical social and political thought and my later interest in Caribbean studies. The history of European expansionism has in reality been the history of European ethnocide against native peoples, as witnessed to by a long record of European anticolonialist thought that goes back to Las Casas. But one has to live in Africa or India or the Caribbean (as did Las Casas himself) to comprehend in any full sense the meaning of that grim truth.

A number of personal acknowledgments are in order. Some of these essays were conceived during my Harvard period, and it gives me pleasure to record the graduate friendships of those days: Bernard Crick, Dante Germino, Melvin Richter, Harry Eckstein, Severo Colberg, and Antonio Gonzalez.

Other essays, again, were written in their original form when I taught, earlier, at the University of California at Los Angeles; and I recall with equal pleasure my friendship there with Richard Schier and Sidney Wise, both of whom helped to introduce me to the pagan subculture of southern California, revealed so richly in the books of one of my favorite Anglo-American authors, Raymond Chandler. My general interest in socialist thought, of course, predates that American period of residence, going back to the time when as a young Welsh undergraduate I lectured to Workers Educational Association audiences of South Wales miners; and it was an interest originally stimulated by two of my grammar-school sixth form masters in the West Ebbw valley, Harry Lewis and Walter Tidswell, who introduced me to the Left Book Club of that time. It is the genius of the grammar-school system, both English and West Indian, that it produces remarkable teachers who leave a permanent imprint on the students who come under their influence. Finally, I take the opportunity to recall the memory of the late Leo Huberman who, as Monthly Review Press editor, was willing to publish my books at a time when the corporate business publishing firms and the prestigious university presses alike were too timid to accept radical manuscripts. Apart from being an uncompromising Marxist, he was a gentle and humane person, the very epitome of what a socialist should be. He was the kind of man whose death makes the rest of us feel that, in some way, we have lost a part of ourselves.

—Gordon K. Lewis

August 1, 1977
Trujillo Alto
Puerto Rico

[Chapter 1]
The Eighteenth-Century Background: The Debate on Empire and Slavery

It is a curious aspect of Sir Leslie Stephen's monumental *English Thought in the Eighteenth Century* that, apart from a passing reference to Burke on India and the free-trade controversy with reference to the American colonies, it quite omits any discussion of the contemporary debate on the issues of slavery and empire. It is an equally curious aspect of another definitive book by another English scholar—J. W. Allen's *History of Political Thought in the Sixteenth Century* of 1928—that, while including chapters on England, France, and Italy, it omits any reference to Spain and consequently any discussion on what was perhaps the most seminal debate of the century: the meaning of the New World discoveries for European thought, as it was thrashed out by the Spanish jurists and theologians of the time. Those omissions are in part understandable. Stephen's work, published in 1876, appeared at a time when the slavery issue had become a forgotten controversy and the new wave of later Victorian imperialism was yet to come. The Indian Mutiny of 1857 and the Jamaican Morant Bay "rebellion" of 1865 had been the last occasions in which English public opinion had been aroused on matters of race and empire, while Disraeli's Crystal Palace speech of 1872 had to await another generation before it bore fruit in the jingoist popular imperialism of the 1890s. In much the same way, Allen's work appeared at a time when even educated Englishmen were more concerned with what empire meant in India or Africa than what it meant in the American hemisphere. So, the study of po-

[13]

litical thought in the English universities meant—as it means even today—the study of More, Erasmus, Bodin, Calvin, Luther, and Machiavelli, rather than the study of those Spanish thinkers and writers, from Las Casas and Sepulveda to Solorzano and Avendano, who attempted to determine what the conquest of the Indies meant for the old, traditional problems of obedience and authority; for, indeed, it is not too much to say that the momentous debate between Las Casas and Sepulveda as to whether the New World aboriginal peoples were justified in rebellion against the conquistadores is causally and ideologically related, by a continuity of historical experience, to the modern-day debate on the relationship between the European societies and the Third World.

But there is even more to it than this. The strain of *insularismo*, of an inward-turned "little Englandism," has always been present in the English outlook, of all social classes. Imperial expansion and insular prejudice went hand in hand. Whether it is the young aristocrat doing the grand tour in the eighteenth century, or the Victorian middle class visiting the European spas, or the new working-class tourists of the post-1945 period discovering the European popular resorts for the first time, there are present the same linguistic poverty, the same condescending astonishment at foreign habits, the same ability to travel abroad without suffering the indignity of an enlarged imagination. Politics and thought have exhibited a similar pattern. The old British ruling class chose not to listen to Burke and so lost the North American colonies, while a century later they chose not to accept Joseph Chamberlain's grand scheme of a world-wide federal imperialism. The rising middle class, in its turn, became a byword for bourgeois philistinism, and Matthew Arnold's lament on that score was echoed by every European visitor from Taine to Dibelius. The working classes, finally, have been more nationalist than internationalist in their ideology, as the history of the British Labour party only too clearly shows. Even academic England has not escaped this parochial temper, so much so that the study of the United States itself only became academically respectable in the twentieth century, while up to the present moment Latin American studies, not to speak, say, of Caribbean studies, continue to suffer a Cinderella status in the universities. The decline of Britain as an imperial power after World War II has gone hand in hand with a decline of concern for causes of freedom elsewhere; so, the prolonged Vietnam war failed to generate the militant sympathy of the British trade-union and progressive movement that, earlier, the Spanish Civil War had generated, while the presence, after the 1950s, of a new, colored immigrant minority in the national life has been met, not with the interracial fraternalism that it had every right to expect, but with an ugly racism infecting all social levels. There has been, as it were, a chronic failure on the part of the English people to develop a cosmic view of things. Public opinion, both popular and educated, has remained dismally unaware of the fact that what is called "Western civilization" has always been only one culture form among a global host of non-European civilizations, and that many of those other civilizations have been possessed of a historical antiquity predating the Western forms by centuries. So, to take examples of exceptions that prove the general rule from the Victorian period alone, it is not generally known, even now, that when Carlyle came to write his scurrilous antiblack *Discourse on the Nigger Question* in 1849 he was answered by the younger Mill in a reply which anticipated in a remarkable fashion all of the key questions of the later "race relations" discussion—the problem of environmental impact on cultural development, the genetic issue, the relationship of slavery to social behavior, the nature of "race" itself, and the rest—or that Macaulay, for all of his self-congratulatory Victorian chauvinism, eloquently defended the practice of racially mixed marriages and the social capacities of Negroes in a now forgotten article in the *Edinburgh Review*.

That general English temper, without doubt, has been pervasive and long lasting. At every turn, certainly since, say, the period of the Napoleonic Wars, allegiance to any international cause has been sacrificed to considerations of

[15]

"practicality" or "national interests" or "reasons of state." Yet at the same time it would be erroneous not to admit that, also at every turn, there have been elements of the better aspects of the national temper, whether it be in the record of radicalism or Christianity or socialism, that have valiantly resisted the temptation to put patriotism, in whatever guise it has come, before the common interests of peoples the world over. In typical English fashion, they have come from all groups and classes, and they have certainly not been identical in any ideological sense. Burke opposed the North American war but supported the war against revolutionary France. The Society of Friends led the campaign against the slave trade but on principles more conservative than radical. The Christian Socialists of 1848 fought for the ideal of an international working-class fraternalism, but they were far from being socialists in the Marxist sense. There is hardly anything in common between John Bright, who opposed the Crimean War on grounds of free-trade liberalism, and George Lansbury, who opposed the war of 1914 because he identified his socialism with pacifism. Some of the campaigns for freedom have been single-handed, like Lord Shaftesbury's struggle for factory legislation, or Florence Nightingale's heroic struggle for decent nursing, or Bradlaugh's rationalist defense of free thought. Others have been more organized efforts, most noticeably the long history of the sort of republican populism that stretched from Wilkes, through Cobbett, on to the Chartist upheaval, fighting against the old regime of church, state, and aristocracy. They suffered all of the ostracism which the English national Establishment has developed into a fine art: as one American wit has put it, the Americans defeat their enemies, the English disqualify them. But to the degree that they succeeded they made England a better place to live in; and to the degree that they influenced the world outside, the world itself a better place to live in.

The prolonged debate that accompanied the abolitionist

campaign against the slave trade and, after that, against West Indian slavery itself spans the period between the 1760s and the 1830s that saw the disappearance of the first British Empire and the beginnings of the second British Empire. First and foremost, of course, it was a debate on the phenomenon of slavery, seen as at once an anti-Christian and an antinatural phenomenon. But it was also, to a lesser degree, a debate on the physical presence of the black person in England itself, thus anticipating the debate in the England of two hundred years later on the presence of the twentieth-century Caribbean-Asiatic immigrant. It started, to all intents and purposes, as we know from Clarkson's definitive account, in the unlikely Oxford of the 1780s, characterized, as it was, by political latitudinarianism and intellectual torpor, as we know, again, from Gibbon's account of the university at that time in his *Autobiography*; just as unlikely a place, indeed, as the later Newmanite Oxford of the 1840s out of which emerged the Christian Socialist movement. In both cases, of course, it was an Oxford tempered, as it were, by London. Yet the fact demonstrates how, in characteristically English fashion, radical and progressive movements have originated in what seem to be the most unpropitious of places.

It is true—again by matter of introduction—that the English abolitionist movement was only a part of a general European critical assault upon slavery; the record has been conveniently summarized in Marcel Merle's collection of texts, *L'anticolonialisme européen de Las Casas à Marx*. The elements that went into that body of thought were many and varied, ranging from the religious and the sentimental criticisms of slavery to the economic and the utilitarian criticisms. The French critics, as Professor Seeber's study shows, tended to emphasize the economic-utilitarian critical approach, yet sharing with the English and American critics the sentimental approach, as can be seen in the rise of the genre of *littérature négrophile*. The English critics, differently, tended to emphasize the basic religious criticism, of, that is, the paradoxical maintenance of Negro slavery by nations ostensibly

[17]

Christian, thus following, albeit in Protestant terms, the great example of the *obra lascasiana* of the sixteenth century. If, then, in France, the tone of the antislavery literature, following Montesquieu, was one of sceptical rationalism, in England it was the tone of Christian liberty, emphasizing the simple truth that the Christian ethic, with its insistence on the equality of all men, made slavery inexcusable. Voltaire's early popularization of the virtues of the Pennsylvania Quakers, in his *Lettres Philosophiques* of 1734, marked the beginning of the French admiration for the Quaker view of slavery as well as, of course, for all things English, including the English Constitution. If, then, the English debate did not give birth to a grand, comprehensive work such as Las Casas' *Historia de las Indias* or Raynal's *Histoire des Deux Indes* it managed, even so, by way of book, pamphlet, sermon, and, not least, personal example to enlist a national public opinion in support of the cause of the slave which in the long run probably did more to help him than the writings of the philosophes.

The beginnings of the movement go back to the late seventeenth century. It is certainly present with the visit of George Fox to Barbados and Jamaica in 1671, during which, through the medium of meeting-house sermons and conversations in private houses, that great stalwart of the cause admonished owners of slaves to treat them as human beings, to inculcate in them respectable habits of marriage, and to set them free after a considerable term of service, if rendered faithfully. Richard Baxter's *Christian Directory*, published two years later, admitted the legitimacy of slavery if based on voluntary choice, poverty, or imprisonment by act of war, but clearly declared inadmissible any form of slavery arising out of the slave trade, which the author openly denounced as piracy. That note of protest thereafter disappeared for some fifty years or more, overwhelmed by an age of complacency following the Revolution of 1688. It reemerged slowly in the second quarter of the eighteenth century with John Wesley in the English field, and John Woolman in the American. Wesley's first American visit of 1737 suggested to him the

[18]

strategy of conducting religious lessons on the plantations of friendly disposed planters, thus becoming the genesis of the missionary endeavor in the American plantations. Woolman's *Journal*, in turn, makes it clear that in his investigations he managed to talk with slaves who spoke some English, as well as making enquiries with ships' captains engaged in the trade, thus anticipating the firsthand investigatory research that became the hallmark of the more organized abolitionist movement a generation or so later. The Quaker contribution, thus early on, is significant because it was as much concerned with the corruptive impact of slave ownership upon the slave owner as it was with the intrinsic anti-Christian character of the institution itself; and a chapter in Woolman's account concerned itself with the morally debilitating influence of the trade upon the young mariner-apprentice boys who learned their art in the African slavers.

This early religious contribution to the prolonged discussion on the place of slavery in Western civilization can, of course, be easily exaggerated. It has been conventional wisdom to speak of the Quaker opposition to slavery. Yet it was, in the beginnings, the opposition only of a minority within the movement; Quaker slaveholders were much in evidence in Barbados at the time of Fox's visit; and it took a full century after that visit before the English Quaker congregation finally made traffic in the trade a bar to membership. The Moravians, in turn, held slaves without much disturbance to conscience in the early Danish Virgin Islands, and the head of the movement, Count Zinzendorf, himself sought to justify the institution. The Moravian mission in Dutch Surinam, indeed, went on to become in the next two centuries one of the largest business enterprises in the tropical colony, being only outmatched, in the twentieth century, by the North American bauxite companies. The British Society for the Propagation of the Gospel likewise had its own slaves, albeit under trust, in the West Indian colonies, which helps to explain why the Church of England, to the very end, was officially hostile to the emancipatory movement. It was, indeed, the deist convention of the French Revolution, and not any of the Christian nations, that first abolished slavery in 1794, almost a full century before the Spanish nation abolished it in Cuba in 1886.

Yet when all this is fully acknowledged it remains true that it was the resident missionary like William Knibb and James Phillippo in Jamaica, and John Smith, the Demerera martyr, in British Guiana, who fought valiantly to put Christianity at the service of the slave masses rather than the slave masses at the service of Christianity. They belonged—to use Troeltsch's famous distinction—to the sects rather than to the churches. They helped, not least of all, to make Christianity, in its best sense, a part of popular West Indian religious life, so that right on into the present period of the twentieth century the vocabulary of politics in societies like Barbados, Antigua, and Jamaica has remained Christian while in the metropolitan center itself politics has lost its biblical-fundamentalist basis. The old-fashioned biblical imagery of the Pentecostalist cults and the new Marxist-Leninist imagery of the national political parties, this is to say, still walk hand in hand in the present-day Caribbean, whereas in Britain they have long parted company. Or it is another way of emphasizing this difference to say that whereas in the advanced capitalist societies of Europe Christianity has long lost its early revolutionary meaning, in the Caribbean, both Protestant and Catholic, that message still lives, founded on the insistence of the original Christian revelation that the message means, above everything else, salvation for the poor and perdition for the rich. The early Christian sectarian missionaries in the New World set that message within the framework of their assault upon the monstrous institution of slavery; and although at times they thought in ameliorative rather than in abolitionist terms, they left behind them a legacy that still lives in Third World societies like the Caribbean.

This constituted, essentially, the early beginnings of the rise of the religious-humanitarian assault upon at once the slave trade and slavery itself that culminated, in 1807, with the abolition of the trade, and in 1834, with the abolition of slavery. Yet it is worth recalling that the black presence in England predates those movements by at least two centuries or more, a fact only obscured by an orthodox Whig history that has seen national development in terms of the growth of the insular "island race." The Elizabethan royal proclamation of 1601, with its complaining note about the high numbers of "Negroes and blackamoors" in the kingdom, and its stern recommendation of deportation, indicates that by that time a noticeable black community had settled itself in Shakespeare's London, immediately occasioned by the royal encouragement of the triangular trade with West Africa and the new American lands and the return of absentee planters with their retinues of black retainers. Throughout the seventeenth century this influx accelerated: black servants in the service of royal favorites at court, enslaved domestics, servants to ships' captains, even free, independent sailors, as well as exotic specimens brought from the New World for gentlemen's households, not to mention the escaped slaves. Most of them were the human flotsam and jetsam of English Caribbean expansion, living a precarious life in a society which even for the native English poor meant a terrible struggle for survival, gravitating to the unspeakable warrens and alleyways of riverside London, where they came to constitute, perhaps, the first of the black ghettoes of European society. There were, of course, the privileged sectors; the coachmen, footmen, and pages of ladies of fashion, dressed up as black dandies, replete with Oriental trousers, turban, and scimitar, to illustrate the status of their employers; as a phenomenon, they survived well into the eighteenth century, as many of Hogarth's whimsical prints colorfully illustrate. There were even Negroes of patrician African birth who had prominent places in the courts of the Stuarts, and the sharp eye of diarists like Pepys and Evelyn noted them with uninhibited curiosity. Dryden is said to have been beaten by Rochester's Negro servant; and that particular story, indeed, exemplifies how throughout the century the scheming, trusted black servant played the role of confidant in the life of social and sexual intrigue of his master or mistress, since the type appears as regularly in the Restoration melodramas as it did, earlier on, in the ferocious Anglo-Italianate plays of Marlowe and Beaumont and Fletcher.

The stage was thus set for the eighteenth century, when the black person, both as physical presence and literary stageperson, came to be a conspicuous type, thus making that century perhaps the most cosmopolitan of all in English history. If the assessment of contemporaries is correct—that by 1772, the date of the historic judgment of Lord Mansfield in the Somerset case, some fifteen thousand free Negroes lived in London, to be reinforced after 1783 by the transported ex-slaves from the American colonies who had been promised freedom for fighting on the losing British side— the morbid fascination of the English public with that person becomes easily explicable. In part, it was the Negro servant, the deserted slave, the black laborer who undertook the nauseous tasks of keeping Georgian London clean; the street entertainers, the last of whom survived into the era of early Victorian London, as is shown in the vivid description of the Negro street serenaders interviewed by Mayhew as part of his remarkable description of the London underworld in the 1850s; as well as the variety of black beggars, street vendors, and crossing sweepers described in Pierce Egan's *Life in London* of 1821. Those of them who were servants rapidly became a serious social problem, for, once they deserted as runaway refugees, they joined the motley crowd of the London underworld; and the remarks of Sir John Fielding in 1748 indicate clearly enough that they frequently organized secret societies aimed at self-protection and at persuading other Negroes to abscond: this, perhaps, might be the nearest that the black slave in England came to organizing, as did the American abolitionists in the following century, an underground railroad to spirit Negroes away from slavery to freedom. Fielding's comments also indicate that at least one English law officer of the time attributed the harsh lot of the Negro to the manner in which they were imported and used by their masters with scant consideration of social conse-

[22]

quences. There was always, of course, the danger of recapture of the renegade slave, and the black African Equiano described the horror of that procedure in his *Autobiography* of 1789. It is heartening to note, however, that, as Fielding admitted, the English mob frequently sided with the slave as against the law officers and the slave master; and it is worth adding in that respect that the mob riots of the period, as with the Gordon Riots of 1780, were religious rather than racist in character.

All of these constituted, as it were, a black lumpenproletariat in eighteenth-century England. But even as early as that there was taking place a class-stratification process. The fortunate few who formed an elite group were already present, as noted, in the latter part of the seventeenth century. They became even more conspicuous in the new affluence of the following century. George I brought with him two black favorites from his petty German court, one of them immortalized in some verses of Pope. There were black trumpeters and drummers in some of the Army regiments, dressed up in peacock-colored Eastern-style uniforms, and invariably the delight of the London mob. Above them in the social scale were blacks who had become middle class in their life style; and it is possible that among them were London counterparts of those middle-class blacks in Toronto who were reported by William Lyon McKenzie in the early part of the nineteenth century as being rich enough even to keep white servants. The interracial fraternization that took place was widespread, and we know from the correspondence of Mrs. Thrale that mixed marriages were frequent and socially acceptable. There was, finally, the well-known group of black-brown intellectuals welcomed in the London salons of the period. There was Job Ben Solomon, one of the leading Arabic translators of his time, collaborator with Sir Hans Sloane, the early pioneer of Caribbean natural studies, and a protégé of the Duke of Montagu. There was Ignatius Sancho, well known for his correspondence with Sterne. The same Duke of Montagu financed the education of the Jamaican Francis Williams, who ended his curious career by setting up a school in Spanish Town, Jamaica, and in that very act challenging the basic assumptions of a slave society hostile in principle to literary and educational pursuits, whether pursued by black teacher or white missionary. In similar fashion, the Sierra Leone Company helped finance the education of blacks like Anthony Domingo and the celebrated Prince Naimbanna. Not least of all these was the ex-slave Ottobah Cuguano who worked with the English miniaturist Cosway and composed, in his *Thoughts and Sentiments on the Evil and Wicked Traffic of the Slavery and Commerce of the Human Species* (1787), a full and comprehensive account of the system from firsthand experience.

Equally conspicuous, of course, but in a quite different way, were the returning colonial gentry, the East India "nabobs" and the West Indian planters, coming "home" after years of exploiting their colonial estates to buy a country seat, marry into the county aristocracy, and found a family. The picaresque novel of the century is full of the type. As good a description as any is that penned by Smollett in *Humphrey Clinker*, satirizing the figures of the arriviste West Indian planter and overseer, as well as the East Indian clerks and factors, all of them devoid of breeding or taste, loaded with wealth they did not know how to use, currying favor with the highborn, and utterly intoxicated with pride, vanity, and presumption. Even in the midst of Beau Nash's Bath they stood out as an arrogant and brutalized set of men. There is hardly a book or play of the period that did not regard the type with open disdain. The young German pastor Charles Moritz, who wrote an engaging account of his travels through England in 1782, described seeing Foote's play *Nabob* in a rowdy London playhouse, with the main character being a foppish young man who had inherited an immense East Indian fortune, contemptuously denying any knowledge of his early school friends, and surrounded by a fawning company of would-be philosophers seeking his favor. The general attitude was summed up in the remark attributed to the fawning servant in a play, *The West Indian*, that achieved a momentary popularity in the 1770s: "He's very rich, and that's sufficient. They say he has rum and sugar enough belonging to him, to make all the water in the Thames into punch." It is only with the historic decline of the privileged status of the West Indian sugar economy after the period of the Napoleonic Wars that the type disappears from the literary scene, so that after, say, Thackeray, there is little heard of him.

But for the period of the golden age of sugar he left his mark on English society. He became, to begin with, in the shape of the "West India" interest, a potent force in the politics of the period. Fashionably, he bought a parliamentary seat, cultivated friends at court—the legendary Beckford of Jamaica became a personal friend of Chatham—and through the agency of the West India Committee, the guardian of West Indian propertied interests in London, defended the protected status of West Indian sugar against the growing free-trade political economy. He and his kind became, indeed, perhaps the first of organized parliamentary lobbies, so much so that the agent for Massachusetts reported in 1764 that there were fifty or sixty West Indian members of Parliament who could turn the balance any side they pleased. They were aided, in turn, by the hard core of some thirty members of the pro-Hastings party, the so-called Bengal Squad. It is the final testimony to the continuing power of the lobby that as late as 1834, when the metropolitan commercial capitalism had finally decided to jettison the West Indian sugar economy, it could still persuade the Westminster Parliament to grant it a parting compensatory gift of some £20 million, none of which went to the freed slave. Economically, all this is to say, the repatriated planters and merchants brought back with them a repatriated wealth that went into the bloodstream of commercial capitalism at home. "Of West Indian riches," a writer in the *Edinburgh Review* in 1804 noted caustically, "it is more especially true, that they are apt to make themselves wings, and fly away."

Culturally, it was a different story, for if the West Indians left any mark on English society it was hardly of a cultural kind. The art of combining slavery with the arts is a Greco-

Roman achievement that the West Indian planter class never learned. The testimony of every observer who visited the West Indies during this period—Père Labat, Lady Nugent, Père du Tertre, Humboldt, "Monk" Lewis—agrees in painting the portrait of a master-slave society in which the life of the plantation "great houses" centered upon hard drinking, dancing, insipid conversation, and sexual excess. Every traveler agreed in the observation that drunkenness, when it existed, was the vice of the white group, not of the "free coloreds" or blacks. The master who attempted to be humane to his slaves, like "Monk" Lewis in his Jamaican estates in the years following Waterloo, rapidly discovered that he would be vilified by his fellow planters as dangerously Jacobinical and that his society would be shunned. Nor was this accidental; for the essence of slave society, in the words of a Creole apologist concerned, on the whole, to defend the institution, was one based on fear, and fear supersedes right. The social organization of the plantation economy, in effect, involved a quasi-military rule to be ready at any time for the ever present danger of slave rebellion; and it is only necessary to read a document like Lady Nugent's Jane Austen-like *Journal* written in her period as governor's wife during the Anglo-French war to be made aware of how much the fear of servile revolt was a brooding omnipresence in the daily life of the planter class, requiring the almost continuous presence of a friendly naval squadron or of reliable "home" regiments to allay its terrible presence. It was thus no accident that sailors like Nelson and Rodney became the darlings of the Caribbean plantocracy; and the friendships formed in the planter clubs of the islands repeated themselves once the rich exiles returned home.

In every sense of the word, then, the sociocultural impact of the newly domiciled returning planter was reactionary to a degree, even by the easygoing standards of Augustan Toryism. He brought with him, one, his slave-based wealth and, two, an obsessive racist hatred for the West Indian black person. The wealth became the basis of a new conspicuous consumption fabulous even by contemporary standards, attested to most famously in the vulgar architecture of the Fonthill Splendens country seat that Beckford built for himself out of his Jamaican fortune. There were, of course, as in any ruling class, notable exceptions. The Codringtons left behind them the lasting monument of Codrington College in Barbados; the Tortolan Quaker Thomas Humphreys helped found the Institute for Colored Youth in Philadelphia; and "Monk" Lewis' *Journal* revealed an almost anthropological curiosity about Negro song, dance, and folklore. But these were exceptions. The moral and mental level of most was that of Thackeray's Joseph Sedley; and the absentee West India planter became as much the target for domestic lampooning as did the retired Indian army "old hand" in the later history of the empire.

It is wise, of course, not to overstate the case. Slavery and its massive profits, after all, were a national economy unthinkingly accepted by most of the leading minds of the century. The merchant princes of Bristol and Liverpool were as much its conscious agents and beneficiaries as their Creole counterparts. Postlethwayt's dictum in his propagandist book, that the British Empire was "a magnificent structure of American commerce and naval power on an African foundation," was the gospel of the day; and the assault upon mercantilism was based less on moral outrage against slavery than on a reasoned utilitarian economic liberalism. The abolitionist leaders themselves, Wilberforce, for example, accepted to the letter the unstated assumptions of Puritan economics. Nor is the thesis tenable that the planter wealth was responsible for the ostentatious luxury of the age, which was so indignantly castigated in books like Brown's *Estimate of the Manners and Principles of the Times* (1757), for it would be difficult to argue that all of the targets of that indictment —the decay of learning in the universities, the self-seeking corruption of politics, the shameful state of the church, the national love of affluence, and the rest—could be seen as the end result, so to speak, of a grand colonial Creole plot to

[27]

subvert the spirit of the nation. The eighteenth century, after all, was passing through a profound transformation, away from a semifeudal society to the new society of commercial capitalism, with the new business spirit replacing the old spirit of noblesse oblige. The slavery system was an integral part of that transformation, and accepted as such by most opinion of the day. Later Caribbean scholarship has argued, as in Eric Williams' persuasive *Capitalism and Slavery*, that slavery was only ultimately abolished in the Caribbean because new economic forces finally made it an unprofitable enterprise, and that the old planter class itself facilitated the abolition by its inability to respond innovatively to those forces, thus converting that class, as it were, into the villain of the piece. That is undoubtedly true. But it is equally true that, reactionary as they were as a class, the West Indians only reflected the general spirit of the age when they argued that slavery represented vast and important property interests that ought not to be lightly interfered with. The abolitionist leaders themselves shared that sense of the sanctity of property, which helps to explain why their campaign took some long sixty years or more to succeed.

Or, to put all this in a slightly different way, all elements of the contemporary thought accepted commercial capitalism as the mainstay of the national greatness and prosperity. The free-trade economists, following Adam Smith, were against slavery not because it was immoral but because its protected status violated their doctrines. The abolitionist leaders, in their turn, accepted the basic principles of commercial enterprise but claimed that the slave trade and, later, slavery, were violations of the moral ideas on which all commerce should be based. There was only one minor strand of economic thought—that of the few English writers who were influenced by the French school of Physiocrats—that failed to fit into those categories. For the leading principle of the Physiocrat writers once accepted—that agriculture and not commerce constituted the sole form of productive labor in the economy—it followed that commerce, and its artificial obsession with the balance of trade, should be replaced by a reinvigorated agriculture governed by a centralized planning regime. It followed, too, that the slave trade being almost the purest form of commerce, its continuation, as well as its economically evil effects, should be attacked. A handful of English writers did in fact launch such an attack from that viewpoint, summed up as well as any in William Spence's widely read *Britain Independent of Commerce* (1808). The so-called gains of commerce, Spence argues, are really only the profits made by the importer or exporter. What little real gain, benefiting the nation, that takes place is offset by the nonproductive expenditure on luxury goods that has helped encourage the moral decline of manners (an echo of the argument of "Estimate" Brown). West Indian rum and American tobacco only serve to debilitate the population. The expenditures of the East India Company outrun its profits; at the same time, by evidence of the West Indian planters themselves, the profitability of the West Indian trade has declined catastrophically over the last twenty years. All this, Spence concludes, demolishes the argument of the importance of colonial possessions; while, with reference to the Caribbean holdings, he adds the telling argument that the possible success of the St. Domingue black revolt can only lead to similar slave revolts in all of the islands.

The Physiocratic argument, inevitably, could gain no hold in England. For whereas the French bourgeoisie were faced with an *ancien régime* that stifled trade and commerce by a network of repressive regulations, the English bourgeoisie were already well on the way to demolishing the apparatus of tariffs and navigation laws based on commercial jealousy. Yet the interesting aspect of the Spence argument is that, as with Adam Smith, it attacked slavery not because it was immoral or un-Christian but because it was uneconomic, although they arrived at that conclusion from different premises. There is the familiar attack upon the follies of the planters. There is the equally familiar criticism of the waste and luxury generated by the importation of unnecessary colonial products. But there is singularly absent any appreciation, first, of the fact that colonial wealth was based on the surplus value emanating from slave labor or, secondly, of the sub-human conditions under which the slave worked. Once again, it was left to the Christian-humanitarian movement to bring the ethical judgment to the forefront of the debate.

In retrospect, it is easy to see that the debate on this entire issue was one of the seminal debates of the period. An examination of its course makes it clear that it was conducted on two levels: first, the particular level at which the legitimacy of the trade and the character of the slave person were debated; secondly, the general level at which slavery simply became a phenomenon that illustrated the growing culture contact, after the discovery of the Americas, of Europe with the peoples of the continent, as well as those of Africa and Asia. The two debates, of course, were by no means separate, since both of them were rooted in the single historical fact of the European voyages that became the genesis of the slave trade, beginning, perhaps, with the African Negroes brought back to Portugal as early as Gonçalvo's Guinea expedition of 1443. Yet they generated different challenges to the European mind and spirit. The slave trade and slavery challenged the European doctrines of liberty, first in their Christian form and, after that, in their secular form. The growing awareness of the new worlds challenged the provinciality of the European mentality, its arrogant Europocentrism so much stimulated, after 1600, by the growth of nationalism, and which equated its own outlook with universal and eternal principles. The Dutch culture historian Henri Baudet has described, in his brilliant essay, "Paradise on Earth: Some Thoughts on European Images of Non European Man" (1965), how all this reflected itself in a marked dualism in the European attitude to the newly discovered outside world:

Two relations, separate but indivisible, are always apparent in the European consciousness. One is in the realm of political life in its broadest sense, in the atmosphere . . . of concrete relations with concrete non-European countries, peoples, and worlds. This is the relationship that freely employs po- litical, military, socioeconomic, and sometimes missionary terminology. It is this relationship that has also, in general, dominated the pens of the historians who have recorded the history of our Western resistance and of our expansion. The other relationship has reigned in the minds of men. Its domain is that of the imagination, of all sorts of images of non-West- ern people and worlds which have flourished in our culture— images derived not from observation, experience, and percept- ible reality but from a psychological urge. That urge creates its own realities which are totally different from the political real- ities of the first category. But they are in no way subordinate in either strength or clarity since they have always possessed that absolute reality value so characteristic of the rule of the myth.

Both of those elements—of the reality that flowed from the physical confrontation with the transported African slave, and of the myth that his exotic background excited in the European reader—are powerfully present in the eighteenth- century discussion, with both of them being further encour- aged by the universalist, antihistorical temper that so deeply marked the mental climate of the century. The discussion of the reality expresses itself, generally, in the sphere of social and political theory, contributed by both the proslavery and abolitionist camps; that of the myth expresses itself, more characteristically, in the sphere of the novel, the theatrical play, the edifying verse.

As far as the first debate is concerned—that of the moral and legal legitimacy of slavery—the early apologists accepted the conventional classical view, based on the ancient world, that slavery was the result of war. Hobbes added to that his own view that since civil society was founded on the habit of obedience fed by fear, any state of human dependency, in- cluding slavery, was preferable to anarchy. Locke added to that the qualification that only lawful war justified slave status, since slavery was a "vile and miserable" condition alien to "the generous temper and courage of our nation"; but he failed to ask the embarrassing question as to whether the English slave-raiding wars on the West African coast were lawful or unlawful; and none of the lesser English writers who followed his argument asked themselves whether a slave revolt could be justified as that last act of rebellion of an oppressed people against a tyrannical government with which Locke himself had justified the Revolution of 1688. The heart of Lockeian theory, in any case, was that of consent: at the back of any government there existed, as he saw it, an active citizen body for whom obedience is conditional upon that government's just behavior. The difficulty of applying that doctrine, based on natural law, to any slave society was, quite simply, that the slave person, legally, was no more than an item of capital equipment, and therefore—in a phrase used by Edmund Burke a century later, in 1789, in a speech to the House of Commons on the trade—dead as to all voluntary agency. Only Dr. Johnson, of the leading minds of the century, broke through that dilemma by openly condoning slave revolt, dramatized in the toast that he proposed, on a visit to Oxford, to "the next insurrection of the Negroes in the West Indies," an episode which Bryan Edwards reported in tones of scandalized horror. There was, this is to say, a fatal flaw in the Lockeian liberal ideology. It revealed itself—to anticipate by a century—in the intellectual debate of the American War of Independence. For Locke and his ideas were the main apologetic of the colonists, and Tom Paine's influence appears to have been the main force in the founding of the first American Anti-Slavery Society. Yet the slave-holding colonies successfully excluded slavery from the final agreement on the new federal constitution in the Philadelphia constitutional debates; and there is no discussion, suggestively, of the slavery issue in the *Federalist Papers*.

Yet in many ways Locke was ahead of his time. His thoroughgoing rationalism went ill with an England that was still profoundly religiotheological in its assumptions. The clerical argument, therefore, that slavery was consistent with, indeed justified by, religion and Christianity was accepted well into the Age of Reason. A divine will had imposed slavery upon the world for purposes inscrutable to man.

The aboriginal American Indian and, after him, the transported African slave laborer, had been enslaved in order that they might be converted to Christianity. The theme had been introduced in Columbus' first enthusiastic letter to his royal Spanish patrons, and it became the official apologetic of the Spanish regalist theologians who saw the new "Atlantic era" as the ordained opportunity to rescue the American-African savagedom from its pagan heathenism into the fold of Christ. This theme was to become later transmuted into the myth of the pseudo-Africa from whose hell the captured slave had been providentially rescued in order to be received into the Christian faith. But that was after 1750 or so; and for the first half of the century the English religious world was far more preoccupied with a rearguard action against the steady advance of the deistic movement. There were, even so, probably hundreds of obscure Anglican parsons who preached the Christian message for the slave, collected in tomes of sermons long since forgotten; and the agitated conversation in Goldsmith's *The Vicar of Wakefield* is one example which indicates that for the ordinary clerical mind the slave was in the same category as the English village laborer who, both of them, must submit to a servitude ordained by the necessary inequality of social life and structure. The slave was thus not yet seen as a special case. Attitudes were still ambivalent, an ambivalence nicely revealed in Boswell's *Journal*, in which, on one of the few occasions in which he dared to disagree with Johnson, he defended slavery as a marvelously humane institution yet at the same time, as a Scotsman, could proudly acclaim the decision of the Scottish Court of Session to decide affirmatively in the cause of the Negro Joseph Knight.

It is tempting to make out of all this the thesis that the real enemy of slave freedom was the organized Christianity of the period. Yet that is too simplistic an interpretation. Slavery, in fact, like other later issues in English politics—votes for women, for instance, or imperialism itself—was an issue that made nonsense of traditional party or ideological divisions. Logical inconsistency only too often marked the attitude of the leading minds of the age. Dr. Johnson, admittedly, was consistent in his stubborn, commonsensical Toryism: as he asked in a famous question, Why should the American colonists demand freedom if they were prepared to maintain slavery? The internal inconsistency of Lockeian liberalism, on the other hand, has already been noted, and it repeated itself throughout the century. Hume, in a celebrated essay, saw something of the diversity of national characters in environmentalist terms. Yet in the same essay he penned a footnote in which he insisted, without proof, upon the natural inferiority of the Negro race, possessing nothing, according to him, of manufactures, arts, or sciences. In any case, he added, not one of the Negro slaves dispersed throughout Europe had indicated any symptoms of ingenuity. Thomas Jefferson, again, was almost certainly deistical in his religious beliefs and liberal in his political theory. Yet that did not prevent him from writing, in his *Notes on Virginia*, one of the most offensive of antiblack passages, regarding the Negro in America as inferior not only to the white man but also to the Amerindian; the Negro, he concluded, was incapable of any thought above the level of plain narration, and with misery enough among them there was no poetry. In the American case, furthermore, that general prejudice was carried into the nineteenth century, infecting all movements of social thought, including the social gospel movement in the churches.

Coming back to England, it was the same story. Gibbon, the superb anti-Christian skeptic, could excoriate early Christianity for its acceptance of slavery but was at the same time hostile to the antislavery movement of his own day: "But in this rage against slavery," he wrote peevishly to Lord Sheffield, "in the numerous petitions against the slave trade, was there no leaven of new democratical principles? no wild ideas of the rights and natural equality of men?" Adam Smith, likewise, demolished the case for protectionist mercantilism in his monumental treatise, thus striking a fatal blow at the privileged position of the West Indian sugar planters within that system. But when he came to deal with slave labor it was mainly to insist upon its productive inefficiency as compared with free labor rather than to emphasize its essential inhumanity. On the other hand, it was Burke who managed at one and the same time to compose his massive reactionary diatribe against the French Revolution and to put together in his speeches of the Warren Hastings trial the most formidable chapter in the history of English anti-imperialistic literature as it concerned the sordid record of the East India Company. When, this is to say, in sum, a deist historian like Gibbon—whose famous chapter on Christianity remained for a century a mainstay of rationalist argument—could be on the proslavery side, and a mystic conservative like Burke—whose political theory really amounted to a doctrine of obedience to things as they are—could be on the antislavery side, it seems clear that both of the legends that have arisen—the conservative argument that Christianity freed the slave and the rationalist argument that Christianity did nothing to free him—manage to state a half-truth only.

This is not to be seen, as many European critics have seen it, as typical English hypocrisy. The explanation is twofold. In the first place, educated England in the eighteenth century was concerned, primarily, with the fight against a neo-feudalistic state, a corrupt church, and a grossly inefficient national economy, seeking to replace it all with the specifics of utilitarian theory. Secondly, that fight was largely a middle-class movement, in the service of the new, emergent bourgeois class of merchant and trader and industrialist. Its main article of faith was the sanctity of property. To attack that principle—whether it meant the emancipation of the West Indian slave or of the English laboring poor—was to attack the very foundations of society itself; and it was logical, from that viewpoint, that abolitionists as socially conservative as Wilberforce himself should have been regarded by the Liverpool and Bristol slave merchants whom he sought to convert to his views as a dangerous social leveler. That was the lesson of the pregnant sentence of the Scottish writer Adam Ferguson, that "he who has forgotten that men were originally equal easily degenerates into a slave." That, of course, was the sentence of a mild Scottish professor of philosophy, a sort of pinchbeck Montesquieu, and by no means reflected an egalitarian strain in English social theory that had, in fact, died out with the Levellers and Diggers of the Cromwellian period. But the analogy was never far from the consciousness of the new bourgeoisie; and with the advent of the French Revolution and the panic that it unleashed in the English ruling class it became a pathological conviction that slavery emancipation abroad meant certain social revolution at home. The equation, of course, was a gross libel on the motives, essentially Christian and conservative, of the abolitionist campaigners; and it was left to Paine—who is credited with having first used the phrase "the religion of humanity"—and the radicals and pre-Marxian socialists who came after him—to establish definitively the necessary unity of the struggle of both oppressed white and oppressed black.

Much of all this, of course, was the prelude to the real drama. For it is only after 1770, or thereabouts, that the final and decisive confrontation between the proslavery and the antislavery forces takes place. Clarkson's great *History* still remains, even today, the authoritative account of the antitrade movement. It has been fashionable to deride the religious-humanitarian element of the movement; Macaulay's sneering contempt for the saints of Exeter Hall was not unlike, later, Lytton Strachey's amused satire on the Victorians. But no one can read the record of the men who led the battle for abolition after 1783, both in Parliament and in the country, without a profound respect for the sense of stricken Christian conscience that converted what had been, hitherto, a disparate conglomeration of fine poetic-literary indignation into a highly efficient movement of at once parliamentary maneuver and national propagandist agitation. All of the four men who, in the 1770s and 1780s, put the movement together—Ramsay, Clarkson, Granville Sharp, Wilberforce, none of them, incidentally, being Quakers—represent that type of English-man who, from time to time, emerges to arouse the English people to a noble cause. All of them, in different ways, experienced that road-to-Damascus revelatory experience which has been so common to the English religious experience. Granville Sharp became converted to the cause on being confronted with the escaped slave Jonathan Strong, which persuaded him to educate himself in the law as a means of upsetting the negative Law Officers' ruling of 1729, with the result that he managed, almost singlehandedly, to argue the later Somerset case against the powerful opposition of Blackstonian legal conservatism; his reward, in Clarkson's phrase, was that after that victory the poor African ceased to be hunted in English streets as a beast of prey. James Ramsay brought to the cause a different ingredient, that of the Anglican minister who had spent nineteen years himself as a resident minister in St. Kitts and who provided, in his volume on the *Treatment and Conversion of African Slaves in the British Sugar Colonies*, a firsthand account of what slavery actually meant; and a report all the more authoritative because it frankly recognized that the conventional recipe of Christianizing the slave was absurdly inappropriate in a situation where slavery made the Christian virtues, on the part of either planter or slave, comically anomalous.

Wilberforce's was a different story. By birth and education a privileged person, he passed through, like his friend the younger Pitt, the usual experience of his type: casual education at Cambridge, the enjoyment of the social life and gambling of the London clubs, an easy parliamentary apprenticeship which might easily have graduated him into the prime ministership itself. All this was changed almost overnight with his encounter with his old schoolmaster Isaac Milner and with Captain Newton, erstwhile captain of a slave ship and himself now a repentant remorsefully aware of the enormity of his calling; the first encounter converted Wilberforce to piety, the second to a recognition of his life work. Clarkson's conversion, perhaps, was the most memorable of all. As a Cambridge undergraduate he entered for the 1785 Prize Essay in the spirit of an innocent undergraduate contesting for an idle academic honor; and he himself described vividly how, on reading up on his source materials, especially the American Quaker Anthony Benezet's *Historical Account of Guinea*, there was slowly borne upon him that a window had been opened up on a new and horrifying world which, to begin with, he had seen only as a literary subject. There followed, as with Wilberforce, an agonised *crise de conscience* as he found himself torn between the considerations of worldly advancement, this time in the Church of England, and the strident call of duty. The die was cast; and once the decision was made, his life became, in his own phrase, not so much a trial for academic reputation, as for the production of a work which might be useful to injured Africa.

The subsequent struggle was a war on two fronts. There was, first, the campaign to persuade the pre-1832 unreformed Parliament to legislate for abolition. That it took some twenty-five years to obtain the 1807 antitrade act and some sixty years to obtain the antislavery act is a measure in itself of the lethargy and indifference that met the reformers. Their parliamentary spokesman, of course, was Wilberforce; and it was fortunate that he had as powerful allies the younger Pitt and, after his death, Fox himself, both of whom imperiled their careers to espouse a thoroughly unpopular cause. They had to bear the weight of a parliamentary membership on the whole persuaded by the proslavery propagandists; it was a rare member, indeed, who, like Sir William Dolben, member for Oxford University, was willing to board a slave ship and see for himself. There was, of course, the great pillar of strength that was Burke. The genius and talent of the House, beyond doubt, was on the liberal side; to read Wilberforce's speech of 1789 introducing the report of the Privy Council committee, or Pitt's speech of 1792, with its impassioned defense of Africa, or Brougham's speech of 1810 against the contraband slave trade (once Parliament had accepted the abolition of the trade in 1807), or Grenville's speech of 1814 against the foreign slave trade, is indeed to read the House of Commons at its best and noblest. By comparison, the contributions of their opponents, many of them members from the English slave ports, starkly revealed the intellectual poverty of the antiabolitionist phalanx; and it was a typical eighteenth-century touch that one of the arguments of the opponents was to cast aspersions on the credibility of the witnesses presented by the abolitionist side on the ground that many of them were nothing more than simple mariners while the planters had presented highborn witnesses including Admirals of the Fleet. In this way, in Clarkson's caustic comment, the House of Commons was called upon to adopt the preposterous maxim of attaching falsehood to poverty, or of weighing truth by the standard of rank and riches.

Wilberforce's contribution, altogether, as the commander-in-chief of the parliamentary campaign, was inestimable. It seems irrelevant, then, to argue, as some historians of the movement have argued, that Wilberforce delayed the moment of success because, by temperament moderate and compromising, he relied too much on aristocratic patronage and parliamentary diplomacy. Even one of his ablest lieutenants, Stephen, made the point in his observation that his leader's policy was "to load the shelves of a cabinet minister with laboured memorials, to haunt him with conferences for years, and at last to be turned round by the whisper that a governor stands well with great men, and must not have his toes trod upon." But this, after all, as a reading of the Croker or the Greville *Diaries* shows, was the aristocratic politics of Eldonian Toryism, in which cabinets were made and unmade on the basis, not of principle, but of personal ambition, family influence, the mean ambitions and self-seeking of public men who belonged, with singular exceptions, to an exclusive ring of aristocratic houses. To have attempted a mass agitational movement—in the manner of a Cobbett or a Tom Paine, when the English ruling class had already lost the American colonies, were confronted with the fearful challenge of republican France and, after 1791 or so, the terrible picture of the Haitian black war of national liberation—would have been to invite almost certain disaster for the cause.

[39]

There was, it is true, the other constituency of the rising middle class. It is the supreme merit of Clarkson that he perceived, acutely, that here lay the second front of the movement and that he became its indefatigable organizer. Much of the movement appealed to the sentimental humanitarianism of that class. The drawing room became an abolitionist hotbed. Ladies wore the famous seal depicting the slave donated to the Society by Josiah Wedgwood, often inlaid in gold in snuffboxes or bracelets. Cowper's famous poem was reprinted in book form as a "Subject for Conversation at the Tea Table"; and abolitionist lecturers toured the provinces. The boycott came into favor as a new device; and the cartoonist Gillray did a print of the royal family in an antisugar posture. The local association, the petition of citizens to Parliament, the presentation of the abolitionist play that might be the rage of the moment—all became grist to the movement. England became divided into a series of corresponding societies, many of which provided vital information to the national headquarters. The West India lobby thus became duplicated in the abolitionist lobby.

But Clarkson's real genius lay elsewhere. He was a born detective. A deeply religious man, he was yet instinctively a Benthamite utilitarian in his passion for facts. He knew that victory depended on factual demolition of the planter case. In the phrase used in the *Anti-Slavery Recollections* of James Stephen's son, the market place of a West Indian colony was a sealed book to the British public. For Clarkson, it was urgent to break down that ignorance, an ignorance shared by the vast majority of parliamentary members. We watch him as he rides up and down England, visiting mainly the slave ports of London, Liverpool, and Bristol; persuading ships' captains, many of them the real monsters of the trade, to allow him to examine their ships' logs; interviewing ordinary seamen, first to tell their horrendous stories of the middle passage, secondly to make notarized statements of their experiences, and thirdly to persuade them to appear as material witnesses before the parliamentary investigating committees, often at the price of being victimized by their employers;

visiting the sordid public houses of the slave ports in order to note at firsthand the methods used by slaver captains to impress their unwilling crews; obtaining copies of articles of agreement which documented the fraud employed in that particular aspect of the trade; collecting specimens of the torture instruments used to terrify, sometimes murder, refractory slaves on board passage; assiduously researching in customs houses to make notes of the muster-rolls of slave vessels; and amidst all of this managing at the same time to help in the organization of local committees, as well as cultivating the acquaintanceship of local newspaper editors who might help propagandize the cause. It was a truly herculean task, at times involving the very real possibility of its author being murdered by the dock gangs in the employ of the powerful vested interests of the proslavery mercantile community. It is literally astonishing that by the end of his researches Clarkson had managed to obtain the names of no less than twenty thousand seamen involved in the trade, knowing the life history of each one of them. It owes as much to him as to any other one single individual that the Report of the Privy Council of the Lords of 1788 remains to this day one of the seminal official documents in the history of British public administration; for much of the factual evidence collected in that report came directly from his own researches and the exhaustive memoranda he shaped out of literally hundreds of conversations and cross-examinations.

In doing all this, he exposed in grim detail the case of the proslavery interests. Every ruling class in history has manufactured its own particular "noble lie" with which to rationalize its privilege. But there can be few instances, in the history of the English ruling class, in which mendacity and outright misrepresentation were utilized so irresponsibly as in the case of the catalogue of excuses put together in the cause of slavery by the Anglo-Caribbean segment of that class in the eighteenth and early nineteenth centuries. The general tone was set by the bland assertion of an apologist in the *Gentleman's Magazine* of 1788 that "self-preservation is the primary law of nations and in the present state of things the rigid maxims of morality may sometimes be sacrificed to the claims of national policy." That permit to lie led to all of the myths and half-truths about both the slave trade and slavery itself. There was the argument that the trade was the nursery of British seamanship; Clarkson showed, by careful statistical analysis of the rate of crew fatalities, that it was rather its grave. There was the argument that the transported African prisoner found the middle passage to be little less than an Elysian retreat; the publication of the famous print of the slave ship *Brookes* by the London Committee, with its plan illustrating the gross overcrowding of its black cargo, immediately laid the argument to rest. A further question begging theme of the slave lobby tract literature was the much-overworked argument that slavery was simply an indigenous phenomenon of the intertribal rivalries of the West African barbaric kingdoms, for which the English trader, who was simply a middleman, could not be held culpable; the thesis formed a large part of, for example, Robert Norris' *Memoirs of the Reign of Bossa Ahadee, King of Dahomey* (1789). The argument had in fact been anticipated by Wadstrom's description of his own Guinea voyage published in the same year, *Observations on the Slave Trade . . . ,* and fully refuted by the factual description in that book of how the British and French traders had in fact enlarged a local trade into an international commerce. It was left to Clarkson, once again, to put the final nail in the coffin; and there are few pages in his memoir more enthralling than his account of how, in the best manner of a Poirot or Maigret, he boarded fifty-seven men-of-war in the English ports in the search, finally successful, for the seaman who could provide him with a firsthand eyewitness account of the trader marauding expeditions up-river in the Calabar region.

The legend, indeed, of the trade as a purely domestic West African phenomenon was only made possible because of the vast ignorance of the continent during the period. The age of African exploration proper had yet to come, even though the books of both Wadstrom and Benezet had already been published, drawing as they did on African evidence, as well as

Alexander Falconbridge's *Account of the Slave Trade on the Coast of Africa*, published in the same year (1788) as that of Wadstrom, and containing a graphic firsthand account of the slaving coastal forts. Indeed, some fifty years earlier, a similar account had been published in the form of Captain William Snelgrave's *New Account of Some Parts of Guinea, and the Slave Trade* (1734), by an author who had been deeply involved in the trade but was conscious of its atrocities, without being, so early on, a conscious abolitionist. It is not too much to say that these few books almost inaugurated a new historiography that perceived slavery to be part of a common Atlantic history. But they were pioneer works, as far as the African point of the triangular system was involved. For the eighteenth and early nineteenth centuries it was the West Indies that held the limelight. For every traveler, then, who made the Guinea trip there were literally dozens of visitors to the Caribbean colonies, most of whom, entertained by the fabulous hospitality of the planter class, added by way of pamphlet or book or magazine article to the vast proslavery literature.

That West Indian contribution to the entire debate, indeed, merits a special notice. The West Indian historian Elsa Goveia has documented the continuing expression and defense of the proslavery creed on the part of the West Indian historians of the century in her exhaustive analysis, *A Study of the Historiography of the British West Indies to the End of the Nineteenth Century* (1956). Some of them were particular studies, like Atwood's *History of Dominica*, Poyer's *History of Barbados*, Dallas' account of the Maroon rebellion in Jamaica, and Sir William Young's account of the campaign against the Black Carib remnant of St. Vincent. Others were more general histories, especially the trio of the Jamaican historians, Charles Leslie, Bryan Edwards, and Edward Long. To these must be added the more general English histories that deal only peripherally with the West Indies: the once-famous histories of Robertson and Oldmixon, and the curious

Account of the European Settlements in America, popularly supposed to have been written in part by Edmund Burke in a moment of financial embarrassment. Some of them were composed by English authors who did not know the islands by personal experience, others by resident English planters and officials Creolized in the islands. Their major importance is that their accounts, most markedly those of the settler-historians, provided the educated English reading public with a general picture of the colonial society that was at once proplanter and anti-Negro, with all the stereotyped caricature of the slave person that naturally accompanied it. For they wrote for an English audience rather than a West Indian society that was, like most slave economies, fundamentally anti-intellectual. They provided vital ammunition to the anti-abolitionist and antiemancipation movements; so much so that the most racist of them all, Long's *History of Jamaica* (1774), became, in Wilberforce's phrase, the veritable bible of the West Indian planter class, as the extensive quotations cited from it in the prolonged British parliamentary debates between 1789 and 1834 make abundantly clear. The planter-historians thus produced, as best as they could, the moral and intellectual apologetic for the planter-society.

The difference of tone between the metropolitan-based writers and the Creole historians is marked, and it demonstrates how residence within the slave society itself tended to modify, at times completely erode, the humanitarian instinct as its terrible pressures made themselves felt. Thus, Oldmixon, Robertson, and Burke all accepted the natural character of the colonial sugar empire, although all of them also criticized sharply a mercantilist policy detrimental to the planter interests. They all accepted the prime role of the sugar economy for the national interests of trade and commerce, although the Burke volume emphasized, in addition, its importance for military defense in the Anglo-French imperialist rivalry of the period. It is in their treatment of the white master-black slave relationship, however, that they reveal a comparative detachment that marks them off from the planter-historians proper. Oldmixon defended the planters against severity of treatment to their charges, but he clearly considered them to be exaggerated rather than baseless; furthermore, he refused to accept, as had earlier writers like Du Têrtre, rigid theories concerning racial differences. Robertson, in turn, saw that slavery could not rest on natural-law theories, but justified it, at most, following Montesquieu, as made necessary by climate rather than by race. The Burke volume, finally, as Goveia remarks, was one of the few works written on the topic that managed to combine advocacy of the commercial interests of the plantocracy with advocacy of the human claims of the plantation slave, thus escaping the bitterness of the humanitarian writers against the planter group, while retaining something of their insistence upon the idea of a common humanity. This is the literature, altogether, of amelioration rather than of emancipation. It had none of the savage, Christian indignation that made Wesley's early denunciation, *Thoughts upon Slavery* of 1744, so memorable in the tract literature. It believed still in the readiness of the planter to accept ameliorative measures from the imperial parliament. Its inner logical contradiction lay in the fact that, one, it hopelessly exaggerated the goodwill of the planter and, two, failed to demonstrate how a recalcitrant Creole ruling group could be persuaded to accept amelioration. It was, in sum, a literature of appeasement. Like appeasement everywhere, it failed because it assumed, mistakenly, a common universe of values between the opposing camps. It attacked, not the system itself, but what it saw as the abuses of the system. It had none of the frank recognition of the more radical wing of the abolitionist groups that only a root and branch destruction of the system could finally terminate the issue.

The planter-historians, by contrast, recognized instinctively that there was no halfway house between slavery and abolition. They were, most of them, educated, even sometimes sensitive men. Yet they lived in a slave society which constituted, quite simply, an island of white persons surrounded by an ocean of blacks, both slaves and "free coloreds." Despite the fact, then, that, as residents, they were perceptive observers of much of the sociocultural realities of the bond-slavery among which they lived—it is still refreshing to read Long's sympathetic account of the social tragedy of the light-skinned illegitimate sons and daughters of Creole white fathers who, educated at young ladies' finishing schools in Chelsea or, as young men, at Eton itself, returned to the island society only to find themselves in a no man's land, and, accepted neither by the white parental society nor by the black plantation-barracks society; or Edwards' critical account of how the special character of West Indian plantation property, being a species of lottery, generated in the planter an attitude to his enterprise quite distinct from that of proprietors of landed estates in England—they were apologists, in the last resort, of the slave-based West Indian social order. Some of them, certainly, acknowledged theoretically the criminality of slavery. Leslie wrote that "slavery is the ruin of society," and Edwards could admit that "so degrading is the nature of slavery, that fortitude of mind is lost as free agency is restricted." But such remarks were nothing more, as it were, than literary acknowledgments to the spirit of the age, and the textual material of the histories reproduced all of the various myths invented by the planter mind to justify the institution: that since slaves were not open to persuasion, compulsion, in Edwards' phrase, becomes humanity and charity; that slavery was actually beneficial since it rescued the slave from a barbaric Africa, by contrast with which the West Indies were a veritable paradise; that if England abandoned the trade it would only mean that the French and the Spanish would take it over on even more profitable terms; and that the admittedly brutalizing character of slavery was due, not to the system itself, but to the stubborn intransigence of the slave himself. That last argument summed up what was an attitude of the Caribbean planter class in general, expressed typically in the observation of a Puerto Rican planter in the following century on the eve of the Puerto Rican emancipation act of 1873 that "the only thing that makes the institution of slavery hateful is the slave himself." It was a line of rationalizing argument tantamount, so to speak, to making the seismograph responsible for the earthquake. And, finally, there was the argument that the colonial slave was in any case treated far better by his master than the laboring poor of England itself were treated by landlord and capitalist at home—a shrewd blow at the capitalist-Puritan ethic of the English Quaker business and commercial class who, by that time, had forgotten the original Quaker teachings on the evil of the acquisition of material wealth.

There are certain leading points about all this that merit further attention. There was, in the first place, the effort to present the colonial master class as a benevolent group, doing the best they could under difficult circumstances. The Simon Legree type of master, as it were, so prominent in the abolitionist literature, was presented as the exception rather than the rule. In any case, it was argued, the English planters were better than the Spanish or the Dutch variant; thus Edwards, regarded as the "moderate" spokesman of the planters, could find no language sufficiently violent to denounce the Spanish extermination of the Indian aboriginal groups in Hispaniola and Puerto Rico and conveniently forget the same indignant note when he came to write of his fellow countrymen in Jamaica. Long, certainly, was scandalized by the miscegenetic habits of the Jamaican planter, but managed at the same time to draw a general portrait of him as a kindly master whose authority over his charges was somewhat like that of an ancient patriarch. This particular apologetic reached its height in Henry Bolingbroke's *Voyage to the Demerary, 1799-1806*, which imagined the rise of a colonial gentleman-class developing the life-style of the English territorial baronage overseas; and that it had its effect in England itself is obvious enough from the huge success that popular plays like Thomas Bellamy's *The Benevolent Planters* enjoyed for a season or more. Yet it is difficult to imagine that it made any real headway against the odium against the Creole that was engendered by the vulgar affluence of the Beckford style and that so offended staid British opinion. The analogy with the North American situation a century later immediately suggests itself, for the effort of the plantation aristocracy of the Old South in the ante-bellum period before the Civil War to paint a similar romantic portrait of Southern chivalry succeeded no more in reconciling the Northern abolitionist forces to the "peculiar institution" of slavery.

The second point to make relates to the problem of the British-West Indian politico-constitutional relationship during this period. All of the planter-historians accepted the Whiggite historiography of the day, based on the Lockeian theories of the limitations of the sovereign power, but now applied to the imperial relationship. They defended the rights of the colonials and of the colonial assemblies as the guardians of popular rights against at once the claims of the Westminster Parliament and the abusive behavior, as they saw it, of a local overweening alien executive in the form of colonial governors and their executive councils. They saw themselves as communities of white English settlers entitled to all of the civic and constitutional rights of Englishmen overseas. Long, writing before the American Revolution, denied that the Crown could claim absolute powers over the colonists; Edwards, writing after that event, denied that Parliament could claim such powers; and they both based their argument on the theory of generic federal consent within the imperial relationship.

Why, then, did not the West Indian colonies follow the American colonies in a war of independence against an imperialism unwilling to accept that interpretation of the relationship? The answer, quite simply, is that the argument for colonial independence was fatally compromised by the coexistence of legal enslavement within the society. The fear of slave rebellion made absolutely necessary the protective arm of the British naval-military force. The instinct of Creole nationalism gave way to the instinct of property. It is true that minor recalcitrant groups, like the Caribs of St. Vincent and the Jamaican Maroons, could be deported; and the respective histories of Young and Dallas anticipated the policy of forced resettlement which, after the Civil War, was to become the American method of destroying the tribal cultures of the Plains Indians. But such a policy was impossible to apply to the black mass of the West Indian plantation economy as a whole, constituting as it did the labor army of that economy. The threat of slave rebellion, then, had to be met by the control mechanisms of terror, repression, and punishment outlined in the gruesome detail of the slave code legislation of the period. The outcome of all this was the erosion of any American spirit of resistance to the imperial metropolis. "The North Americans," wrote an English visitor to the region in 1825, "indeed were too much for us, the West Indians may be crushed by a wave of Mr. Canning's hand." There thus grew up the notorious reputation of the West Indies as the most loyalist of all of the imperial colonies; and that loyalist mentality infected all of the various leadership groups of West Indian society up to the last period of post-1945 dismantlement of the empire: the plantocracy itself in the golden age of sugar capitalism, the "free colored" group after emancipation, the nationalist political movements between World Wars I and II of the present century.

The third point to make is that the planter-historians, along with the English hack copyists who produced a vast pamphleteering literature based on those accounts, managed to put together a whole catalogue of stereotyped caricatures of the Negro person as stupid, incredibly lazy, cowardly, mendacious, grossly sexualistic, and possessed of an animalistic nature. Edwards could declare himself no friend to slavery, but almost in the very same breath declared cowardice and artful dissimulation to be the chief vices of the slave; while he could dismiss the musicological folklore of the plantation life as nothing more than songs "fraught with obscene ribaldry, and accompanied with dances in the highest degree licentious and wanton." Long, far more racist, perceived the Negro as completely bestial, evoking physical disgust on account of his phenotypical characteristics. Taking a hint, perhaps, from the ingenious speculations of that earlier intellectual curiosity Lord Monboddo, he saw the black person as forming a separate human species akin to the orangutan, both of them forming, in his view, man in a lower state

[49]

of nature, leading him to the oft-quoted observation that an orang-utan husband would be no dishonor to a Hottentot female; an observation, in its moral offensiveness, only equal to his further observation that successful procreation of children between mulatto male and female was biologically impossible. To read passages such as these is to enter, indeed, into the mindless labyrinth of the white racist psyche; and the fact that, as in Long's case, they were promulgated under the guise of a pre-Darwinite theory of the fixity of species did not in any way disguise the racial fear and hatred which were their real psychological foundation. It is true that this sort of Creole literature was far more benign when it came to discuss the rising mulatto middle class. But the motive there, too, was suspect; for it saw that group as a more culturally Anglicized segment that could play the role of socially conservative buffer between white master and black slave. The argument was, in fact, a typical expression of the imperialist policy of playing off one set of colonial interests against another in order to make imperialist exploitation less troublesome. It only remains to be said, in fairness to that line of argument, that it has proved to be prophetically correct in the subsequent social history of the West Indies; for what Long aptly termed the "pride of amended blood" has made the Creole brown bourgeoisie the most reactionary of all the segments of the West Indian plural society, right into the modern postindependence period.

The fourth and final point to emphasize about all this is that the general portrait it painted of the black person was, anthropologically speaking, hopelessly simplistic. It showed him as he had become shaped by the grotesque perversions of the slavery condition, so that the distinction between nature and social convention that forms so much a part of the eighteenth-century philosophical debate was arbitrarily forgotten. Edwards himself saw something of the dilemma when he wrote that "it is no easy matter to discriminate those circumstances which are the result of proximate causes, from those which are the effects of national customs and early habits in savage life," but he failed to recognize the radical

[50]

implications of the distinction. It was left to the English critics to formulate the conclusion. Both Clarkson and James Beattie, the latter in his *Essay on the Nature and Immutability of Truth*, recognized clearly that the real answer to Hume's thesis of the innate inferiority of the Negro was to invoke the environmentalist theory. It was the total depressing effect of slavery, Clarkson argued, that produced the characteristics of plantation behavior, for it was hardly to be expected that intellectual genius should flower in a situation in which there was nothing to awaken abilities or excite expectations. To suppose such genius to emerge, Beattie continued the argument, would be just as rational as to suppose any private European person was a member of an inferior species simply because he had not raised himself to the condition of royalty. The importance of this line of attack was inestimable, since it challenged the theory of immutable typologies of racial character that has always been an integral component of racist thinking. It challenged, equally, the other component of the racist thesis that there is a law, as it were, of civilization which condemns separate races to static roles within the framework of history. The answer lay in the alternative theory of the historical evolution of peoples so much at the heart of European liberalism; and it received its most noble expression in the impassioned oration of Pitt at the end of his Commons speech in the debate of April 1792, in which he conjured up the vision of a new and rejuvenated Africa which, released from the cancerous excrescence of the trade, would benefit from science and philosophy to build up, ultimately, its own unique contribution to the family of nations.

There had to be challenged, finally, the racist assumption that there existed collective group-personalities based on a superiority-inferiority scale, making it necessary to deny the possibility of individual exceptions. That explains why the abolitionist camp made so much of the educated Negro; and why, in response, Long felt it necessary to write a separate chapter, full of amused contempt, on the figure of Francis Williams, the Jamaican native who—as already noted—was put through a course of English education by the Duke of

Montagu in order to prove the intellectual capacities of a colored person. The best that Long could bring himself to say was that the Latinate compositions of Williams were no better than what might have been expected from a middling scholar at the seminaries of Eton or Westminster, the worst to quote Hume's comment that a black student, thus educated, could become nothing more than a parrot who speaks a few words plainly. Long could even manage, unfairly, to laugh at Williams because of his habit of composing laudatory odes to successive Jamaican governors, despite the fact that such fulsome dedicatory prefaces to the aristocratic patron was the common practice of the eighteenth-century world of letters. The black person, clearly enough, who succeeds, socially or intellectually, in the success game according to the norms established by the dominant white society, cannot be tolerated because he exposes the central principle of racism, which is to stigmatize a whole racial group in order to justify and facilitate its exploitation.

This, altogether, constituted the corpus of prejudice, at times racist, at times more moderately cultural, that the abolitionist movement had to confront and answer. The detail of the abolitionist struggle has already been noted. It is worth noting, however, as a footnote, the theoretical elements involved in that movement. They were, essentially, two: one—that of an outraged Christian conscience; and, two—that of a doctrine of imperial trusteeship which received its most magisterial expression in the speeches of Edmund Burke in the famous Warren Hastings trial and the indictment of English rule in India. The religious element must be stressed. It appealed at once to Christian conscience and Christian theology, the theological component receiving a typical expression in Granville Sharp's curious tract, *Law of Retribution*, which argued, using the Old Testament texts, that the plagues of Egypt and the captivity of the Jews had been the punishment meted out by the divine providence for the offense of slave-owning in the ancient world. That line of orthodox theological argument could not commend itself to either the freethinking deist or radicals like Wilkes and Cobbett. But the point to make is that neither of those movements, deism or radicalism, contributed much to the cause of the slave, except in very minor and secondary terms. To be a freethinker, as in the cases for example of Hume or Gibbon or Jefferson, was in no way to be a racial egalitarian; while the radical movement throughout this period, as the authoritative volumes of Professor Maccoby show, was mainly concerned with the domestic struggle of popular liberties against the monarchy, the church, the territorial aristocracy, and the old corrupt parliamentary system. In the case of radicalism, indeed, Cobbett, in his splendid letter to Wilberforce, properly condemned the abolitionist leader for his indifference to the English poor yet spoiled his argument by going on to assert that Wilberforce's charges against the West India planters were completely false and misrepresentative of the true facts.

The two elements of the movement—the Christian ethic and trusteeship—were, of course, intermixed, for the one flowed from the other. The religious argument possessed, of course, its limitations. It underestimated the powerful economic interests involved, for despite Smith's argument on the inefficiency of slave labor, the West Indian sugar economy continued to yield vast profits to the end, both to the more successful planter and the metropolitan creditors who financed him; and the various schemes propounded by the abolitionist movement to replace the slave trade with a substitute commerce based on African arts and crafts were economically unsound. Its leaders were only too frequently overconcerned to assuage the planter interest and, in their eagerness to deprecate opposition, could even manage, by a sort of intuitive self-deception, to persuade themselves that slavery and the slave trade were two separate evils and that it was impossible to attempt to overthrow both at the same time. Their general attitude to the slave person was as sociologically naive as that of the plantocracy itself; for it saw him and his type as children-people who could only be redeemed, first, by freedom, and then by evangelical Christianization. They knew nothing of Caribbean culture history, of the fact that, since the very beginnings of the transatlantic trade, the uprooted West African slave populations had come to constitute a vast black underclass of the plantation district that stretched from the southern United States to Brazil, generating a new Creole Afro-Caribbean subterranean civilization, expressed in folklore, music, and religious cults, as completely unknown to the English abolitionist as it was to the Creole planter.

Their vision, then, of a new West Indies was that of the missionary mentality. They were as horrified as any West Indian planter by the idea that the slave might emancipate himself through the mechanism of the slave revolt; and there was not wanting, indeed, the type, like Lord Holland who, as himself an absentee West Indian plantation proprietor, supported abolition on the ground, hopelessly mistaken, that the end of the trade would mean the end of island black rebellions. Clarkson's curious correspondence with the Haitian Creole Emperor Henri Christophe revealed the same narrow English view of Christianity as the final recipe for the colonial tragedy. The view was summed up in the *History of the West Indies* published in 1811 by one of the first of the English cleric-historians on the region, Thomas Coke. He parted company with the abolitionists, it is true, on slavery, for he perpetuated the orthodox view that all human conditions, however evil, are imposed by a divine will inscrutable to man; a religious quietism that left the slave with the cold comfort of the assurance that he could "praise God in the furnace of affliction." But both of the religious outlooks, humanitarian and quietist, agreed in the claim that the moral and social regeneration of the West Indian person lay in the acculturating force of European Protestant Christianity; and how deep and lasting was the impact of that claim upon the society can be gauged from the fact, to take a single instance, that when, later on, the West Indian-born Edward Wilmot Blyden came to publish his essay of 1887 on "Christianity, Islam, and the Negro Race," that remarkable anticipation of the theories of Negritude and black pan-Africanism envisaged the retention of the Christian creed, albeit fully Africanized, in its prophetic vision of the black future.

Yet when all has been said about the limitations of the Christian movement against slavery it remains true that of all the various elements of eighteenth-century England it was the religious element that played the most important role in the abolitionist campaign. Before that, the typical attitude toward slavery was either the orthodox religious view that it was divinely preordained or the orthodox secular attitude that it was, however unfortunately, simply a necessary part of the social order of things. It is worth noting, in that latter respect, that whenever a reference in the earlier literature of the period was made to slavery it was usually invoked as a stick with which to beat one's political opponents in the scurrilous political struggles between different political factions. Thus, to take an example, one of the earliest references in the literature is to be found, at the very beginning of the century, in the anonymous satire on *Reformation of Manners* of 1702, written in the manner of Dryden. The author is clearly concerned to vilify the record of the Restoration monarchy, with all of its vices and corruptions. He castigates the court favorites who have been granted lucrative monopolies, after the style of the African Company, in the trade:

> Others seek out to Afric's torrid zone,
> And search the burning shores of Serralone . . .
> The harmless natives basely they trepan
> And barter baubles for the souls of men.
> The wretches they to Christian climes bring o'er
> To serve worse Heathens than they did before.
> The cruelties they suffer there are such
> Amboyna's nothing, they've outdone the Dutch.

This is typical English eighteenth-century factional verse. Its real targets are the author's political enemies: the old Tory of the Stuart cause, the court favorites, the commercial monopolists, not to mention the hated Dutch commercial enemy. Slavery, and the slave, are simply used as symbolic elements with which to dramatize the argument. It is the chief merit of the Christian assault later on that it brought the slave to the very forefront of the issue, concerned with him as a fellow human being, as a fellow Christian caught in the tragic web of life. Nothing can really cancel out that contribution.

It was left to the great figure of Burke to combine the Christian and secular arguments into the grand theory of imperial trusteeship. For Burke, as has been well pointed out, was the true founder of the third British Empire. His leading principle was that of imperial responsibility, and he applied it impartially in his magisterial statements on the respective causes of the American colonies, Ireland and India. He did not participate much in the slave-trade controversy. But the leading principles he enunciated in those other great controversies applied, if only inferentially, to that other one. "My lords," he told the impeachment committee of the House of Lords, "to obtain empire is common; to govern it well has been rare indeed." Good government, here, meant two things. First, it meant the impartial application of the great universal laws of justice and right. "God forbid," Burke argued further, "that when you try the most serious of all causes, that when you try the cause of Asia in the presence of Europe, that a narrow partiality of justice should so guide us, that a British subject in power should appear in substance to possess rights which are denied to the humble allies, to the attached dependents of this kingdom, who by their distance have a double demand upon your protection, and who by an implicit . . . trust in you have stripped themselves of every other resource under heaven." He recognized that the original conquest of India under Clive had been unjust (just as the abolitionists agreed that the original despoliation of the West Indies, by England as much as by Spain and France, had been unjust). But he saw, too, albeit reluctantly, that the English power could not now easily withdraw (just as the abolitionists saw that the only consequence of the withdrawal of the English power from the

Caribbean, following the example of the American Revolution, could only have had the consequence of delivering the slave population even more securely into the power of the plantocracy). The least the imperial power could now do, Burke continued, was to seek the loyal approbation of its subjects. "To this at least," he argued of the English conqueror, "he is strictly bound—he ought to govern them as he governs his own subjects. But every wise conqueror has gone much further than he was bound to go. It has been his ambition and his policy to reconcile the vanquished to his fortune, to show that they have gained by the change, to convert their momentary suffering into a long benefit, and to draw from the humiliation of his enemies an accession to his own glory."

The second principle of imperial government sprang from Burke's reverence for established forms, for historical civilizations, for, in brief, the historical legacy of the past. "If," he continued, "we undertake to govern the inhabitants of such a country [India] we must govern them upon their own principles and maxims, and not upon ours. We must not think to force them into the narrow circle of our own ideas; we must extend ours to take in their system of opinions and rites, and the necessities which result from both; all change on their part is absolutely impracticable. We have more versatility of character and manners, and it is we who must conform." Just as the offense of the Paris revolutionaries in 1789 had been to destroy needlessly the complex edifice of old French society, so it was the great sin of Hastings and his cronies to have contemptuously ignored the political institutions and the ingrained social customs of the old Mogul Empire. There was a law of historico-cultural continuity that had been recklessly violated in both cases. It had been argued by the defense, Burke went on, that the company and its servants had not been any more oppressive than the native princes, that Indian society was so barbarous that, by comparison, the practices indulged by the Hastings regime were excusable. The answer was that Mohammedan society, in reality, was an ancient civilization replete with its own morality, religion, law, and concepts of social propriety; the real barbarity was the English imperial insolence that rode over it roughshod.

Burke, clearly, was the first English statesman to comprehend the moral import of the problem of subject races. That Hastings himself was acquitted is perhaps immaterial. The great lesson of his impeachment—that there existed a compact within which the colonial subject has rights and the imperial master obligations—had been established. Burke, perhaps, did not apply it to the West Indian situation because the West Indian slave society, having been created as it were, *de novo*, out of the African transplantation, possessed none of that ancestral pre-Colombian culture system that was known to the European mind, in Peru and Mexico; nor did there exist at the time any real knowledge of the sophisticated older African tribal civilizations that predated the arrival of the European in the sixteenth century. The most that can be said is that Burkean trusteeship became the operative ideal of the English colonial administrative class which, after emancipation, took over the responsibility for West Indian government; and the Governor Eyre case of 1865 showed that many liberal Englishmen had learned the Burkean lesson. But this, even so, was the world of the socially conscious colonial officer, whose very real dedication to the peoples he ruled was ultimately destroyed by the vested interests of the economic forces of imperialism: the West Indian planter, long after emancipation; the white East African settler; the British industrial investors in India; the oil corporations in the Arab sheikdoms of the Middle East. The West Indies, of course, were the worse losers in that imperialist game, for having been originally cultivated by the British mercantilist commercial capitalism as sources of capital accumulation they were abandoned by the new British laissez-faire industrial capitalism of the nineteenth century as other, alternative sources became more profitable.

This, then, all in all constitutes the primary relationship

of the contact between the Old World and the New World in the area of politico-economic-military relationships mentioned by Baudet in his suggestive essay. It remains to look at the other, secondary relationship of which he speaks, that of the impact of the New World of Asia and the Americas upon the literary-cultural imagination of Europe during this period. As the Mediterranean era gave way, after the sixteenth century, to the new Atlantic era, the age of discovery, there emerged the tremendous movement of the European response to the new worlds opened up by the wondrous travelers' tales that flourished in the three centuries after the pioneer voyages of the Spanish and Portuguese discoverers. It was a response of astonishment, admiration, above all curiosity, that finally flowered in the eighteenth-century cults of romantic exoticism. The voyages of discovery, from the early collections of Hakluyt and de Bry on, gave rise to a whole new literature of romantic utopianism. The ingredients of that movement were varied; in part, it was that of a pessimistic nostalgia, going back to the medieval theme of a forever irretrievable golden age, in part that of a more optimistic vision which became, in effect, the basis of a vigorous, radical criticism of European society, starting with books like Bacon's *New Atlantis*, More's *Utopia*, and Campanella's *City of the Sun*, through the mode of the extraordinary voyage like *Telemaque* and *Robinson Crusoe*, and culminating in the Rousseauistic back-to-nature movement.

The new American-Antillean world revealed in the histories of the Spanish conquistador-historians, the Chinese vogue started by the Jesuit travelers—which received a fresh impetus from the account of Lord Anson's reception at the imperial Chinese court during his tremendous voyage around the world—Montaigne's *Livre des Coches* that was composed on the basis of information about Brazil derived from Villegagnon, the earthly paradise of Tahiti described in Bougainville's account of his voyage to the South Seas: all of them combined to draw for the eighteenth-century reader the general image of mythical peoples, primitive children of nature inhabiting heaven-like countries, free from all the ills that afflicted European life. It was a genre that lasted for three centuries or more. A typical example, in the English case, was the popular series, entitled *The World Displayed: or a Curious Collection of Voyages and Travels*, published in twenty volumes or more during the decade of the 1770s, which included, among much else, Francis Moore's travels to the inland parts of Africa, Joseph Pitts's description of Mahometan Mecca, Dr. Shaw's travels through Barbary, Jonah Hanway's travels through Russia and Persia, Père du Halde's excursion into China, Sir Henry Middleton's voyage to the East Indies, and Commodore Roggewein's expedition to the Antartica southern lands, all of them, in the editors' words, presenting "entertaining descriptions of many places, which, tho' not yet resorted to for the sake of commerce, are well worthy of the notice of the curious." Even today, the modern reader, by an act of imagination, can enter into that earlier age, when the whole, unknown world lay before it, waiting to be discovered and explored. It is the age when the mutineers of the *Bounty* could, as it were, disappear from the face of the earth, to build a new life in an unknown Tahiti-like island. It is the genesis, so to speak, of the Shangri-la element in the Western imagination. It is an age now passed; and the modern reader, again, on looking back at it, must feel the regret that overwhelmed Alexander at Persepolis when he realized, at the end of his tremendous career, that there were no more worlds left to conquer.

All this literature—both the factual travel accounts and the romantic fantasies based on the accounts—carried certain general themes. It pitted nature against art, eulogizing the splendors of life in the American forest or on the Pacific island as against the evils and corruptions of organized civil society. It was critical of property, rank and dignity, religious intolerance, the sexual customs of the Old World. It compared the pacifism of the natural man with the barbarous warfare of contemporary Europe. It eulogized the Arcadian peace of rural life against the evil character of life in cities. It contrasted the contentedness of the "savage" with the restless *ennui* of European man; the simple forms of natural government with the corrupt courts of the *ancien régime*; the supposed communism of natural society with the gross contrasts of wealth and poverty in European society. At every point, man in the state of nature was deemed happier and more fortunate than man in the state of conventional society. It is true that there were skeptics, like Voltaire, who ridiculed all this as idle dreaming, and critics like Condorcet who refused to accept it as invalidating the general European spirit of optimistic progress and reason. At the same time, it constituted a particular and powerful element in the social thought of the century, based psychologically on the truth that, in Huizinga's phrase, a culture wishing to be free of itself experiences a perpetual longing for the uncivilized.

For the student of race relations—which is inextricably connected with this general theme of culture contact—much of this possesses important implications. The cosmopolitan temper of the Age of Reason revealed itself here at its best. Its attitude to the new-found worlds and peoples had little of the traditional Europocentrist bias. It brought to their study, rather, all of the attractive traits of the Enlightenment: its voracious curiosity about the new and the novel, its passion for reason and justice, its ruthless dissection of antiquated institutions, its enthused discussion of every new idea, however odd or iconoclastic, its determination, above all else, to subject everything to the spirit of rational analysis. It saw the Negro, the Indian, the Asiatic, as equals in the great army of humanity; and it embraced, indeed created, albeit in a frequently romanticized form, the Chinese mandarin, the Egyptian philosopher, the Abyssinian potentate, as fellow philosophes engaged in the debate on the ideal society. It put into the mouths of those idealized figures its own criticism of its own society, in the manner of Swift's Gulliver attempting to explain to the astonished King of Brobdingnag the barbarities of eighteenth-century European society and manners. It was willing, eagerly, to learn from others. It was, in some ways, a cult of primitivism; but it did not commit the fatal mistake of equating primitivism with savagery. It enlarged European sympathies. Not least of all, it generated the beginnings of a whole new series of intellectual disciplines based on the experience of the world as a whole and on the new intercontinental contacts: Oriental studies, the science of languages, the comparative study of religion and culture, the science of archaeology. Europe, altogether, was willing to sit at the seat of other civilizations. Burke, in the passage already quoted, had spoken of the cause of Asia being tried in the court of Europe; the cause of Europe was now tried in the court of Asia.

Much of all this, it is true, was French rather than English. The English bourgeoisie, having effected the Whig compromise of 1688, was not placed in the position of the French revolutionary bourgeoisie before 1789. It was characteristic, then, that it was a French writer like Raynal who, in a prophetic passage of his great book on the *Histoire philosophique et politique des établissements et du commerce des européens dans les deux Indes*, anticipated the rise of a black Spartacus in the Caribbean slave society who would lead his people to freedom (a prophecy fulfilled a brief generation later with the outbreak of the Saint-Domingue war of black liberation). It was characteristic, too, that Clarkson should have had to journey to the Paris of 1789 to meet colored deputies from Saint-Domingue who had been accepted as overseas members of the new revolutionary assembly; thus reflecting, it is worth emphasizing, the profound difference in racial attitudes between French and British colonialism that has persisted right into the twentieth century, so that it has been possible for a black African deputy to become president of the French Senate while it would be unthinkable to imagine that present-day English public opinion would accept the presence of a black West Indian as a member of the Cabinet.

Yet eighteenth-century England—as already noted—was no less agitated than France by the theme of non-European man. The difference was that the French debate was more analytical and philosophical, the English debate more romantic and sentimental. Studies like Wylie Sypher's *Guinea's*

Captive Kings (1942) and, to a lesser degree, more amateurish studies like Verle McCullough's *The Negro in English Literature* (1952), have fully annotated that debate. Verse, drama, fiction, all contributed to a vast antislavery literature which, although lying outside the mainstream of social and political theory, at the same time remained a remarkably continuous theme in English literary annals throughout the century. All the poets of the age—Pope, Thomson, Savage, Cowper—wrote on the theme, culminating in Wordsworth's ode to Toussaint L'Ouverture. Chatterton wrote his *African Eclogues* based upon his knowledge as a resident of the Bristol of the trade. Blake, taking a hint from the Song of Solomon, wrote his "Little Black Boy." In the realm of the theater there was the astonishing long life of the Oroonoko legend, starting with Aphra Behn's early novelette of 1688 and going through innumerable theatrical productions throughout the following century; Garrick is said by Davies to have made his first appearance, in Ipswich, in one of them. Plays like Bickerstaff's *The Padlock* brought in the new ingredient of the realistic Negro who attempts some of the earliest Negroid English in the history of the English theater; while later plays like Colman's *Africans*, based in part upon the *Travels* of Mungo Park, introduced a new serious sociological note about the cultural realities of Africa conspicuously lacking in the extravagant heroics of earlier efforts. In the sphere of the novel the contribution played on a whole gamut of themes and aspects. It began with novels like Defoe's *Captain Singleton* which, although by no means an antislavery tract, managed to present, under the stimulus of its author's genius for imaginative verisimiltude, perhaps the first account in English fiction of an attempted uprising on an African slaver. The genre then continues in the various novels of Mrs. Scott, Henry Mackenzie, Charlotte Smith, Mrs. Inchbald, and the anonymous *Adventures of Jonathan Corncob*, all of them full of the sentimentalizing manner of Sternian whimsy. It ends with the type of novel, like Robert Bage's *Man as He Is* and William Godwin's *St. Leon*, in which an attempt is made, not always successfully, to marry the antislavery theme to that of Jacobinical egalitarianism.

All this, obviously enough, was composed of a vast variety of attitudes and sentiments. There was real indignation; even the urbane Addison could write an impassioned plea for the plantation slave in one of his *Spectator* essays. There was much impressive realism in the descriptions of plantation life, often based upon what the author had read or heard about from the colonies. There was not even wanting the author who, following the philosophes, was ready to incite the Negro to revolt, as is evident in the eloquent fury of James Montgomery's *The West Indies* and its invocation of some future Genghis Khan of Africa who would rouse his people to insurrection. There was, too, the occasional playwright or versifier who saw clearly enough, although perhaps in no culturally scientific form, that the private defects of the slave-person were anchored in the social nexus of the plantation system, thus unknowingly anticipating the Prospero-Caliban, colonizer-colonized debate of the modern period.

Even so, notwithstanding all that diversity of attitudes, throughout it all there ran a single, preeminent note: that of sentimental pity, of what Sypher aptly terms the "delectable anti-slavery tear." For eighteenth-century England was the age of feeling. An age essentially satisfied with itself, it could afford to find relief and entertainment in the cultivation of its finer feelings as an amusing luxury or a pleasing diversion, in the kind of "sensibility" gently satirized, later on, in the novels of Jane Austen. Whether it was the class of the idle rich or the new middle class craving for spurious excitement in the new bourgeois novel of the times, it became for them a fashionable fad to play at the game of sympathy with the poor and oppressed. The virtuous instinct that is patently spurious; the portrait of a fictitious misery that is devoid of genuine sympathy for the victim; the shallow bathos of mood; all of the cant, that is to say, that Dr. Johnson so justly castigated, became the general character of the movement. Its typical audience was that of the "man of feeling"; and the muckraking hacks of Grub Street, following the example of Sterne and Smollett and Richardson, cultivated it as a profitable literary field.

The West Indian slave provided a perfect theme for all of this. He was black; he was, in a geographical sense, safely remote; he was the epitome of sublime suffering. The theme was a literary goldmine and worked for all that it was worth. To read through the popular journals and the critical reviews of the 1770s and 1780s is to catch the full flavor of the theme and all the set pieces that it cultivated. It is full of stock characteristics. There is the pseudo-Africa of an idyllic tropical life from which the Negro has been torn by the depredating slave-catcher, contrasted with the equally pseudo-Africa of the proslavery propagandists who saw the Negro as being rescued from a tropical hell of cannibals and tigers. There is the primitivistic note which contrasts the ennobled African in that paradisical Africa with the cancerous evil of European "civilization." There is the portraiture of the poor Negro as he yearns for the lost African home, much of it composed in a spirit of insincere, even silly neoromantic manner that anticipates the American songs, in the following century, of Stephen Foster. Just as Richardson, in the *Clarissa Harlowe* to which Rousseau's *Nouvelle Heloise* owed so much, prolongs the exquisite agony of a feminine martyrdom, exhausting practically every movement of the pathetic vocabulary of the times, until the sympathy of his reader becomes so involved that it is difficult to distinguish between delicious excitement or painful distress, so the sentimentalist proslave poets and essayists memorialized the theme of a slave martyrdom. Legend piles upon legend. There is, most popular of all, the Oroonoko story of the princely Negro treacherously enslaved and who shows that, in his wit and refined manners, he is equal to the gentlemen-courtiers of the best of the European salons. There is the equally popular Inkle-Yarico story, appearing in its English form as early as Ligon's history of Barbados (1657), in which appears the classic heartrending story of unrequited love—the native girl who befriends the stranded English sailor and is callously sold

[65]

by her lover into slavery. There are the endless variations on the theme of the "dying Negro" who can expire nobly, defiantly, sometimes in tones of fiery passion and desperate resolution, and sometimes even—like Christ on the hill of Calvary—with pious forgiveness of his white torturers. Courage in servitude, resolution to die rather than submit to slavery, stoicism, filial reverence, benevolence, the powerful capacity to love—all of these are invoked to argue the antislavery case. Most of it, with the minor poets, is conducted in the Arcadian Popean style, in the mock-heroic manner that anticipates the Byronic romantic posture of the next century. Cowper and Blake, it is true, rose above that manner in their respective contributions, and Southey's simple ballad stanzas on the theme of the remorseful English sailor who had participated in the trade were done in the convincing manner of "The Ancient Mariner." Yet, all in all, the main impression is that of an insipid, imagined noble savagery which, frequently removed from reality, opposed to the opprobrious epithets used against the slave by the proslavery writers romantic effusions, enforcing, in Sypher's apt phrase, an ethical principle by an operatic gesture.

Clearly enough, there is little that is radical or democratic here. There is the idealization of the slave-person; even Edwards, Creolized pro-planter writer as he was, tried his hand at the theme of the "Sable Venus." There is the Christian-humanitarian theme that all men are equal, that the black person, like the white, is an individual capable of feeling, stoic resolution, natural poetic genius, and sagacity of mind. But no radical conclusions are drawn from this, in the Rousseauistic manner; that that is so is evident enough from the difference between Clarkson's prize essay of 1785, with its basic appeal to pity, and Rousseau's Dijon prize essay on the origin of inequality in society, with its neosocialist attack upon property as the prime source of social discord. The English poet, Pratt, for example, who invokes the Voltairian hatred for Christianity to argue the case that the introduction of the Christian religion destroyed a superior native African religion strikes a rare note indeed. It is frequently only the cruelty of the planter to his slave charges, not slavery itself, that is lamented, as can be seen in the melodramatic *Paul et Virginie* of Saint Pierre, which was translated into English by Helen Maria Williams while she was incarcerated in the Luxembourg prison during the Robespierrian period of the French Revolution.

And this, after all, is understandable enough. Eighteenth-century England was a deeply class-conscious society; as, indeed, modern England still is. Its ruling class was not prepared that readily to admit that, as a species of mankind, it was not in all ways superior to a menial black slave. There must have been many of them, most of them, perhaps, who contemptuously dismissed, as did Dean Tucker, the "noble savage" as a myth since, on investigation he turned out to be a barbaric creature with a club and scalping knife. Nor, as a ruling class, was it yet prepared to accept the Burkean lesson—as the acquittal of Hastings showed—that an English colonial administrator should be brought to account for the treatment he imposed upon an inferior non-European race. It perhaps disliked the figure of the West Indian absentee planter and the East India nabob; but the dislike was not so much based on a revulsion against colonial subjection as on a distaste for individuals who—in the manner of Lord Chesterfield's correspondence—could not deport themselves in polite society with the taste and dignity required of a gentleman. A similar note—of class prejudice against the colonial parvenu—was struck by Adam Smith in the long paragraph in his *Theory of the Moral Sentiments* in which he compared the Spartan discipline and courage of native peoples with the effeminacy of European society. But it is difficult to believe in the sincerity of the argument, especially when it appears in a volume in which the plangent rhetoric of the style obscures its inner poverty of thought. The real point Smith wished to make was different: that slavery was objectionable because it subjected native peoples to the rule of the lowest form of Englishman, the well-known "poor white" element of West Indian colonial society. His frequently quoted passage, then—"fortune never

[67]

exerted more cruelly her empire over mankind, than when she subjected those nations of heroes to the refuse of the jails of Europe, to wretches who possess the virtues neither of the countries which they come from, nor of those which they go to, and whose levity, brutality, and baseness, expose them to the contempt of the vanquished"—must be read in that light.

That quotation, indeed, illustrates how much the whole question of slavery and the slave trade was seen by the eighteenth-century mind in terms of social class: a natural attitude granted the almost universal acceptance of gradations of social station as ordained by universal laws of nature. At the same time, of course, it was an evasive mode of argument. For it overlooked the fact that the real profits of slavery and the trade went to the groups, in the ruling class of the time, of the finance houses, the bankers, the trading magnates, the aristocratic absentee owners. The legend, then, that slavery was simply an oppression practiced by a white lower class against a black servile class must be seen, in the sociology of the problem, as one of the first efforts to advance a theory of scapegoating; that is to say, of making the "poor white" overseer or accountant the villain of the piece. The argument must have eased the conscience of many a Bristol or Liverpool factor or of the elder sons who inherited the fortunes of estates that had the foundations of their opulence in the exploitation of the West Indian slave. The "poor white" person involved in that exploitation, as a matter of fact, was almost as much its victim as the slave himself; a truth evident enough from a reading of the accounts of their experience that some of them wrote; not to mention the glimpses that we catch of them, as far as the French Caribbean is concerned, in the accounts, sometimes done with real compassion, of writers like Père Du Têrtre, Charlevoix, and Père Labat. Socially ostracized both by the gentility of the "great house" of the individual estate and the denizens of the slave barracks, they led a dismal and lonely life. They were despised by the one group because they lacked the attributes of a gentleman, and by the second group because they lacked the attributes supposedly appropriate to a white man. Not even a Jonathan Wild or a Tom Jones—the archetypal social adventurer of humble origins of the picaresque novel of the century—could have made much headway in such a tight, closed world. The Smith passage makes that abundantly clear.

Nor, if truth be told, were the abolitionist campaigners and the antislavery littérateurs themselves immune to this world outlook. Many of them moved in the same social circles inhabited by Lord Chesterfield's idealized gentleman. The liberty they claimed for the slave was as often as not a merely spiritual liberty. The only equality they were prepared to admit was, again, as often as not, the leveling power of death. The French radical like Rousseau was seriously demanding a social revolution; they merely asked for a moral reformation. If he weeps over a prisoner, remarks Sir Leslie Stephen of Sterne, he has no desire to destroy the Bastille. Poets like Hannah More wept over the slave in like fashion. The genuine abolitionist and, after him, the genuine emancipationist, were, admittedly, not guilty of that offense, for they seriously intended the termination of both the trade and the slavery institution itself. Yet even they were trapped in the dilemma of strategy, for they could not concede the unpleasant truth that the slave might have been capable of organizing freedom for himself, after the manner of the "black Jacobins" of Saint-Domingue. They underestimated, consequently, the contribution that the great slave revolts of the period made to the decline of the planter class. They thus failed to recognize the truth that it was no accident that the final emancipation act of 1834, in the case of the English-speaking Caribbean, followed only three brief years on the heels of the Jamaican slave rebellion of 1831. How much they shared the general fears aroused by the Saint-Domingue revolt, indeed, can be gauged from the fact that although Brougham advocated amelioration (after having supported abolition of the trade) in his 1803 *Enquiry into the Colonial Policy of the European Powers*, at the same time he urged the restoration of French rule in the Caribbean on the ground that independence in any one of the islands would endanger every European power possessing interests there: and, suggestively, it took him another twenty years or more for his apprehensions to subside sufficiently for him to become a leading spokesman in favor of the termination of slavery itself.

It is tempting to see all this—the point has been noted earlier —as just another expression of English hypocrisy, almost as if the abolitionist leaders were simply another version of Dickens' character of Mrs. Jellyby. The accusation has been most recently stated in a book like Jack Gratus' *The Great White Lie*. But to so argue is to overlook the basic fact that the reformers were men shaped by the spirit of the English eighteenth century. It was a deeply conservative spirit, convinced that happiness was independent of birth or wealth, and that existing institutions, however wrong in detail, were essentially right in general character. The poets like Pope and the essayists like Dr. Johnson reflected that complacency in their insistence that there was a moral lesson teaching mankind that there was only a small part of life which kings or law might hope to cure. The abolitionist-emancipationist leadership generally shared that conviction of the sanctity of existing institutions. That perhaps explains why they were never able to offer a satisfactory answer to their opponents' argument that the condition of the West Indian slave was no worse, and possibly even better, than the lot of the ordinary soldier, sailor, and village laborer in England itself. Only a social critic who took an openly socialist attitude, as did Mably in the French debate, that both conditions were part of a more general slavery suffered by all working classes in the general system of the time could have responded in any satisfactory way to that argument.

The final commentary that surely must be made is that whatever their motives—pity, indignation, Christian conscience or even possibly guilt—the reformers felt slavery to be so monstrous an offense that they were prepared to override the eighteenth-century gospel of prudence in their determination to bring it to an end. They sought, in Clarkson's phrase, to establish the principle that commerce itself should have its moral boundaries. For half a century or more they managed to place and keep the figure of the slave-person— his situation, his character, his destiny—at the forefront of the English political debate. It is an achievement, in retrospect, all the more remarkable in the light of the important role that the slavery economy played in the transatlantic commercial system of the period, not to mention the enormous property interests involved in its perpetuation. Granted their own limitations, granted, even more, the temper of the times, that was no mean achievement. It could hardly be expected that they could have done more.

It is interesting, looking at the overall picture, to note the ascriptive role that the black person played, or rather was obliged to play, in the age of European expansionism after 1600 or so. "The portrait of the negro," in the words of the *Report of the Committee on the African Institution* of 1807, "has seldom been drawn but by the pen of his oppressor, and he has sat for it in the distorted attitude of slavery." The remark was specifically addressed to the proslavery literature of the period. But it applies, more generally, to the general image of the Negro as he appeared in the European literature of the larger time period; as, that is to say, he appeared through the distorting spectacles of the white European mind. It was, in general, an unsympathetic image, going back, perhaps, to the Judeo-Christian ethic which implanted into the medieval mind the sharp contrast between black and white, between sin and virtue, between the children of darkness and the children of light. It received further expression in both the travel literature and, later, the abolitionist literature, in the temptation to paint the picture of a syncretic Negro-Indian, a regalized hero-figure who is not so much Negroid as almost neo-Grecian in his physiognomy. This confusion about color and race runs the whole gamut of the period: from the Shakespearean Othello who is a dark Ethiope rather than a full-blooded Negro, through Columbus'

[71]

description of the Arawak Indians he met on his first voyage, gaining fresh impetus with Mrs. Behn's Oroonoko who is the extraordinary, handsome, regal African par excellence, running on, finally, to the legendary Indian of the James Fenimore Cooper novels. There is little anthropological reality about this recurring theme; the distinct impression is gained that the author in each case wishes to prove to the reader that the Negro hero is not really Negroid at all. The whole exotic creed of the "noble savage," indeed, is infected with this indefiniteness about color. Like God with Adam, the European writer on the theme recreated the Negro within the framework of his own European scale of values.

The general tone of anthropological naivete is worth further emphasis. Not, of course, to condemn it, for anthropology as a professional discipline had to wait until the following century to emerge; but merely to note it. As far as the anti-abolitionist groups were concerned, the mere fact that they used a euphemistic term such as "the African trade" indicated sufficiently that they were unwilling or incapable of seeing the sociology of slavery in any scientific terms. As far as their opponents were concerned, they were tempted too easily to see the slave-person through a romantic looking glass. That can be seen, just to take one further example, from the character of the prints and engravings included in their literature. To look at them is to feel that one is in the presence, after the manner of Watteau, of idyllic tropical landscapes, in which the white masters and their ladies appear as Caribbean equivalents of the gay cavaliers and their insouciant mistresses of Versailles, with the slaves playing the role of innocent, bucolic peasants. One reviewer of Marcus Rainsford's *Historical Account of the Black Empire of Hayti* (1805) noted, similarly, how its illustrations portrayed the Negro in European phenotypical fashion, so that he became, as it were, a white with his face blackened. The same delusive portrait appears—as already noted—in the versifying efforts of the period. One illustrative example is the picturesque poem, "The Sugar Cane," composed by Dr. Johnson's friend James Grainger in 1764. Its depiction of slaves dancing escapes the indictment of men like Long and Edwards that it is all sexual orgy. Yet at the same time it becomes, in his hands, a sort of West Indian village Maypole dance. There is sympathy, even admiration, in the sketch. But the framework of reference is still English. It was logical then that the same author, in his poem of two years later, "Advice to the Planters of St. Christopher," should go no further than merely to exhort the planter class to treat the slave with tender mercy.

Inevitably, the real victim of this European structure of thought and attitude was the Negro. It was difficult, after all, to recognize the "noble savage" in the deculturated, detribalized Negro slave of the plantation economy. It was easier to see him in other mythologized figures: Voltaire's Chinese atheist philosopher, the Persian hero of Montesquieu's *Lettres Persanes*, the Red Indian of the French Canadian *voyageurs*, the innumerable utopias and El Dorados inhabited by folk-peoples who appeared to be more Caucasian than African as their authors described them. The marriage of science and philosophy that came out of the seventeenth century erected a grand design of nature in which the Negro was placed very much at the bottom. Defoe's *Robinson Crusoe* —the book so beloved of Rousseau's *Emile*—makes that eminently clear. For it was less an epic of primitive life than a celebration of the heroic exploits of the *homo faber europeanus*, using his inventive civilization as a means of survival. Its basic assumption was that of a neoevolutionary view in which the bands of *mauvais sauvages*, the rescued native Friday, and Crusoe himself embody the different stages in the growth of civilization. Only its tropical setting, facilely invoking the European dream of the idyllic island paradise, away from it all, made it seem to its reader to be something else. Nor should the fact be overlooked that its author, with characteristically ingenuous candor, admitted openly that the foundation of his hero's early wealth was his brief adventure as a slave-owner in Brazil, thus illustrating how accurately he portrayed the assumption of the public opinion of his day that slavery belonged to the natural order of things.

Robinson Crusoe thus contained at least two basic in-

[73]

gredients of racist thinking. The first was the treatment of differences between various human groups, racially interpreted. The second was the aspect of the story which can be seen as a story of primitive capital accumulation based upon Crusoe's rescue from his wrecked ship of the products of his European economy and their deployment as weapons to cultivate the island, once he has a subordinate labor supply in the form of Man Friday, along capitalist lines. It was left to the later Caribbean planter-historians and their English allies to add the further ingredient: the assumption that the Negro, defined in negative terms, was inferior because biologically he was incapable of the power of reason and of the ability to understand moral precepts (the ready assumption in Defoe's novel that the Carib Indians he encountered were cannibals, a fact never historically proved, is typical). Underlying all this, finally, there was the fixed notion of the "white bias," the unchallenged presumption that the lighter the skin shade the more likely the possibility of social acceptability. That bias, along with its crippling psychological bondage, became the cardinal principle of Caribbean society under European rule, accepted both by the white plantocracy and the Creole multilayered pigmentocracy; and that the bias survived both emancipation in the nineteenth century and independence in the twentieth century is testimony to its success in shaping the Caribbean communal psychology.

All this, in sum, constitutes the contribution of the eighteenth century to the modern, seminal debate on race and color. When all of its limitations have been noted it remains true that its reputation as the "age of reason" was not an empty one. It was ready and eager to look at non-European peoples in a spirit of genuine curiosity. It no doubt tended to romanticize those peoples, as the legend of Quashie-Sambo, the regal slave whose honor is so delicate that he cannot tolerate punishment, sufficiently shows. But it was willing to listen to the black and brown voices, and to recognize that there were cultural and spiritual values in the non-

European civilizations absent in Europe. To speak of the English case alone, it is suggestive that for all of his prejudice Boswell's omnivorous curiosity led him into a lengthy correspondence with Dr. Johnson's Negro servant Francis Barber, a correspondence now located at the Yale University Library. The eighteenth-century mind, at its best, believed in the capacity of reason to change opinion; and the abolitionist movement can be seen as a modern campaign to force legislative change through the pressure of an informed public opinion. The well-known story of the actor George Cooke in his confrontation with a hostile Liverpool audience nicely illustrates that point. Hissed for appearing drunk on the boards of the theatre in that slave-trade town—where, as one visitor noted in 1795, "almost every order of people is interested in a Guinea cargo"—he pulled himself together and said venomously over the footlights that he had not come to be insulted by a pack of men every brick of whose detestable town was cemented by the blood of a Negro; and it says much not only for the magnanimous spirit of his audience, but also for the change that the abolitionist movement had helped foment in their opinions, that he was loudly cheered for his act of defiance.

But there was more to it even than this. The debate of the period was throughout a cosmopolitan, international debate. The French philosophes and the English abolitionists were agents in a common cause. Raynal had a profound influence in England, and his *History of the Two Indies* ran through some eighteen English editions. The numerous French translations of *Oroonoko* similarly influenced French opinion. Clarkson read Benezet; the remarkable Frenchman Baron de Vastey wrote a series of books ardently defending the newly independent Haitian kingdom against its European detractors; and Wilberforce became an international name—an English visitor to Barbados in 1825 noted the use of the remark "you Wilberforce nigger, you" in a street brawl in Bridgetown. There was a close connection between the English abolitionists and the Paris group *Les Amis des Noires*; and Thomas Day dedicated his famous "Dying Negro" poem to Rous-

[75]

seau. Joseph LaVallée's French novel, *Le Nègre comme il y a peu des Blancs*, was translated by the American black "blue stocking" Phillis Wheatley who, along with Francis Williams, helped to provoke the minor controversy over Negro literary talent; and Necker's *Treatise on the Administration of the Finances of France*, with its lament over the slave trade, was translated into English.

Nor must sight be lost of the special and quite different contribution made by those French writers of the period who were excited by the new republican experiment after the American War of Independence. All of them—Raynal himself in the North American passages of his book, Mably in his *Recherches historiques et politiques sur les Etats-Unis de l'Amérique septentrionale* (1788), Chastellux in his *Voyages dans l'Amérique septentrionale dans les années 1780, 1781 et 1782*, and Brissot in his *Nouveau Voyage dans les Etats-Unis de l'Amérique septentrionale, fait en 1788*—wrote more or less as fervent Physiocratic admirers of the new America. Yet all of them, from what they saw on their travels, drew profoundly pessimistic conclusions for the future of the republic. Mably perceived, with socialist prescience, that the rise of a commercial bourgeoisie in the American cities already presaged an inevitable class struggle between rich and poor, along the old European lines; social envy, he writes, is an incurable disorder incident to all free states in which property is very unequally divided. Brissot, by contrast, recognized property as a natural right; yet even he deplored the rise of trading-commercial cities in which an original natural equality is being subverted by the poisonous spirit of capitalist accumulation. Chastellux, more aristocratic in his taste, added to that an acute appreciation of the disappearance of the older simplicity and discipline of the Boston and Philadelphia Quakers under the growing pressure of wealth and luxury. Most of these critics, moreover, related the betrayal of their anticipations of a democratic, rustic America to the additional corrupting influence of slavery. The Virginia planter gentlemen, Raynal noted, gave themselves up to that effeminacy and ostentatious entertainment so common in countries where slavery is established; a condition, he added, that could only be ended by a gradual emancipation of the slave after reaching twenty years of age, and readiness on the part of the white population to intermarry with the nonwhite. Chastellux, in turn, saw how the Southern land proprietary system made slavery necessary, with both economic and racial inequality resulting: "It is not only the slave who is beneath his master," he observed, "it is the negro who is beneath the white man." Even Brissot, the most optimistic of them all, noted with disgust how the social character of the Southern states wore the imprint of slavery; they seem, he remarked acidly, to enjoy the sweat of slaves. It was left to Mably to draw the more daring of conclusions from all this. Rather than reproach the Americans for holding slaves, in the indignant manner of Raynal, he saw slavery as simply a variant of the wage-labor that characterized the emergent bourgeois society. Inequality is everywhere; and there is no real distinction between white indentured servant and black slave. "I beg to remark," he wrote, "that the liberty which every European believes himself to enjoy is nothing but the possibility of breaking his chain in order to give himself up to a new master. Want here makes the slaves; and they are the more miserable, since no law provides for their subsistence."

This general picture, with its accompanying vignettes— the French philosophe arguing in the Boston homes or riding in the Shenandoah valley, the English abolitionist debating in the Parisian salons, the Moravian and Methodist missionaries sending their reports home from the islands— dramatically underlines the truth that this was truly an international controversy. How much so can be more fully appreciated if it is compared, briefly, with the attitude to race and slavery in the following century. The general tone of the eighteenth-century attitude had been sympathetic and can possibly be summed up in a series of affirmative statements: that the ideals of primitivism and progress require, even demand, humane treatment of the slave; that the slave, as a human prototype, might claim an innate equality with, if not a superiority to the European; and that, even more, the virtues discovered in these New World peoples, if copied, might improve the character of European society itself. The attitudes of the nineteenth century lacked that sympathetic tone. The impact after 1789 of the twin forces of nationalism and democracy replaced the older, universalistic history with the nationalist, chauvinistic, inward-turned histories of Guizot and Thierry and Macaulay. In the particular English case, as Dr. Williams has pointed out in his *British Historians and the West Indies*, it led to an apologetic reinterpretation of the abolitionist-emancipationist movement—from Victorian historians like Green and Acton to more modern historians like Egerton and Carrington and Coupland—in which everything was seen, simplistically, as the triumph of English morality and conscience in the service of culturally childlike peoples who were incapable of doing anything for themselves. They wrote, in Williams' caustic phrase, almost as if Britain had introduced Negro slavery solely for the satisfaction of abolishing it.

It was a similar story in the world of Victorian literature. Slavery emancipation in the 1830s seems to have been accepted by Victorian public opinion as the happy ending to a sad story, to be conveniently forgotten. Thackeray is about the last novelist to note at any length the black presence; and in his story of the Osborne family who saw nothing objectionable to their scheme to marry off their son to the "woolly Miss Swartz" from St. Kitts as a means of replenishing the family fortunes there is to be heard, perhaps, the last note of the older racial tolerance. After that, the Negro almost completely disappears from English verse and fiction. Dickens, admittedly, wrote against slavery in his *American Notes*. But that can plausibly be seen as nothing more than a minor note in the general anti-American animus of the volume as a whole. The characteristic tone of the Victorian writer on race reverted, in fact, to that of the earlier planter-writers. Trollope, in his *West Indies and the Spanish Main*, reproduced all of the bitterness, mythology, and racist animosity of Long, seeing the West Indian islands almost as if they were a sort of black, subhuman overseas parish of

[78]

Barchester Towers. Froude, in his turn, in his book *The English in the West Indies*, did the same, seeing the Negro as so lazy and ill-disciplined that his only salvation lay in the efficient application of the authoritarian Indian system of imperial rule to the islands. The grand rage of sympathy and enthusiasm of the eighteenth century was thus replaced by the impregnable insularity of the Victorian mind. It was almost as if the tremendous outpouring of the earlier period, of play, essay, book, pamphlet, and poem—put together in the remarkable compilation of the American scholar Lowell Ragatz, *A Guide for the Study of British Caribbean History, 1763-1834, including the Abolition and Emancipation Movements*— had never existed.

There is one final point of importance to be made. Imperialism everywhere corrupts. When it is allied to slavery, it doubly corrupts. Clarkson saw that with reference to the master-slave relationship on the individual sugar estate: "You cannot exercise an improper dominion over a fellow-creature," he wrote, "but by a wise ordering of Providence you must necessarily injure yourself." Burke saw it with reference to the wider field of relationships between the colony and the metropolis: "Today," he observed in the Hastings trial, "the Commons of Great Britain prosecute the delinquents of India. Tomorrow the delinquents of India may be the Commons of Great Britain." James Stephen repeated the warning in his book of 1826, with its suggestive title, *England Enslaved by Her Own Slave Colonies*, with its insistence that the imperial parliament had long been too servile to the Caribbean plantocracy and that it was now high time to abolish West Indian privileges and enact the ameliorative legislation which the island assemblies of themselves would never countenance.

Of the fact that the imperialist spirit, with its powerful prejudices, both cultural and racial, left its mark on the English mind there can be little doubt. The Caribbean and, later, India became forcing-houses from whence arbitrary notions of government were transplanted into England itself.

[79]

It was no accident that two of the most powerful critics of the ideology of democracy in the following century—Fitzjames Stephen and Sir Henry Maine—had learned their anti-democratic prejudices as members of the India Viceroyal Council. The Hammonds, in turn, have pointed out in a chapter of one their remarkable books that the arguments that were used by the new industrial capitalist class to justify the child labor of the new factory system were almost identical with the arguments that had been used earlier by the slavery interests to justify West Indian slavery. Most lasting of all, perhaps, the habit of empire generated in the English populace as a whole a series of negative and hostile stereotypes about non-European peoples which have been recently annotated in V. G. Kiernan's book, *The Lords of Human Kind: European Attitudes to the Outside World in the Imperial Age.* That compendium of racial bigotry, cultural arrogance, religious disdain, ignorance, and paranoid fear lay dormant for the best part of the nineteenth and twentieth centuries, permitting the English, of all social classes, to persuade themselves that they were the guardians of liberal civilization. It has taken the post-1945 wave of Asian-Caribbean immigration into the England of the present day to resurrect those hitherto repressed feelings and to give them new expression in the form of a popular racist politics along American lines. It is, as it were, the return of the native. It means, inescapably, that the last chapter on English empire and slavery has yet to be written. It may well be that when that chapter is written it will have to end with the depressing conclusion that if Europe has been the cradle of civilization the Caribbean has been its graveyard.

[Chapter 2]

From Aristocracy to Middle Class:
Bulwer-Lytton's England and the English

1832 marks the watershed between the England of the *ancien régime* and that of the middle-class Victorian civilization. Politically, the rule of the territorial aristocrat gave way to that of the newly enfranchised town bourgeoisie. Economically, slave-based capitalism, within the protective framework of the old mercantilist system, gave way to the new laissez-faire factory-based industrial capitalism, although there still remained scattered throughout England dozens of Mansfield Parks, owned by men like Jane Austen's Sir Thomas Bertram, created out of the West Indian sugar estate and its accumulated capital. Philosophically and culturally, the world of the Duke of Wellington's Toryism gave way to the world of Gladstonian Liberalism. It was a transition that converted England into the workshop of the world and, in so doing, created a capitalist world market which finally broke down the isolation of even the most distant peoples. The world outlook of the eighteenth century, which was still excited by the possibility of other, unknown worlds waiting to be conquered, was replaced by a nineteenth century of bourgeois complacency, convinced that Europe, with its science and industry, was the undisputed master of the whole world.

In England, of course, the principal doctrinal architects of the new movement were the Benthamite-utilitarian thinkers, running from Adam Smith and Ricardo to the elder and younger Mill. Among them, they put together the system of philosophic radicalism. In part, it is true, it was a defense of the new prototype of the businessman and factory owner, eager to expand his entrepreneurial genius free from the trammels of the state power. But, in part, too, it was a movement which, as both Halevy and Dicey have shown in their monumental studies, was concerned with the national patrimony as a whole. The idea of the welfare state was in fact logically secreted in the "greatest happiness of the greatest number" principle; just as, indeed, with equal logic, the idea of negative government of the Herbert Spencer school was secreted in the Benthamite dogma of the natural identity of interests in the social process. These two leading concepts, indeed, came to constitute the leading contradiction of the philosophical-radical school; a contradiction that received its final expression in the political thought of the younger Mill who advanced, almost simultaneously, the objections of the liberal idea against the claims of popular democracy and the objections—especially in his later work—of the socialist idea against the philosophy of the laissez-faire state.

Yet for the period between the French Revolution and the middle of the nineteenth century it was the more positive side of the creed, based on the principle of the artificial identity of interests requiring, necessarily, the intervention of a wise legislation, that carried the day. A whole group of Benthamite disciples, both within Parliament and outside, conducted a campaign of reforming zeal in at least half a dozen fields of first-class importance—education, legal reform, colonial administration, factory legislation, the reform of the civil service. Contemptuous, like their master, of fictions such as natural rights or the social contract, they married moral principle with organizing genius. The two Mills themselves in the India Office, Southwood Smith in the Poor Law Commission, George Cornewall Lewis at the War Office, Sir Henry Taylor and James Stephen at the Colonial Office—all combined the radical application of disinterested intelligence to the art of government with an administrative zest that outraged both aristocratic sinecurist and Cobdenite businessman alike. They converted the careful accumulation of facts and statistics into a new science of government, so that factory inspectors like Leonard Horner and medical officers like John Simon gathered together the material of the famous Victorian Blue Books which Marx used later on as evidence to buttress his tremendous indictment of industrial capitalism in *Capital*. They married theory to practice: Austin elaborated out of his naval experience a theory of sovereignty in which the ability to enforce command became the essence of government, while the younger Mill discovered in his experience at the India Office principles of efficient public administration which the ancient universities were quite incapable of providing. They obtained a new prestige for the public servant; the growth of the English civil-service machinery throughout the rest of the century was in fact nothing much more than the serious application in practice of the principles outlined in Bentham's fertile *Constitutional Code*. They thus made it possible, all in all, for Liberalism, later in the century, to absorb Green's theory of social rights and the Fabian ideas of efficient, centralized administration with a minimum of ideological embarrassment. They may themselves have dissented from that final outcome. That the outcome was implicit in large sections at once of their philosophical assumptions and their practical achievement is, however, beyond doubt. They laid, indeed, the foundations of modern England.

The philosophical foundations, of course, were set by the great names. But a small group managed to write books which have become minor classics; Henry Taylor's *The Statesman*, for example, and Cornewall Lewis' *Government of Dependencies*. To those must certainly be added Edward Bulwer-Lytton's *England and the English*, published one year after the 1832 Reform Act, which was indeed its immediate stimulus. Its history has been one of curious neglect. The neglect, to some extent, was due to the English distrust of philosophical analysis; the younger Mill has assured us that at the date of its publication the book was far ahead of the public mind. To some extent, too, the neglect was due to that English sense of complacent self-satisfaction which Lytton himself noted: the English people, he tells his reader, would fight for the cause for which Sidney died on the scaffold but would not for the life of one of them read a single chapter of the book in which he informs them what the cause was. In addition, Lytton wrote as a pungent critic of the new middle-class civilization that was being ushered in after 1832; for despite his philosophical radicalism he was essentially—as befitted a littérateur and novelist of the Regency period—a sort of pagan aristocrat horrified at the alliance of technological genius and cultural illiteracy which was the hallmark of the *nouveaux riches* of the day. In one way, indeed, the book is nothing much more than a brilliant conversation between its author and Prince Talleyrand, to whom it was in part dedicated, upon the follies of the English bourgeois way of life. In the great peace that followed the Napoleonic Wars, then, he was not listened to any more than Henry Adams was listened to in the Gilded Age of post–Civil War America.

Yet no book summarizes so brilliantly and pungently the nature of the national life and character as they passed through this transitional period. There are times, as Lytton remarks in his apologia for the book, when it is necessary for an Englishman to write about England. Lytton was admirably suited to fill that need. Born into the lower county gentry, once settled in London he had access to both high society and the literary world and was intimately acquainted with the pre–1832 demimonde of aristocratic profligacy, parliamentary intrigue, and moral corruption. He used his immense industry to write his novels around that world, so that most of the central figures of those novels are, characteristically, brilliant and dazzling young aristocratic reformers seeking to improve its quality. He did not allow the patronage of that world to corrupt him, nor permit himself the life-style of a man with a great fortune and powerful family connections, both of which he lacked, which could only have meant—as it did with Sheridan before him—a tragic self-destruction. Yet he did not entirely escape that trap, and both his son and his grandson in their respective memoirs, and Michael Sadleir in his *Edward and Rosina*, have described how his unhappy marriage to a woman determined to have all that comfort and luxury could give her made him, like Sir Walter Scott before him, a writer driven desperately to maintain a standard of living he could ill afford. There was, again, the experience of his parliamentary career to draw on. That career in itself, first as a Benthamite radical and secondly as a Disraelian democrat, would have been enough in itself to satisfy most ambitious men. His impassioned speech of 1838 in support of the motion to terminate the ill-advised apprenticeship system in the West Indian colonies was termed by O'Connell one of the best he had ever heard in the House; and Holyoake has left a spirited description of how, in the 1855 debate on the newspaper stamp tax, Lytton, for all the world looking like an elegant lounger, rose to make a brilliant speech that was credited with clinching the victory for the forces arrayed against the "taxes on knowledge." To achieve such a reputation was no mean feat in an age of parliamentary giants. All in all, Lytton brought to his analysis of English prides and prejudices a remarkable variety of gifts. As Horne remarked, *England and the English* was more the work of the man of the world, and the member of Parliament, superadded to the thinker.

The book itself is divided into five major sections. The first, dedicated to Talleyrand, presents a view of the English character. The second deals with the revolution in society and manners stimulated by the tremendous impact of the Napoleonic Wars. The third, dedicated to the outstanding Scottish educator Dr. Chalmers, surveys the field of national education and the influences of morality and religion. The fourth section, dedicated to the elder Disraeli, treats of what Lytton terms the intellectual spirit of the times and includes some penetrating analyses of literature, drama, art, and the sciences. The fifth section is entitled "A View of Our Political State." As appendices, there are included an essay on Bentham's political philosophy, especially written for the occasion by John Stuart Mill, a brief study of James Mill, and Lytton's own further elaboration of his farseeing scheme for the reform of the educational system. All of it carries Lytton's characteristic style: analytical rather than impulsive, elaborately circuitous rather than direct, refined rather than simple, systematic rather than instinctive. It is a style that makes the superb social commentator rather than the first-class novelist; that perhaps explains why, reading his once-popular novels today, it is difficult to understand that in his own day he was classed with Dickens and Thackeray.

It may be promulgated as a general thesis that the English character has been shaped, historically, by the mingling of the aristocratic ideal of gentlemanly chivalry with the Puritan notions of the successful middle class. Lytton saw this clearly, so that the outstanding quality of the book is its acute perception of the nature and consequences of that intermarriage. His argument is an excoriating criticism of both those elements. He was too much a man of the world to take a Podsnap-like pride in the national achievement and too much of a bohemian aristocrat to care for the middle-class religion of social respectability which, he notes, comes to dominate English life after 1832. The special habits of that religion he acutely analyzes as dubious virtues. "The sense of independence," he writes, "is often the want of sympathy with others." The victory of the Calvinist economic virtues creates a social dullness: "It is evidently the nature of commerce to detach the mind from the pursuit of amusement." It generates the notorious selfishness of the acquisitive society; commenting favorably on the Owenite effort to challenge the associationist psychology, he remarks that "the unsocial life is scarcely prolific of the social virtues." Nor is he content to accept the simple thesis, in the manner of Comte, that these are the necessary and inevitable items of a permanent national character. They are to be traced, rather, he argues, to the social and political alliance of bourgeois and aristocratic influences that was the outcome of the French wars. The English habit of reserve is really the curious outcome of the invisible class fences of a complicated class society, for the absence of readily identifiable distinctions breeds a morbid fear of being snubbed, itself the foundation of social reticence. The adoration, in turn, of "common sense" is simply the pathological obsession of a successful business world afraid of radical challenge; its panegyrists are in reality referring to "our general indifference to political theories, our quiet and respectable adherence to the things that are." The fundamental root of all this—whether one speaks of the old territorial oligarchy or of the rising middle class—is the institution of private property. "The root of all of our notions," Lytton tells Talleyrand, in making a distinction between English and French national vanity, "as of all our laws, is to be found in the sentiment of property. It is *my* wife whom you shall not insult; it is *my* house that you shall not enter; it is *my* country that you shall not traduce; and by a species of ultra-mundane appropriation, it is *my* God whom you shall not blaspheme."

Lytton clearly dislikes both segments of the English ruling class. Yet it is the central theme of his argument, which runs throughout the whole book, that it is the pervasive influence of the aristocratic spirit that, more than anything else, has corroded and poisoned the pattern and spirit of the national life and character. It is true that he does not write with the impassioned hatred of Cobbett or the eloquent fury of Carlyle. His style is more that of the teasing, acute critic, writing with an almost Addisonian urbanity. But the indictment is nonetheless serious for that. To portray him, as did Carlyle himself in his satirical portrait of Lytton in his *Sartor Resartus*, as a mere aristocratic adventurer in literature, is to misapprehend completely the earnest purpose of the book.

It is Lytton's favorite thesis that English life and manners can only be understood within the framework of the general historical fact that since 1760 or thereabouts the changes that have taken place have compromised the social dignity and, to some extent, the political power of the aristocracy and at the same time have increased its social influence. It is not royal power, but aristocratic power, he urges, that we have to fear, for "the power of the king is but the ceremonial to the power of the magnates." Ever since the Revolution of

1688 the aristocratic influence has spread itself, as an unseen monopoly, throughout all the affairs of state. The Reform Act of 1832 has simply compelled the aristocracy to become more circumspect in the exercise of that influence. That it has been able to do this Lytton traces to two factors that distinguish the English aristocracy from its continental counterparts. First, it has been a local, land-based group, rather than a court entourage. Its members, then, mix more readily, and with more seeming equality, with other classes, as their hospitality, their field sports, their agricultural and county meetings, their assiduity in "keeping up the family interest" show. "Without the odium of special privileges, without the demarcation of feudal rights, the absence of those very prerogatives has long been the cause of the long establishment of their power." At the national level, that has meant the high degree of representation of the aristocrat in Cabinet and Parliament; at the local level it has meant the social government of the country through the alliance of the squirearchy and the clergy. All political power must have a social base. The social base of aristocratic power, for Lytton, is the immense wealth of the landed gentry, distributed throughout every parish and county of the nation. That is why, he tells his liberal friends, the rule of the new industrial middle class would still remain an aristocracy of shopkeepers. That is why, too, he tells the doctrinaire republican like Paine or Godwin, their proposed abolition of the monarchy would have a similar result. For the English aristocracy is not, like the French before 1789, the mere shadow of a royal court. It is, rather, a separate class with its own property basis. "In any republic you can devise," he admonishes, "men with this property will be uppermost; they will still be your rulers, as long as you yourselves think that property is the legal heir to respect." Nor, he adds, does mere electoral reform make any substantial difference to this. The reins of power, after 1832 as before, are still in aristocratic hands. Government still remains a combination of "the spirit of democracy in the power of obtaining honours and the genius of an aristocracy in the method by which they are acquired. The highest offices have been open by law to any man, no matter what his pedigree or his quarterings; but influences, stronger than laws, have determined that it is only through the aid of one portion or another of the aristocracy that those offices can be obtained." It is a pregnant observation. It explains the political success of Sir Robert Peel in one generation just as it explains, although perhaps to a lesser degree, the political success of Disraeli in another.

The second explanatory factor, for Lytton, was perhaps more important. For he writes as a perceptive social psychologist. He sees that the real reason for continuing aristocratic power lies in the communal psychology of the English themselves:

> You may sweep away the House of Lords if you like; you may destroy titles; you may make a bonfire of orb and ermine, and after all your pains the aristocracy would be exactly as strong as before. For its power is not in a tapestried chamber, or in a crimson woolsack, or in ribbons and stars, in coronets and titles; its power, my friends, is in yourselves; its power is in the aristocratic spirit and sympathy which pervade you all. In your own hearts while you shout for popular measures, you have a reverential notion of the excellence of aristocratic agents; you think rich people alone 'respectable'; you have a great idea of station; you consider a man is the better for being above his fellows, not in virtue or intellect, but in the good things of life.

The result, he continues, is the ingrained snobbishness that afflicts all classes as a national disease. It produces the arrogance of the *nouveaux riches*. "The road to honours is apparently popular; but each person rising from the herd has endeavoured to restrain the very principle of popularity by which he has risen. So that, while the power of obtaining eminent station has been open to all ranks, yet in proportion as that power bore any individual aloft, you might see it purifying itself of all democratic properties, and beautifully melting into that aristocratic atmosphere which it was permitted to attain." The aristocrat, all this is to say, is not to be regarded as the villain of the piece. He, as much as those he uses and exploits, is the victim of that "sneaking kindness for a lord" from which no Englishman, of any social level, ever completely escapes. The end result is a schizoid national personality. The political ideas, whether expressed in terms of liberalism or popular democracy, are progressive; but the social spirit is reactionary. It is that underlying tension between political ideology and social behavior which has probably caused the European reputation of the English as a race of hypocrites.

The comparison with de Tocqueville—whose book on America was published only a few years later—immediately comes to mind. For whereas the leading thesis of *Democracy in America* is that all aspects of American life and behavior are rooted in the democratic principle, it is the leading thesis of *England and the English* that the species *homo anglicanus* can only be fully understood in terms of its subjection to the aristocratic principle. The comparison goes even further. For both authors are suggestively ambivalent in their attitudes to the societies they are describing. For just as de Tocqueville sees in the American democratic principle at once the regenerative force of a new society and a threat of standardized mass rule, so the Englishman sees in the aristocratic principle at once a false moral standard creating all of the fossilized incrustations of the national character and evidence of the fact that by accommodating itself to the demands of other classes to become, as it were, new members of the club, the English ruling class has thereby saved itself from revolution. The reform which removes abuses, he notes, prevents the revolution that avenges them. Emerson noted the same truth in his book on *English Traits*; and Lytton would have fully agreed with the American's shrewd observation that the history of the English aristocracy has been the history of an aristocracy with its doors open.

The rest of Lytton's book is a prolonged description of the implications of all this, in social life, art, science, politics, and literature, replete with anecdotes, lively pen portraits of typical character types, and sustained moral analysis. There is, to begin with, he tells his reader, the multilayered ranking order of social status, the shifting shades of graduation so subtle and refined that they baffle practically every foreign visitor. "As wealth procures the alliance and respect of nobles, wealth is affected even where not possessed; and, as fashion, which is the creature of an aristocracy, can only be obtained by resembling the fashionable; hence each person imitates his fellow, and hopes to purchase the respectful opinion of others by renouncing the independence of opinion for himself." This, in turn, generates the English habit of reserve, since, nobody being really fixed in society, except the very great, whose self-esteem is almost a law of nature, everybody must tread carefully in the social acquaintanceship he chooses to cultivate. "In any advance you make," Lytton warns the social climber, "to a seeming equal, you may either lower yourself by an acquaintance utterly devoid of the fictitious advantages which are considered respectable; or, on the other hand, you may subject your pride to the mortification of a rebut from one, who, for reasons impossible for you to discover, considers his station far more unequivocal than your own."

These considerations, Lytton continues, are the foundations of fashion and society. For he knew the London salon and the country estate as well as anyone; and his observations, at once amused and acid, reveal the experience of the insider. He matches Thackeray in his portraiture of "vanity fair." The vast wealth of the aristocracy produces all the vulgarity with which "a mind without culture amuses an idleness without dignity." There is the grand tour, which has made the young English nobleman abroad a synonym for reckless extravagance. There is a diplomatic service which, because of aristocratic patronage, is filled by the same type, so that "we have enrolled as the diplomatic representatives of the nation stray specimens of erratic imbecility," disguised under the rubric of "eccentricity." There is the open, scandalous marketing of elder sons and marriageable beauties in a society "crowded with the insipid and beset with the insincere." There are the fops, the dandies, the upper-class scroungers, the Beau Brummels who, if they are intimate with the Prince Regent, can become the arrogant dictators of dress and manners, the society hostesses who lavish their attention not on the most agreeable member of a family, but on the richest. There is the incessant rivalry of ostentatious hospitality among the lowborn rich—the nobility who trace their origins from a rich merchant or a successful lawyer—and the arrogance of the genuinely hereditary great who, incensed at the conspicuous consumption of these newly rich, try to emulate and surpass it with their own high-life style. There is the vast system of government patronage which secures appointments in the church, or the government department, or the army, for the worthless son; and there are few chapters more revealing in the book than those in which Lytton describes how it is absolutely impossible, in the French or the Prussian fashion, for an ordinary soldier to rise, through the ranks, to the positions of higher command in the army, or how, in the church, the aristocratic system of patronage produces a national clergy which is politically reactionary, socially respectable, and intellectually decadent, since it is their function not so much "to win the sympathies of the cottage as not to shock the prejudices of the drawing room." There remains to note—to complete the picture—the dismal fact that while with the French it is the indispensable accomplishment of a gentleman to speak the language well, in England such an accomplishment is regarded with suspicion; a phenomenon which Lytton traces in part to the bad teaching of the "public school" system. To know Latin and Greek, he observes, is a great intellectual luxury, but to know one's own language is almost an intellectual necessity.

In all of this, Lytton is clearly annotating the typical characteristics of a postwar period of change. Just as later, in the post-1918 and post-1945 periods of English life, the Napoleonic Wars had unleashed new social forces. Wars, as Marx said of revolutions, are the locomotives of history. A new class of money-barons, whose wealth had been made in the wartime prosperity period, formed a new aristocracy of money competing with the old aristocracy of breeding (which Lytton undoubtedly idealized in his account). The titled exclusive, in Lytton's phrase, is replaced with the socially ambitious *roturier*. The new wealth attempts to ape the outward trappings of the old; the social race becomes more aggressive, more competitive, more vulgar; a mad pursuit of pleasure replaces the older restraint; the parvenu breaks down the old walls of caste. "Throughout Europe," in the words of one of the more perceptive writers of the fashionable novel of the time, "it was holiday time for people intent on promoting the greatest happiness of the smallest number." There was added to all this a new national temper that had become used to following the great events of the prolonged war with France and the tremendous career of Napoleon, creating a public opinion eager for excitement; and it is to that postwar feeling that Lytton attributed the tremendous popularity of Byron's "Childe Harold" among the expanding reading public.

The old class structure, in brief, with its fixed ranks and notions, was in complete disarray. It was being replaced, first, by the rising industrial and commercial bourgeoisie and, second, by the emerging town proletariat as the type of the village laborer gave way to the type of the town laborer. Lytton recognized the significance of both. It is true that he did not know either class at first hand, as Dickens, for example, knew the middle class and Mayhew (in his remarkable social documentary of the proletarian underworld of London, *London Labour and the London Poor*, of 1851) knew the growing London lumpenproletariat; his world, rather, was that of the London demimonde, and throughout his life he was known as the epitome, in his own mannerisms, of the scented dandy. Yet he was a social observer of keen perceptions. Of the new middle class he was not overly enthusiastic. Yet he saw their earnestness, their philanthropic spirit, their dedication to work and improvement. He dislikes their English pragmatism, which leads to a "practical" spirit that knows nothing of first principles in social organization: "if you could speak to him out of the multiplication table," he observes of the type, "he would think you a great orator." But he appreciates their educational system, in which their schools pay serious attention to religion and vocational training, and he has high praise for the new foundations of London University and King's College in which a new curriculum emphasizes medicine and chemistry aimed at filling the growing middle-class professions. What he dislikes most, perhaps, is the Dissenting Puritanism so much the enemy of recreation and entertainment. His special chapter, indeed, on the character of the English Sabbath constitutes a damning indictment of the morbid Sabbatarianism which gradually became the hallmark of Victorian England. The absence of decent, respectable places of entertainment—such as the popular tea gardens of the continent—means that the poor must seek consolation for their weekly toil either in the conventicle or the alehouse, usually the latter, thus generating the reckless drunkenness of the working class noted throughout this period with astonishment by every French and German visitor. Here, certainly, Lytton is writing of the new shopkeeping class of the Bounderbys and the Gradgrinds in much the same spirit that Talleyrand sought to combat the uncouth arriviste society of the revolution and the empire with an effort to renovate the exquisite aristocratic manners of the *ancién regime*.

Yet Lytton, in fact, is too English to be simply a counterpart of the aging, cynical roué of the Congress of Vienna. Nothing illustrates his liberalism better than the sections of his book that deal with the working class. He sees the poor as the victims of the system he is analyzing. Shut off from social intercourse with classes above them, they do not feel themselves to be members of a national community of common concerns. They are made to feel that poverty is a crime. Lytton is one of the first of English authors, even before Engels, to use the evidence of the parliamentary hearings on the first Factory Act of 1831 to illuminate the state of the new industrial laboring class. Before Dickens, he sees that it is the children of that class who are the foremost victims of the system. He appreciates, too, how the operation of the old poor-law system, based upon a principle of punitive legislation, actually encourages pauperism because it subsidizes laziness; the operation of the Poor Laws, he notes, is the history of the poor. Failing reform in this field, he adds, especially a reform that takes the care of the poor out of the hands of the old corrupt parochial administrative system, the only result can be the "fierce cries of a Servile War," an ominous phrase that presages the rise of Chartism a decade later. There are few pages of Lytton's whole book which blaze so much with real fury as his portraiture of the town poor. The child has no young dreams; he breaks at once into the iron realities of life. Once a young man, he resorts, in desperation, to gin and narcotic drugs as the horrible cements with which to repair a shattered and macerated frame; and his wife is driven to the crude operation of abortion in order to avoid a further burden.

Yet underneath all this degrading poverty Lytton sensed the presence of an emerging working-class civilization. He notes the growth of the trade union, the mechanics' institutes, the political clubs among the more intelligent and serious elements of the factory-operative class, the general thirst for education and the habit of serious political discussion that characterizes all of those institutions. He sees, even more, that they represent the best elements of the old English tradition of freedom. "It is their voice," he writes generously, "which is heard the earliest, and dies the latest, against Wrong in every corner of the globe; they make to themselves common cause with spoliated Poland, with Ireland dragooned into silence, with the slaves of Jamaica, with the human victims of Indostan: wherever there is suffering, their experience unites them to it; and their efforts, unavailing for themselves, often contribute to adjust the balance of the World." He cites in particular their support in the case of Queen Caroline and also their support of West Indian slavery emancipation; and he includes a moving description of a parliamentary election meeting in a manufacturing town in which the popular audience rousingly rejected the argument of the Tory candidate that emancipation would mean additional taxation for themselves. It is the generous benevolence of spirit, Lytton adds, which makes the workingman the real representative of that character of national honor of which the old aristocracy was once the custodian. It is a spirit all the more remarkable because it is met by the ruling class with hostility and repression: "The very essence of our laws has been against the social meetings of the humble, which have been called idleness, and against the amusements of the poor, which have been stigmatized as disorder." "For I know not how it is, Sir," Lytton concludes his argument on this point, addressing himself directly to Talleyrand, "but it seems to me, that wherever a man is very active on some point of humanity, he always finds himself surrounded by the great body of the English people."

Even more. For it is at this point that Lytton joins hands, albeit briefly, with the radical movement of the period. He sees that the new political theories of the time come from the bottom, not the top, of the social layers. He sees, too, that it is the dissenting sects, like the Wesleyans, and not the established clergy, who identify with the popular side. From the larger historical perspective, he sees that it is from the lower classes that the great minds of England have been recruited. He cites, as a particular example of that general thesis, the social origins of the Church of England itself. Latimer was a yeoman's son; Barrow the son of a London trader; Clarke was a plain citizen of Norwich; while the great divines like Warburton, Hooker, and Tillotson came from the ranks of the middle class. "In fact," he concludes, "the births of our great divines may be said to illustrate the principle of every powerful church which draws its vigour from the multitude and languishes only when confining its social influence to a court." He could, of course, have cited equally appropriately the humble social origins of the radical leaders of his own day, from Paine onward to Francis Place, Samuel Bamford, and William Lovett, not to mention Cobbett himself. That he did not do so was probably due to the fact that his forte was more that of the historical novelist than the political activist. Yet his contribution to the popular cause was nonetheless real because of that, and it was in keeping with his popular sympathies that one of his most successful novels, *Rienzi*, was built around the romantic figure of the fourteenth-century plebeian, Nicola Rienzi, who quelled the turbulence of the rival Roman patrician houses and finally fell a victim to the fury of the very Roman mob which had first raised him to power.

The section of the book on the intellectual spirit of the times follows logically from all this. Lytton sees the major phenomenon of the times as the rise of a new public opinion based, one, on the growth of popular education, both in the working and the middle classes and, two, on the rapid expansion of the reading public. His entire discussion of the state of literature, the arts, the press, and science, is impregnated with an awareness, as a practicing writer himself, of that truth. There is the growth of a popular press mainly antiaristocratic in its sentiments. There is the development of the cheap publications that appeal to the more intelligent working-class reader, with their social significance for the expansion of knowledge: "As the extension of the electoral franchise gave power to the middle classes, so the extended circulation of the press will give power to the operative." There is the decline of the aristocratic patron, which means that the writer and artist must seek new and wider popular audiences. There is the new democratic tone of the novels of Sir Walter Scott and the poetry of Wordsworth, both of whom have sought their inspiration in the experience of the ordinary man. It is true that Lytton at times regrets much of this, for it seems to him that the extension of the reading public leads to superficial writing, both in the press and in authors: "the time is come when nobody will fit out a ship for the intellectual Columbus to discover new worlds, but when everybody will subscribe for his setting up a steamboat between Calais and Dover." At the same time he rejects the easy conclusion that this is proof of the degeneracy of literary talent. It is, rather, he emphasizes, a proof of the enlarged world of readers.

There has grown up, more particularly, a new relationship

between politics and literature. The new phenomenon of the periodical literature, as reflected in the quarterlies of the period, has opened up a new field of opportunity to the author, a revolution that Lytton traces back to the success, in the previous century, of the *Tatler* and the *Spectator*, and continuing with the growth of that very special English type of author—like Swift, Bolingbroke, Goldsmith, Chesterfield, Dr. Johnson—who used the journal essay to write on the political issues of the day, untrammeled by the financial bondage of the author of books to the individual publisher. This results at once in a new literary popularity and a new economic independence for the essayist and reviewer: Southey, Sydney Smith, Macaulay, and all of their lesser imitators. It is the rise, essentially, of a popular court of letters as distinct from a world of authors dependent on aristocratic patronage; and Lytton adds to his examples the figures of Leigh Hunt and the elder Disraeli, both of whom, he asserts, inherit and pursue the liberalizing movement bequeathed by the Johnsonian era. The same lesson is drawn from the increasing freedom of the press, with its character of exposing the abuses of power and predisposed to the reforming spirit. "In those crises," Lytton writes at this point, "which constantly occur in political affairs, when the popular mind, as yet undetermined, follows the first adviser in whom it has been accustomed to confide, when, in its wavering confusion, either of two opinions may be reflected, the representative portion of the press has usually taken that opinion which is the least aristocratic; pushing the more popular, not to its full extent, but to as great an extent as was compatible with its own interest in representing rather than originating opinion." A new reading public, at the same time, gives rise to new tastes, so that the fashionable novel which titillated its readers with the secret life of the world of high society gives way to a new, muckraking, American-style magazine literature of malicious gossip and personal abuse: the forerunner, clearly enough, of the "yellow press" of the later, more fully capitalist mass media.

Much of all this, albeit with certain misgivings, Lytton

approves. He sees it as the expression in the arts and belles-lettres of the new reforming currents of opinion that he traces back, in their origin, to the revitalizing force of Bentham. But he realises that it is still a movement not yet fully assured of victory. That is why he comes back, again, to the pernicious influence of the aristocratic contagion. "The English," Halevy has written, "were a nation of manufacturers and merchants governed by an aristocracy who made it a point of honour to appear ignorant, indeed to be ignorant of the economic foundation on which rested both the national greatness and their own." Lytton particularizes and illustrates that general condemnation. There is, he points out, the sad state of patronage. There is a Royal Academy which, instead of being a public body fulfilling its original purpose of encouraging the arts, has become an aristocratic clique which pays handsomely the portrait painter like Lawrence but, according to rumor, prevented Wilkie's indignant painting *Distraining for Rent* being engraved lest it excite unpleasant feelings toward the country gentleman. There is, again, a Royal Society, most of whose aristocratic members know as much about science as they do of fishmongery. Lytton proves the charge with interesting statistical material. In 1827, out of 109 members who had contributed to the Society's *Transactions*, only one was a peer. He compares the handsome rewards of income given to French scientists by the various French institutes and academies with the miserable pittance on which most of their English counterparts must manage to survive; there is as much scientific genius in England as in France, but being more honored in France it is more generally cultivated. "I am nothing here," the author quotes a scientist acquaintance as saying, "I am forced to go abroad sometimes to preserve my self-esteem." Research into the first principles of scientific investigation is thus discouraged for want of public financial support. All that takes place is applied technology.

Lytton, furthermore, sees all this as part of the general anti-intellectual spirit of English life. It leaves literature and science to the efforts of those who, because of private means, can afford to cultivate their own eccentric interests. For the rest, it is a capricious system of patronage which in Lytton's expressive phrase, sets Michelangelo to making roads and employs Holbein in designs for forks and saltcellars. The genuine scholar receives nothing but ridicule. There is, indeed, a special form of English ridicule. The Parisians laugh at bad manners, the English laugh at any man professing exalted intellectual enthusiasms. The English visits of Voltaire and Rousseau in the previous century had made them social lions; today it is different. "We do not laugh at vulgar lords half as much as at the generosity of patriots, or the devotion of philosophers. Bentham was thought extremely ludicrous because he was a philanthropist; and Byron fell from the admiration of fine ladies when he set out for Greece. It is the great in mind, whom a fine moral sense never suffers to be the object of a paltry wit. Francis I forbade his courtiers to jest at Ariosto; and Louis XIV declared a certain general unfit for high office, because he had evinced the mental littleness of laughing at Racine." The fashionable patron, in brief, does everything for the fashionable. Everything else is left to chance and accident.

What is the answer to all this? For Lytton does not write merely as the jaundiced observer, but as the zealous reformer. The first, leading principle from which he starts is that of the positive state, of a directive government replacing the anarchy of the laissez-faire theorists. "The great mistake of modern liberalism," he writes, "is to suppose that a government is never to interfere, except through the medium of the tax-gatherer." "To unite, then," he adds, in neo-Hegelian fashion, "the people and the Government, to prevent that jealousy and antagonism of power which we behold at present, each resisting each to their common weakness, to merge, in one word, both names in the name of the state, we must first advance the popular principle to satisfy the people, and then prevent a conceding government by creating a directive one. . . . I would wish that you should see the Government educating your children, and encouraging your science, and ameliorating the condition of your poor." Out of this there will grow up a new sense of national citizenship in which each individual will feel himself an integral part of the national community, in which his personal dignity at once reflects and inspires the dignity of the state. Two main forces, as Lytton prophetically appreciates, make this development almost inevitable. The first is the centralization of power more and more into the hands of the administrative machinery of the state in the future, thus replacing the importance of the legislative branch. The second is the intimate relationship between law and public opinion, in which legislative opinion, as created by parliamentary law, will increasingly shape public opinion rather than passively reflect it.

The main vehicle for this new state, Lytton forcibly argues, must be that of a public system of reformed, efficient education, at all levels. Because, for him, history was the march of intelligence, he felt that the real, lasting index of the worth of a society was the quality of mind, both individual and collective, that it created and the readiness on its part to secure the conditions under which that quality could prosper. His major reform recommendation, it follows, contemplates a complete reorganization of education. There must be a national board of education; there must be a system of labor and vocational schools based on the maxim that education for the working class must mean the inculcation of "a more general knowledge applicable to the daily purpose of life"; there must be a reform of the "public schools" toward the end of terminating their present character as privileged seminaries in which it is less important to be properly educated than to form personal connections with rich and well-connected young men for the purpose of improving one's social status; there must be instituted, after the Continental fashion, special teachers' training colleges, for the real scandal of English popular education is that the schoolmaster is hardly any more educated than his pupils; there must be a root-and-branch reform of the ancient universities, which still remain in the condition of intellectual torpor of the time of Gibbon; and, finally, there must be undertaken a radical revision of educational curricula, based on Bentham's *Chrestomathia*, with its perhaps too formidable but at the same time absolutely necessary scheme of modern studies. All this, Lytton argues, constitutes a challenge to the English ruling class; for "if the aristocarcy would remain the most powerful class, they must continue to be the most intelligent."

In addition to this, the argument continues, the state must become the generous patron of the arts and science, since neither aristocrat nor bourgeois, because of their narrow class preoccupations, will undertake that role. It is the function of the state to foster the artist, the writer, the scientist, and it must utilize its system of public honors to confer prestige upon intellect and not simply upon social eminence without merit. That message was the burden, later on, of Lytton's *Letters to Lord John Russell*. "Do not deceive yourself," he admonished the prime minister, "with the belief that you can make intellectual culture the noble necessity of the community unless you can show to the community that you are prepared to honour the highest results to which culture can arrive." To ensure that end, he urges, in his 1833 book, the institution of life peerages in the House of Lords for men of outstanding ability, the state endowment of university professorships and academic chairs, the conferment of honors for achievement in the literary, artistic, and scientific fields. Nor is this, it is worth noting, simply an argument based on a spirit of intellectual elitism. For Lytton is the aristocratic populist. "The true object of a State," he insists, "is less to produce a few elevated men than to diffuse a respect for all the principles that serve to elevate." A rational and wise system of honors, he admits, may not produce a new Milton or a new Michelangelo. But it would by degrees imbue the public mind with a respect for virtue and intellect and ability. It would show them that society rewards all classes of intellect and not, as presently happens, simply rewards military, legal, and political adventurers on the make only. "It is not for the sake of stimulating the lofty, but refining the vulgar, mind, that we should accustom ourselves to behold rank become the natural consequence of triumphant intellect." This will be a slow process, but it must take place. That Humboldt should be a minister of state on the continent has not produced new Humboldts, but it has created throughout the circles around him, and therefore throughout the larger society, an attention to and cultivation of the science that Humboldt embodies in his person.

Lytton, finally, has to address himself to the force or forces that will bring about all this. In his section on parties and politics, he outrightly dismisses both Whigs and Tories, for they both represent birth and wealth. His opinion of the House of Commons is equally negative; indeed, his short chapter describing a typical sitting of the House of Commons is contemputously scornful in a manner that only Dickens, somewhat later, could match. He wants, then, a new, independent national party composed of all of those—writers, thinkers, men of bold spirit—who think along genuinely reforming lines. He adds to this the further argument—one peculiar to Lytton—in favor of a popular monarchy, which constitutes, as he sees it, the best preservative from the domination of "brute wealth and oligarchical ascendancy." The general basis of these agencies will be a national educational system which, among other things, will incorporate the English endowed grammar schools with the end result of producing an intelligent citizenry eager to support them.

How does Lytton's book, in its entirety, look from the standpoint of the England of the later twentieth century? It is a book written with wit, urbanity, knowledge. Its perspective is European; indeed, its author is one of the last of the school of English political essayists to possess a European norm of value and comparison, before the tide of Victorian xenophobic, insular nationalism set in. The reforms he suggested were amazingly modern; and his perception of the power of the influence of the aristocratic spirit is attested to by the very fact that many of them still await fulfillment. The purchase of Army commissions was not ended until Gladstone's famous Minute of 1871. The principle of universal education, from the cradle to the grave, was not recognized in statutory form until the Education Act of 1944. The institution of life peers in the House of Lords had to await acceptance by the Wilson Labour Cabinet of the 1964–1970 period. The official recognition of the writer, the artist, the university scholar, as well as the actor and the popular entertainer, only came about during the same period. Yet it would be difficult to assert that the social disease Lytton emphasized so much—the class snobbishness of the national life—has in any real way disappeared. Contemporary England, despite the welfare state and the general loosening of interclass relationships, remains a society of aristocratic influence, business plutocracy, and middle-class insularity. The real criticism of the book, then, is that while recognizing the seminal root of all this in the institution of private property, its author was unwilling to see the necessity of a fundamental assault upon that institution. He thus treated the symptoms, rather than the main cause, of the national life. He seems not to have read any of the neo-Ricardian English socialists or pre-Marxist French socialists, some of whom had already published their work at the time his book was composed. That explains why he could not see that profound social change requires the agency of a social class to force it through, evidenced by the fact that the reform movements of Gladstonian Liberalism and Labour party socialism were in fact based on the support of the developing working-class movement. He himself dreamed of a small group of liberal reformers who would undertake the task; yet, as Professor Hamburger has shown in his book on the parliamentary career of the younger Mill and his Westminster radical friends—*The Intellectual in Politics*—such a group in itself was powerless to change the power structure of the established parties. The alliance of birth and wealth, then, continued as before. A later book, and another neglected

[104]

minor classic—T. H. S. Escott's book of 1886, *England: Its People, Polity, and Pursuits*—noted that fact:

> While thus in one sense it may be said that as a result of its structure the English Constitution is more democratic, inasmuch as it gives the masses more direct power over the action of the legislature, than that of the American republic, the conditions of this structure also ensure a steady and continuous exercise of influences, which if they are not aristocratic are at least anti-democratic, upon the multitude. At the present time the composition of the House of Commons is more dissimilar, perhaps, than it ever was before from the House of Lords. It is plutocratic rather than aristocratic, but the tendency in England is for plutocracy to assume more and more of an aristocratic complexion.

The English ruling class, in brief, continued to be, as it still is, a combination of aristocratic family and capitalist wealth, along with, perhaps, the new element of a middle-class meritocracy.

Because, then, Lytton could not see the new factory proletariat as the agent of his philosophical radicalism, it was no accident that, later in life, he became a Tory Democrat. There were elements of that ideology even in his 1833 book. For in one way the book is a plea to the aristocrat to transform himself and become the leader of a new England. He almost seems to argue at times that if the aristocrat accepts this role it will anesthetize the dangerous ideas of demagogues like Cobbett. Even the educational reforms he proposes can be seen as preparing the worker for a compliant subordinate role in industry and commerce, based on Taine's dictum—in that French traveler's account of England at a later date—that a people that is uneducated will be ungovernable. Lytton's Tory Democracy thus became, as with Carlyle and Dickens, a passionate nostalgia for a way of life in which an enlightened upper class will play the role of Good Samaritan to the masses, as a means of challenging the new mindless commercialism of the business civilization. "A Republic is cheap," wrote Lytton to Forster in 1848, "but

[105]

if ever that hour arrives it shall not be, if I and a few like me live, a republic of millers and cotton-spinners, but either a republic of gentlemen or a republic of workmen—either is better than those wretched money-spiders, who would sell England for one and sixpence."

Tory Democracy, perhaps, was a noble dream. Yet it was stillborn from the start. It was based upon an interpretation of English history that was entirely fanciful. It assumed a capacity of leadership on the part of the nobility by no means justified in terms of its actual record. That nobility was assigned the role of becoming a new Platonic epigoni; in reality, as Lytton himself saw, it was a class of "men without hearts, women without chastity, polish without dignity, and existence without use." Other parts of the scheme assumed, with Lytton, the revival of the power of the monarchy, almost as if he was writing Bolingbroke's *Idea of a Patriot King*. Yet Bolingbroke himself had admitted that such a monarch would be a "sort of standing miracle," a judgment borne out by the dismal record of the four Georges. It is astonishing that Lytton, a century later, could still embrace that fiction, for it is only necessary to read Thackeray's essay of 1850 on the Hanoverian dynasty to realize with what open scorn it was regarded by the public opinion of the day. The same judgment must be passed on Lytton's curious defense of the Church of England. Its deficiencies, he tried to argue, sprang solely from the control of the aristocratic spirit. Yet the very same year in which his book was published saw the beginnings of that Oxford movement which recognized a lot more shortcomings in its church than simply the power of aristocratic patronage in the assignment of livings. It is difficult not to feel that Lytton defended the church not because he himself was a deep religious believer but because, in typical eighteenth-century fashion, he disliked the puritanical fanaticism of the dissenting sects. In all of this, in brief, he was out of touch with the times. He was, as Lord John Russell said of Sir Francis Burdett, "a high prerogative Tory of the days of Queen Anne." In his own schizophrenic way, he was at once a utilitarian liberal and a

Tory Democrat, anxious to change the social character of England. But because he shared, with both those movements, a real fear of the masses, he did not see that the changes he wanted would be brought about, throughout the rest of the century, by forces with which he could have little sympathy: the revolt of the agricultural laborers, Chartism, the free-thought movement of radical rationalism, and the emergent trade-union movement.

[Chapter 3]

From Faith to Skepticism:
The Ordeal of the Victorian
Freethinker

A separate chapter in the development of English freedom belongs to the history of the free-thought movement in Victorian England. For if the eighteenth century saw the deist attack upon orthodox Christianity, the nineteenth century saw, as a logical successor, the rationalist assault upon the same system. No one can read the record of that story without a profound appreciation of the agony that it involved. For the transition from faith to unbelief is perhaps the most agonizing of paths along which a person can move. A universe of discourse they once understood and loved becomes a universe they cease to know. Their assurance that the burden of the mystery of life has been made understandable is somehow lost. They have no longer the inner conviction that the vast concourse around them possesses a final meaning, within the terms of which they have the comfort of consolation. They now pit their reason against social convention, political ostracism, the powerful tradition of ecclesiastical authority which regards the unbeliever as a dangerous *libertin*. On all sides they are surrounded by people, conventions, institutions, which call them back to the path they have deserted and which warn them of the awful retributions of desertion. They experience the poignant anxiety of the Christian who feels his faith irrevocably slipping away. They may insist, as did Pascal, that there is what he termed a silent opinion at the back of our minds which must be the secret standard of all things. They may argue, as did Renan in his revolt against the Jesuits, that they need what he termed an atmosphere of moral feeling that will justify their heresy. Yet, even so, the passage from belief to unbelief is so psychologically shattering that it cannot fail but leave a lasting mark upon both mind and spirit of those who undertake it. And beyond the merely personal trauma there is the realization of the grief and sorrow that they bring to those dearest to them—friends, family, spouse, colleagues—for whom their apostasy must seem the ultimate dereliction of duty and obligation. To others, their new ideology is proof of a sin in which intellectual vanity has overthrown the humility which should be the proper attitude of mankind to the mystery of life. To others, again, especially the guardians of the established political and religious order, they personify a challenge which must be broken lest their example poison the faith of others.

This constitutes, in essence, the history of the English freethinker in the nineteenth century. Its historical background, of course, was the vast movement of rationalistic European thought that had its roots in the new science and philosophy of the seventeenth century. For those disciplines, by their very method and character, undermined from the beginning the traditional interpretation of nature and life sustained by the orthodox religious outlook, both Protestant and Catholic. Early on, the Copernican revolution, carried on by Bruno and Galileo, assaulted the orthodox cosmology, which at every point accepted the geocentric theory. The Newtonian physics did likewise; and although no deist himself, Newton's system, as popularized by Voltaire, inestimably stimulated the freethinking spirit. Descartes, in turn, laid down a good part of the modern materialist philosophical way of thought; while Leibnitz, although no unbeliever, at least wrought a theist, instead of an obsolete orthodox basis for belief, thus indirectly undermining the orthodox position. In England, both Locke and Hobbes, arguing from different premises, presented an unchallengeable claim for religious toleration and a theory of social organization dispensing with the necessity for a state religion of any kind. Even more formidable as a scientific attack upon the creedal foundations of Christianity was the great work of the French Richard Simon, whose critical analysis of, among other things, the Mosaic authorship of the Pentateuch made him the founder, in effect, of modern methodical biblical criticism.

All this laid the foundations for the sweeping deistical movement of eighteenth-century Europe. In England, it saw the growth of a whole movement, at times openly deistical, at times merely pantheistic, that brought into question the whole structure of Christian supernaturalism and patristic authority. Toland and Collins carried forward Locke's idea of a "reasonable Christianity" to more radical conclusions, attacking the old arguments from prophecy and even forcing a ratiocinative habit on the clerical apologists themselves; Shaftesbury called into question the religious basis of morals; and Mandeville, in his famous *Fable of the Bees,* laid the foundations of scientific utilitarianism, with his argument that public virtues were simply private morals enlarged. Hume added to all this his formidable attack upon the absurdity of miracles, as well as a typical eighteenth-century contempt for all religious enthusiasm, so much so that in his ideal commonwealth he made the church a department of the state lest it should get out of hand. Hume, indeed, is the father of the secular-historical school, along with Robertson. The school reached its apogee, of course, in the great work of Gibbon, with its strictly sociological treatment of the rise of Christianity, and its absolutely antitheological examination of the successive waves of religious belief he so utterly disliked. In that sense, indeed, Gibbon stands on a par with the Italian historian Vico, who earlier on had been one of the pioneers in historiography to study the cardinal laws of civilization inductively from its phenomena. And how much this demythologizing process affected educated England is evident enough in the popular novels of the period, in which the clergyman is either portrayed, as in the *Vicar of Wakefield*, as a comical, eccentric, and harmless person, or, as in the later more hostile work of Paine and Cobbett, as a willing collaborator in the alliance of parson and squire that helped keep the English industrial and agricultural masses in thralldom. Certainly by 1760 most of the middle and upper classes had adopted a spirit of religious indifference summed up in the terse Erastian remark of Selden at the time of the seventeenth-century civil war, with all of its dislike for the bibliolatrous warfare of the time: "They talk much of settling Religion; Religion is well enough settled already, if we would let it alone."

In addition to all this—still by way of introduction—two other streams of thought contributed. In the first place, the great voyages of discovery, starting with the intrepid Jesuit missionary-travelers of the sixteenth century, opened up to European eyes pictures of other world civilizations which predated European Christianity historically and often surpassed it in terms of their ethical principles. Secondly, of course, there was the tremendous influence of the French philosophes, who were read as much by the intelligentsia of England as by that of France. Montesquieu's secular treatment of human affairs in his *Esprit des lois;* Voltaire's matchless ridicule of religious claims as not only false but pernicious; La Mettrie's mechanistic philosophy of mind; the vast work of the *Encyclopédie* in which freethinkers like Diderot, D'Holbach, and D'Alembert examined practically every subject under the sun in a pure spirit of scientific enquiry; Rousseau's final chapter of the *Contrat social* in which he demanded a new civic religion that would replace the obscurantist corruptions of Christianity; Volney's *Ruins of Empires* which saw Christian Europe within the framework of a cyclical historical pattern in which all civilizations rise and decline; Dupuis' *Origin of All Cults* which took a new step forward in the mythological analysis of the Gospel narratives; Condorcet's famous essay of radiant belief in progress written at a time when the events of the Revolution seemed almost to mock it: all of them attacked every institution of the age, including the church, with a merciless critique of reason. This, of course, is not to say that they presented a united front. Theirs, rather, was an eloquent luxuriance of new ideas often conflicting with each other. Thus Voltaire tended to think all religions absurd; Rousseau, on the other hand, as his famous *Confession of Faith of the Savoyard Vicar* in the *Emile* movingly shows, wanted a religion of sentiment rather than a religion of dogma. But, collectively, they all agreed that no institution could claim immunity to rigorous examination based on rational enquiry. They all subscribed, as has been well said, to the truth that whereas ancient Greece, with its dialectic discipline, exhorted people to make their beliefs agree with one another, and the churches of organized Christianity ordered them to make their beliefs agree with ecclesiastical dogma, the modern spirit demands that beliefs should agree with facts.

All this, in brief, was the tremendous legacy inherited by the free-thought movement of Victorian England. Yet it was a legacy with a difference. For the panic and reaction generated by the revolution of 1789 in the European ruling classes resulted in a revival of credulous religious thought that stultified the movement for an entire generation. For once Tom Paine stimulated a popular anti-Christian radicalism, combining heterodoxy with democracy, the ruling classes reverted to an orthodox revival on the ground that while religious skepticism could remain a fashionable fad in the salon, it became a dangerous challenge to their vested class interests once it became the fashionable fad of the public house and the mechanics' institute. For the upper-class elite, religion could be accepted as a private matter between the citizen and his church; but with respect to the majority poor, it became an institution necessary for the maintenance of public order against the threat of popular disturbances. The tomes of a Gibbon published at three guineas were comparatively harmless, since they were read by the London merchant or the country gentleman as little more than a pleasurable intellectual excitement. But the three-penny pamphlet put out by a Paine could erode the habit of social obedience in the mind of the intelligent working-class reader. The English and French deists had written for the middle and upper-middle classes. What now took place in England was a popular propagandist movement appealing directly to the multitude, starting with Paine himself and continuing with men like Richard Carlisle, Charles Southwell, William Hone, Robert Owen, all of which finally flowered into the secularist movement of Victorian England.

The panic and the anger of the English ruling class were proportionate to this new challenge. Paine would certainly have been imprisoned had he not fled to America. The radical bookseller like Carlisle was hounded and imprisoned; the radical editor like Foote was broken by the usage of the blasphemy laws; to which was added the further crippling burdens of the old system of suretyship on newspapers, and the disabilities of nontheistic witnesses in court proceedings. The famous Bradlaugh case, again, much later in the century, although finally ending with the acceptance of that great Rationalist lecturer as member of the Commons, showed how the old religious-oath system was used to hamper the political career of the agnostic. Nothing, perhaps, demonstrates the new reactionary climate of opinion more than the fact that, whereas the elder Pitt was reputed in his lifetime to be a deist, no English prime minister after him dared declare himself so, aptly demonstrated by the fact that although Disraeli hated Gladstone's religious cant, he himself was a cynical, power-mad politican too clever to say anything publicly about his sardonic view, privately held, about religion. For Victorian England, indeed, it was almost as if the deistical movement of the previous century had never existed.

This was the background of the new movement of Victorian free thought. It had to start the struggle almost anew as the new bourgeois respectability—even when the old repressive measures had disappeared—made the open expression of heretical views a hazardous enterprise. Economic pressure, social disapproval, the threat of loss of academic employment, all conspired to persuade the rationalist and freethinker to conform officially to the current creeds; punishment, although more subtle than in the earlier period, was equally real. Many of them thus retreated into pure science or scholarly research, preferring comfort to controversy. That explains why, to take examples only, Leslie Stephen could pass from the rigorous evangelicalism of the Clapham sect to an urbane skepticism with almost imperceptible ease, for his mind was cast in the mold of an eighteenth-century latitudinarianism so that his only regret seems to have been that in relinquishing his Cambridge tutorship on grounds of conscience he was closing the door to the comfortable existence of a Gibbon or a Warburton; or why it was only in his later leisured years that Huxley could bring himself to carry on a general conflict with orthodoxy; or why, finally, despite the obvious anti-Christian message of his seminal books, it was possible for the Victorian public to suppose that Darwin, buried as he was in Westminster Abbey, had died a Christian, until it was shown by his posthumous correspondence that he had definitely abandoned theism. The liberalizing thought, again, of men of letters like Matthew Arnold and, later, John Morley, was less shocking than open unbelief because it was based less on the growth of the new sciences identified with the various names of Faraday, Pasteur, and Laplace than on the older tradition in which Bentham and James Mill had applied the rationalistic ethic solely to the fields of ethics and psychology and law. The result, then, was that with Arnold the message simply dwindled into a vague gospel of "sweetness and light" that was bound, by its nature, to undermine the very conformities that he urged upon his Victorian public; and that with Morley it became the rather arid scholasticism of the mere man of letters.

For others, however, emancipation was more tragic. Edmund Gosse's description, in his *Father and Son*, of his father, one of the finest naturalists of his day, deliberately closing his mind to the geological revelations of Lyell and Darwin, showed that even a gifted intellect could continue to harbor childish errors. The suicide of Hugh Miller, who sought in vain to reconcile geology and Genesis, dramatized a rare Victorian method of escape. In the realm of poetry, Tennyson and Browning, Arnold and Clough traced the impact of the scientific-rationalist spirit in an impressive poetry of doubt and world-weariness. If autobiographies like that of the younger Mill seemed relatively untouched by the debate, others like that of Harriet Martineau were evidence of its agonizing character. The early Victorian novelists like Dickens and Thackeray, again, conscious of their middle-class public, said little either of sex or free thought in their work; but the later novels of Meredith and Hardy reveal their authors as writers earnestly concerned with the search for new sanctions of thought and action as the old moralistic postulates gave way under the pressure of the new intellectual processes. The universities, of course, remained indifferent to the turmoil as unreformed eighteenth-century seminaries for the sons of the rich; but there must have been numbers of obscure clergymen throughout Victorian England, having been educated at Oxford or Cambridge, who must have been tempted to embrace the crisis, described by Froude in his *Nemesis of Faith*, of passing over into the secular world from an Anglican church in which subscription to the articles had become nothing more than a necessary observation of the decencies, and of yet being unwilling to sacrifice a comfortable living in order to enter a new world that might perhaps never relinquish its suspicion of the apostate. But few of the clergy accepted that temptation, contented to remain within the narrow-minded, bibliolatrous atmosphere of the Anglican rectory; so that it is not surprising that the amiable, unthinking young curates who crowd the pages of Jane Austen's novels at the beginning of the century were not much different from the clerical figures pictured in Trollope's novels at the end of the century.

The real ordeal of the Victorian freethinker, as a result, was that of two specific classes in the society: one, that of the class of academics and writers usually located outside the ancient universities in the new colleges and institutes established in the years after the foundation in 1828 of the new University College of London; and, two, that of the more intelligent, self-educated workingman of the mechanics' institutes and "self-improvement" societies. They both suffered from the sectarian bigotry and public orthodoxy of their enemies in church and state. Holyoake's *Autobiography* is a record of successive imprisonments cheerfully suffered; and he is of special interest because he gave the name "secularism" to the antireligious cause, while his ordeal at the hands of the law in 1842 was the last trial by jury for atheism in Victorian England. Froude lost his Lincoln Fellowship at Oxford because of the publication of his *Nemesis of Faith*, while Pattison was denied by the same Oxonian conservatism the headship at Oriel that he deserved. Even the Nonconformist colleges were guilty of similar discriminatory behavior, as can be seen in the fact that much later in the century the Free Church College of Aberdeen deprived the great scholar Robertson Smith of his chair because of his heretical work in scriptural research. Indeed, as far as the more professionally academic writer is concerned, the real punishment lies in the fact that they were refused entry into the ancient universities which, until the end of the century and even after, continued to teach theological and philosophical systems made laughably obsolete by the great work of private scholars—including J. M. Robertson—in the anthropological and hierological origins of the Christian cultus, which work brought up to date the brilliant speculations of the earlier merely a priori mythologists in regard to the Christian legend, such as the once-famous works of Dupuis and Volney, with a modern scholarship unavailable to those pioneers. When it is remembered, indeed, that it was the theological scholar John Spencer of seventeenth-century Oxford who was the first to adumbrate the anthropological theory of sacrifice in his *De Legibus Hebraeorum*, and that as late as the end of the nineteenth century a later and intellectually degenerate Oxford did not even possess a chair in sociology, the contribution of the private scholarly freethinker comes to be seen as all the more remarkable.

For the second group of unbelievers—the intelligent workingperson—the ordeal of suffering, in the very nature of things, was more onerous. Police harassment, imprisonment, deportation—they suffered all. Yet it is important to note that most of these victims, at least for the first half of the century, were antireligious in only a vague, unsophisticated sense. Most of them were members of the Chartist movement, the main appeal of which was to an old-fashioned tradition of "freeborn Englishman" in the older radical manner, and whose attitude to religion was not so much deistical or atheist as it was an acceptance of a mythical reading of English history, after the manner of Cobbett's *History of the Protestant Reformation*, in which a romantic Merrie England of popular folklore and popular religion had been destroyed in the sixteenth century by Henry Tudor and the new commercial bourgeoisie. They thought in terms of an evil alliance of landlordry and "priestcraft" engaged in a conspiracy against popular interests; they thus had no insight into the sociological foundations of religion. It is true that an occasional Chartist, like the self-educated scholar Thomas Cooper, could describe in his memoirs how a reading of George Eliot's translation of Strauss's biography of Christ converted him from a Chartist organizer into a rationalist lecturer; but the same memoir also describes how he later reneged to become an independent popular religious speaker. Another Chartist memoir, that of the Lancashire agitator Samuel Bamford, also describes the author's disgust when the great Chartist leader "Orator" Hunt, at their sedition trial, fiercely denied before judge and jury that he had ever read one line of Paine's antireligious theological writings. If, indeed, Chartism had an ideology, it was that of an insular English radicalism, whose heroes were not so much the English deists or the French philosophes as John Ball, Wat Tyler, the Lollards, Wycliffe, Hampden, and Pym; a tradition summed up in Dickens' *Child's History of England* (1852).

At the same time, two points must be made. The first is that there must have been many ordinary working people of the Chartist persuasion who came near to a more definite free-thought attitude, especially those influenced by the three

Chartist leaders—Bronterre O'Brien, George Julian Harney, and Ernest Jones—who identified themselves at once with the deistical ideas of the French Revolution and the atheistical ideas of Marx. There was something of the same anti-Christian spirit in the Chartist poem of Cooper, "The Purgatory of Suicides," written in part under the stress of the horrors of early Victorian prison incarceration. Secondly, in the Victorian class society it was the workingman-skeptic who suffered the most. The middle-class skeptic suffered little more than the mental anguish of the clerical hero of the deistical Mrs. Humphrey Ward's novel *Robert Elsmere*, in which the author traced the confused pilgrimage of her hero through the whole spectrum of Victorian disbelief: Unitarian liberalism, materialism, theism, and agnosticism; and the book itself, although written with eloquent confusion rather than with rigorous precision, indicated how much middle-class Victorian England was obsessed with the crisis of faith. But the proletarian doubter could not afford the luxury of mere dabbling with dangerous ideas. So, the middle-class skeptic suffered no fate worse than that of *Robert Elsmere*. The working-class skeptic suffered, far more deeply, the fate of *Jude the Obscure*.

A general social or intellectual crisis, however, is always more poignantly illuminated by its particular examples. Three accounts of the Victorian effort to reconcile faith and reason—the *Phases of Faith* of Francis Newman, the younger brother of the more famous Anglican apostate John Henry Newman, the *Memoirs* of Mark Pattison, and the life and work of George Eliot—illustrate collectively the agony of the transition from belief to unbelief. All three of them elected to leave a world in which everything they had once cherished called upon them to return, and entered a new world so overwhelming in the weight of loneliness it threw upon them that they were only prevented from return by the knowledge that it would be a retreat to the security of bondage. All three, too, wrote their accounts of conversion as Victorians, with all the Victorian temptation to see everything, even revolt against religious faith, in morally absolute terms.

The figure of Francis Newman has been overshadowed, both in his own lifetime and later, by that of his elder brother, the great heresiarch John Henry Newman. His confessional *Phases of Faith* (1850) does not possess the subtlety, the elegance, the wit, the deep power of sarcasm and invective which makes of the *Apologia pro Vita Sûa* a document of timeless human interest. The younger brother's autobiography, nonetheless, possesses virtues of their own intrinsic quality: earnestness of tone, a scrupulous fairness to opponents, an anxiety to retain as much as possible of the Christian ethic rather than an eagerness to discard, and only discarding when the weight of evidence against a fact or an interpretation of the Christian corpus is so overwhelming that it must be accepted; avoiding, that is to say, the unattractive polemics that marked the attacks of his clerical enemies. Already at Oxford when the Oxford movement of the Tractarians was beginning to introduce a new reactionary neo-Catholic Romanism, he had resigned a Balliol scholarship because of inability conscientiously to accept the articles; and on leaving the university his boyhood dream of service as an Anglican priest had become transmuted into an academic career at Manchester New College and, later, at the London University College. A three-year missionary journey to Syria and Persia had also deeply impressed upon him the lesson that there existed other world religions, such as Mohammedanism, impervious, because of culture and language, to the dogmatic Christian missionary message, and, too, that the sectarian animosities between Christian, Jew, and Muslim he witnessed during his travels pointed to the uselessness of official church-based religions. The journey, indeed, left him with a lasting distaste for religious bigotry, of any color, and a world view, reinforced by his genius for languages, very few Victorians were ever able to cultivate.

And now, after a decade, in the *Phases of Faith*, he sets

out to map the various stages of his gradual rejection of the dogmatic elements of Christianity and his final arrival at a natural religion stripped of prophecy, miracle, and ecclesiastical authority. "I had become distinctly aware," he wrote, "that the modern churches in general had by no means held the truth as conceived of by the apostles. In the matter of the Sabbath and of the Mosaic Laws, of infant baptism, of Episcopacy, of the doctrine of the Lord's return, I had successively found the prevalent Protestantisms to be unapostolic. Hence arose in me a conscious and continuous effort to read the New Testament with fresh eyes and without bias, and so to take up the real doctrines of the heavenly and everlasting Gospel." He accepted—as against later scholarship—the historicity of the Jesus-figure. But he became persuaded that, despite the simple moral beauty of the Christ teachings, the scriptural texts that contained them possessed so many internal contradictions that it was impossible to accept the dogma of their divine inspiration. They were, clearly, of human origin; and, moreover, their various authors had borrowed much of their message from the popular cult religions, such as Mithraism, of the ancient Roman world. The Mosaic cosmogony, in turn, was incompatible with the new science of geology. Nor was the gospel portrait of Jesus completely edifying, for it revealed an itinerant preacher at once evasive, dictatorial, vituperative, and unjust; there was in his message a narrow Hebraic nationalism far inferior to either the Johannine hymn to love or the Pauline international message with its foundations in themes—universal brotherhood, the equality of races, the hatred of social oppression—which originally made early Christianity an electrifying popular message for the poverty-stricken multitudes of the ancient world. "Thus at length it appeared," he wrote, "that I must choose between two courses. I must either blind my moral sentiment, my powers of criticism, and my scientific knowledge (such as they were) in order to accept the Scripture entire; or I must encounter the problem, however arduous, of adjusting the relative claims of human knowledge and divine revelation."

Inescapably, he chose the latter alternative. The choice made it possible for him to see that none of the things that the founder of Christianity had prophesied ever happened. That was why, too, he goes on to argue, history had given rise to a church which the Christ-figure had not foreseen and in all likelihood would not have applauded had he seen it. "I saw," he wrote, "that the current orthodoxy made Satan eternal conqueror over Christ." The subsequent history of the Christian churches seemed to him to constitute a prolonged gloss on that text. Their institutionalization meant that they had developed the passion for worldly power that had seized the Roman state once the great age of the Antonines had passed away. The early Gospel ethic—combining as it did the earlier Jewish and Judeo-Christian apocalypses with the literature of the Hellenistic mysteries—had become an organized dogmatic system, finalized in the acceptance of Christianity by the emperors as the Roman state-religion. For if that move had been understood as a religious challenge to the orientalized Caesarism of the imperial office, in reality it meant that the church had become corrupted by the cynical opportunism that prompted the move. That is why, Newman tells himself, Christian social theory did not denounce slavery as an institution any more than it sought to elevate the status of women in the ancient world. Churches built on dogma became churches built on intolerance. "It is not practically possible," he wrote in one of his numerous pamphlets, "to reach a Christianity in which intellectual doubt is kindly welcomed and candidly satisfied. It is always treated as a sin, and easy faith magnified as a high merit." Nor was this simply the result of the churches accepting the embrace of the state. It was inherent, Newman argued, in the nature of doctrinal dogma itself. It characterized Catholic bigotry and evangelical piety alike. "But upon all those who mourn," he concluded, "for the miseries which bigotry has perpetrated from the day when Christians first learned to curse; upon all who groan over the persecutions and wars stirred up by Romanism; upon all who blush at the overbearing conduct of Protestants in their successive moments of authority—a

[121]

sacred duty rests in this nineteenth century of protesting against bigotry, not from a love of ease, but from a spirit of warmest justice."

Newman's book and pamphlets are not important for their scholarship. Although he made occasional references to the higher criticism of the German and Dutch scholars of the period, he came to his conclusions independently, so that his work carries little of the tremendous persuasiveness of their monumental learning. He failed, like most Victorian Englishmen, to understand the psychological foundations of the Catholic faith. His final position of a moral theism was not in itself intellectually convincing, for, as his more atheistical critics pointed out, he employed reason to discredit the claims of the supernaturalist canons yet retained a theistical position equally vulnerable to rationalist criticism. He did insufficient justice, perhaps, to the element of human nature in religion, to the truth that any religious movement seeking to enlist popular support must become emotionally attractive even though emotional faith may breed intolerance. His elder brother saw that truth when he wrote that the heart is "commonly reached not through the reason, but through the imagination by means of direct impressions, by the testimony of facts and events, by history and by description. Persons influence us, voices melt us, looks subdue us, deeds inflame us. Many a man will live and die upon a dogma; no man will be a martyr for a conclusion." The younger brother likewise tended to underestimate the element of human nature in politics. When, as an example, he argued in his pamphlet *On the Historical Deprivation of Christianity*, that Hooker and the sixteenth-century Anglican divines were better embodiments of the real Christian spirit than were their Puritan opponents, he failed to see that the great Anglican compromise of that period was really based upon an apologetic of raison d'état and not on a genuine conviction of the moral necessity of religious toleration.

Yet, in the last resort, Newman's contribution was positive. His is the story of an educated layman who came to reject an authoritarian religion he felt he could no longer in conscience accept. Each doubt, as it was conceived, was carried to its own logical conclusion. Nor were the consequences of the skepticism evaded. He was estranged from his family; his wife failed to understand him; and in a period when the average Englishman accepted the traditional creeds as the first principle of middle-class civilization he was subjected to scurrilous and virulent attack—as, indeed, Giberne Sieveking's hostile biography of 1913, *Memoir and Letters of Francis W. Newman*, sufficiently shows. There were moments of terrible loneliness. "My heart," he wrote, "was ready to break; I wished for a woman's soul, that I might weep in floods." Yet the emancipation was finally completed, with its central message being the argument for a secularist ethics which would rescue Christianity from the churches; for it was Christianity that had fashioned Christ, not Christ who had fashioned Christianity. To its influence must go considerable credit for the liberalization of the English intellectual climate within which later skeptics like Bradlaugh, Huxley, and Robertson could carry on the debate beyond the point at which Newman had left it; just as in the French case the doubts that Renan expressed in his *Souvenirs* (1883) helped to set the secularist climate of opinion which enabled the French socialists to challenge the central assumptions of the bourgeois Third Republic.

It has been fashionable to see the younger Newman's life in comparison with that of his elder brother, the later cardinal. But such efforts—such as Professor Robbins' book of 1966, *The Newman Brothers*—have tended too easily to see the story as just a human drama, studiously avoiding, in the academic manner, to pass judgment on either side. Yet in the long run it was the younger brother who best served the cause of freedom. For when from the *Apologia pro Vita Sùa* is taken its literary brilliance and compelling intellectual and psychological power it is clear that it constitutes a magnificent surrender of the individual mind to the claims of corporate ecclesiastical authority, first to Canterbury and then to Rome.

The heart of the argument is that of all the great issues that man confronts—poverty, disease, ignorance, social disorder—nothing essentially matters save the perception and acceptance of the road to salvation; that men fulfil themselves, as its author wrote elsewhere in his *Grammar of Assent,* only as they understand that only Christianity "has with it the gift of staunching and healing the one deep wound of human nature, which avails more for its success than a full encyclopaedia of scientific knowledge and a whole library of controversy, and therefore it must last while human nature lasts." Reason, we are told, is too infirm to meet the human burden. It must yield to faith; and, indeed, the "illative sense" of which Newman made so much was based upon little more than the premise of Pascal's famous wager, that the conclusions that reason reaches must conform to the assurances dispensed by the church. The analogy is apposite. For the greatness of Pascal lay, in part, in his immense scientific achievement, especially in mathematics, and in part in a deep psychological insight into the springs of human behavior quite distinct from the tenets of the church he accepted. The greatness of Newman is the superb artistry with which he subordinates so powerful a mind to a church prepared to grant him the promise of salvation at the cost of surrendering the right to use its power against its assumptions; we watch a drama of conscious self-immolation which stirs, like all suffering, the final impulse of compassion.

Against that total surrender the younger brother pitted his own liberal counterargument, for he rightly saw that it meant, as Renan put it, that reason vanishes in the presence of faith. For him, the right of the individual conscience to shape its own conclusions must be paramount. The history of the churches showed him what could happen when that right was denied. "The theory of each church," he wrote, "is the force which determines to what centre the whole shall gravitate. However men may talk of spirituality, yet let them once enact that the freedom of individuals shall be absorbed in a corporate conscience and you find that the narrowest heart and the meanest intellect sets the rule of conduct for the whole body." Institutions are not divine. They are composed of persons as much liable to error as others. To ride over the consciences of their members is a certain invitation to intellectual degeneration. "To scold down free thought," he argued elsewhere, "prepares the corruption of a religion by weakening the minds of the votaries." The elder Newman uncompromisingly accepted the argument, in his dogmatic assertion that "such troublers of the Christian community would in a healthy state of things be silenced or put out of it, as disturbers of the king's peace are restrained in civil matters." For the younger brother such a statement proved to him that contempt of reason was logically inherent in the Roman position, and that the contempt—which it was the final purpose of the *Apologia* to defend—by its very nature encouraged a chiliastic scorn for intellectual investigation and thereby ensured that men who cherished culture and intellect would come to dismiss with contempt a religion that seemed, to employ Gibbon's famous gibe, to identify Christianity with barbarism.

The spectacle of the two brothers thus utterly opposed in their outlooks vividly illustrates with a quite unique poignancy the nature of the Victorian debate. From a common point of departure in the intellectually lethargic Oxford of the 1830s they arrived at conclusions hopelessly irreconcilable. While the one, with his great decision of 1845 to enter the Roman church, surrendered his mind to an organization which, once the Roman honeymoon was over, itself viewed the apostate's intellect with growing suspicion, the other moved forward to a theism which in turn gradually became an activist social gospel. The one flies to the refuge of authority. The other hears and obeys the calls of reason. The elder brother was, perhaps, all the way through the prolonged agony of his road to Rome, temperamentally Catholic. He came to recognize that there could be no halfway house between Catholicism and complete skepticism, since no dogma has been able in the long run to withstand the dissolvent power of skepticism in open debate. The younger man had attempted as far back as the earlier idyllic

Oxford days to understand the other's doubts. But an invisible barrier had arisen between them. Francis was shocked when he finally realized that the Anglican priest had elected for so long to remain with the English church (in the years before 1845) even after he had embraced ultra-Catholic doctrine; and the grief of that discovery accentuated the division. The criticisms he felt were outlined in the memoir that later on in life he composed on the Cardinal, *Contributions Chiefly to the Early History of the Late Cardinal Newman*, a memoir fiercely resented by the English respectability. "He desired," he wrote of his elder, "to return not to the sixteenth century, but to the seventeenth, which can only mean, to the times of Archbishop Laud. My desire was to let all read the New Testament with fresh eyes, not preoccupied by human dogma." "He knew," he continued of John Henry, "that he hated Protestantism, but instead of quitting at once the Protestant Church, he fancied he might stick to it as long as he preferred an impossible Archbishop Laud to an actual Roman pope; instead of leaving it (as so many of the evangelicals) while he could do so, without compulsion." He was thus obliged to look on as his elder, so it seemed to him, inflicted a perversion of character upon himself, a mortal sin, as it were, that not even the final entry into Rome could assuage.

That the younger brother made the more liberating choice is evident enough from their subsequent careers. The elder brother retreated into the peace of the oratory. His real contributions to Christian thought had already been made, and the parameters of his mind seemed to contract as his eminence in the Catholic cardinalate increased. Francis Newman, on the other hand, once his breach with organized religion had been completed, entered into the full life of Victorian liberal causes. He wrote vigorously for those causes, many of them anathema in their own day: the decentralization of Parliament into more democratic local provincial councils; extensive taxation reform in order to build up a genuine welfare social-service state; the reform of local government; the breakup of the pernicious evil of large private estates in order to develop a healthy system of peasant proprietorship;

the elimination of the debarments, both legal and sexual, that made the Englishwoman, of all classes, nothing more than the chattel slave of her husband; the abolition of the evil of the rule of India by a white centralized bureaucracy which allowed no place for the educated native class; votes for women; legal reform; and, not least of all, the control of the barbaric international anarchy of the times by the institution of supranational legal-political bodies able to enforce international peace by means of an effective international police force. In many of these causes, clearly enough, he was far ahead of his times. He anticipated a new society in which social reform would flow from the acceptance of the moral beauty of the primitive Christian ethic. He thus made possible, later on, the growth of an organized socialism that would incorporate many of his ideas, and, at the same time, of a Christian humanism that flowered in the work of classical historians like Gilbert Murray and T. R. Glover.

Mark Pattison's *Memoirs* (1885) are likewise a record of how the citadel of a Victorian faith was undermined by free thought. Their interest, however, is of a slightly different order. For Pattison, in the beginning, had been a member of the undergraduate group of Oxford Apostles, including Frederic Harrison and the Froudes, that had yielded up mind and heart to the Tractarian movement started by Keble and Newman in 1833 and lasted up to the moment of Newman's famous conversion to Rome in 1845. They had all felt the impact of the moral and spiritual transformation that the movement had brought to old Tory Oxford. To be young, at Oxford, and under the powerful spell of the Newman personality, must have been an exhilarating experience. Arnold's later famous pen portrait of Newman, gliding as some spiritual apparition through the aisles of St. Mary's chapel, and rising to preach in beautiful language and enchanting voice one of his great sermons, is to capture in part the hold that the Tractarian leader had upon his young devotees. As Froude remarked of them, they knew no end but to do the

[127]

will which beat in their hearts' deep pulses. From the beginning, Pattison's shy undergraduate spirit responded to the magic. As with the young Leslie Stephen, his had been an evangelical background, and the deep earnestness of the Newmanite group at Oriel appealed to the ingrained sense of piety within him. By 1838, as he confessed, the "ultra-Catholic fanaticism" was his own. He read the church fathers; immersed himself in patristic bibliography; and stayed for a while with Newman himself at the famous Littlemore retreat. For years, as he described it, his reason seemed to be entirely in abeyance.

The passages in the *Memoirs* that describe the young novitiate's emancipation from that condition are curiously vague, almost as if suggesting some odd nervous disturbance. "As I had been drawn into Tractarianism," he wrote, "not by the contagion of a sequacious zeal, but by the inner force of an inherited pietism of an evangelical type; so I was gradually drawn out of it, not by any arguments or controversy against Puseyism, but by the slow process of innutrition of the religious brain and development of the rational faculties." Whatever peculiar experience the language inferred, it is certain that Pattison possessed an intellectual stubbornness denied to a fellow disciple like Hurrell Froude, so that whereas the latter, as his *Remains* show, sacrificed his critical instincts to the romantic medievalism of the movement, Pattison came to recognize its limitations; its intolerance, its unnatural asceticism, its morbid obsession with antiquated theological disputes, its religious conception of the guilt of error as distinct from the philosophical conception of truth for its own sake. By the middle of the century, then, he had broken away, and thenceforth devoted himself to teaching and to the movement of collegiate reform within Oxford, the latter in alliance with radical university reformers like Henry Vaughan, the main aim of which was to overthrow the religious framework of the university. The literary talent that had so far remained unused now fully asserted itself. He failed, indeed, in that sphere, to realize his ambition of rescuing the great sixteenth-century figure of Scaliger, the enemy of the Inquisition, and one of the great pioneers in the scientific treatment of biblical chronology, from the monopoly of Jesuit scholarship. But his fine essay on English religious thought between 1688 and 1750 in the controversial *Essays and Reviews* volume of 1860 was proof of his ability to undertake, what Anglican scholarship has rarely done; a concise history of the development of Anglican first principles. The essay, indeed, brilliantly diagnosed the reasons for the decline of genuine Christianity and the rise of political Anglicanism in the national religious life during that period. The spirit of toleration—that had begun, after all, with the seventeenth-century Anglican writers like Glanvil, Owen, and Hales, and from which Locke drew the arguments for his famous defense—had been overwhelmed by the reactionary mass of the Hanoverian clergy. It was in that sense, Pattison argued, that the publication of Locke's *Reasonableness of Christianity* opened, and the commencement of the Newmanite *Tracts for the Times* marked the fall of rationalism. It is true that Pattison did not elect to become, like Morris or Ruskin, a fighting critic of the Victorian bourgeois civilization. He retreated, instead, like so many others, into the protected corner of the life of the Oxford don; and there is in the *Memoirs* a fascinating portrait of the curious inner life of an Oxford college which, as a literary theme, has had to await the recent fiction of C. P. Snow.

The collision between the liberal like Pattison and the theologian like the elder Newman, indeed, can only be fully understood if it is seen as a dramatic struggle between 1833 and 1845 for the control of Oxford. For the Newmanite influence threatened, for a generation, to destroy the university as a real center of learning. Newman's analysis of the development of Christian doctrine was academically antiquated. He knew hardly anything of the work being done by Bauer and Strauss in the *Origines Christianae*. He was ignorant of the complex sources of Christianity in Judaism and Hellenism. His vast knowledge of his own church was theological rather than social. Everything dealing with the social and natural sciences he viewed with disdain and fear, for

[129]

he saw them as the fruit of the "spirit of lawlessness" that had come in with the Reformation. That intellectual myopia so truncated the academic curricula that Lyell recorded how, after 1839, the one or two students who took the lectures in Asiatic studies did so for no better reason than the expectation of a Boden scholarship in Sanskrit; while, later on, Jowett was to describe Newmanite Oxford as a school deficient in German, possessing only an inadequate knowledge of Kant and Hegel, and with a supreme contempt for the intellectual tradition of Locke. Liberalism, in brief, was a heresy to be rooted out; and there are few pages of the *Apologia* more revealing of their author's inquisitorial spirit than those in which he tells how it slowly dawned upon him that his Victorian Anglican church was really nothing more than the reincarnation of the great heresies of the fourth century.

Between such opposing camps there could be no *via media*. One had to be destroyed by the other. Looked at in this way, 1845 was not only the climax of Newman's long and tortured pilgrimage to Rome. It was also a signal that reason had finally won out against faith in the struggle for the soul of Oxford. There were those who felt regret; it was as if, in Gladstone's graphic phrase, a great cathedral bell had suddenly ceased tolling. Others saw more frankly the tremendous import of the event. Pattison wrote:

> The truth is that this moment, which swept the leader of the Tractarians, with most of his followers, out of the place, was an epoch in the history of the University. It was a deliverance from the nightmare which had oppressed Oxford for the last fifteen years. For so long we had been given over to discussions unprofitable in themselves, and which had entirely diverted our thoughts from the true business of the place. Probably there was no period of our history during which, I do not say science and learning, but the ordinary study of the classics was so profitless or at so low an ebb as during the period of the Tractarian controversy. By the secessions of 1845 this was extinguished in a moment, and from that moment dates the regeneration of the University. Our thoughts reverted to their

proper channel, that of the work we had to do. As soon as we set about doing it in earnest we became aware how incompetent we were for it, and how narrow and inadequate was the character of the institution with which we had hitherto been satisfied. We were startled when we came to reflect that the vast domain of physical science had been hitherto wholly excluded from our programme. The great discoveries of the last half century in chemistry, physiology, etc., were not known even by report to any of us. Science was placed under a ban by the theologians, who instinctively felt that it was fatal to their speculations. Newman had laid it down that revealed truth was absolute, while all other truth was relative—a proposition which will not stand analysis, but which sufficiently conveys the feelings of the theologians towards science. More than that, the abject deference fostered by theological discussion for authority, whether of the Fathers, or the Church, or the Primitive Ages, was incompatible with the free play of intellect which enlarges knowledge creates science, and makes progress possible. In a word, the period of Tractarianism had been a period of obscurantism, which had cut us off from the general movement; an eclipse which had shut out the light of the sun in heaven. Whereas other reactions accomplished themselves by imperceptible degrees, in 1845 the darkness was dissipated, and the light was let in in an instant, as by the opening of the shutters in the chambers of a sick man who has slept till mid-day.

From thereon, it was only a logical step to the university reforms of 1870 which made possible the entry into the university of, among other things, the teachings of the school of social liberalism of T. H. Green and his followers.

Few eminent Victorians, to come to the figure of George Eliot, embodied so attractively in their person and their work the life-force of rationalism. Her intellectual progress from the Midlands evangelicalism of her youth to a final position of passionate agnosticism, in addition to her consensual marriage with George Henry Lewes, brought her family estrangement, desertion of friends, and much social humiliation. But

[131]

she accepted it all with stoical cheerfulness; and it was characteristic of her generous and gentle spirit that she should have been more concerned about the disturbing impact of her apostasy upon those she loved than about what it meant for herself. Her abnegation of her inherited faith, indeed, was undertaken less as an act of defiance against religion and society than as a regretful necessity she could not deny. Her strong sense of duty to conscience, so typically Victorian, and her willingness to forgive those who could not forgive her, so typically Christian, elicited even from a shocked Victorian respectability a reluctant admiration.

The sources of her agnosticism were varied, mainly the historico-critical work of the German Higher Criticism and the new sociology of Comte and Herbert Spencer. She thus chose to counteract the Tractarian influence by making known to the English reading public, both through her translations of the work of Strauss and Feuerbach and through her own novels, the new currents of thought that were stirring on the Continent. Her fiction, particularly, once she was established as a major writer, helped dramatize the essentially private character of the erosion of belief, since, along with Meredith, she was one of the pioneers of the modern psychological novel. Both the elder Newman and Froude—the one in his *Loss and Gain*, the other in his *Nemesis of Faith*—had attempted to present religious controversy in the guise of fiction. It remained for a great artist to show them that, in that sphere, success required something more than thinly disguised argumentation. It is in the novels, then, rather than in an academic treatise or an autobiographical memoir, that her intellectual odyssey has to be traced.

"For my part," she wrote rather ponderously to a friend in her youth, "I wish to be among the ranks of that glorious crusade that is seeking to set Truth's sepulchre free from a usurped domination." Other influences apart from those mentioned helped her fulfil that ideal. The novels of Sir Walter Scott helped her to see—although Scott would have vehemently denied it—that there was no necessary connection between religion and virtue. The general spirit of writers like Carlyle and Emerson, who did not so much attack religious convention as ignore it, reinforced her growing doubts. An early introduction to Lessing's *Nathan the Wise* exposed her to the twin currents of eighteenth-century humanist thought: the lesson of the *Aufklärung* that the religion of the wise man is the religion of tolerance, and the Rousseauistic plea that real religion requires not the assent of reason so much as the simple feelings of the heart. Those general influences were quickened, in 1838 and 1841 respectively, by the reading of two curious English pioneering works of radical biblical exegesis: Isaac Taylor's *Ancient Christianity and the Oxford Tracts*, and Charles Hennell's *Inquiry Concerning the Origin of Christianity*. Both books, written largely in ignorance of the German scholarship, were destructive of accepted belief. The first took issue with the Tractarian propaganda to prove that the corruptions of ecclesiastical bureaucracy in the early church had emerged as early as the third century and could not therefore be regarded as the consequence of the imperial acceptance of Christianity as the state religion, thus refuting the Anglican temptation to blame everything on Rome. The second argued that the great legend of the Christian epic had to be seen, not as divinely inspired, but as the romanticized mythology of historical episodes in the life of the ancient Jewish people under the imperial oppressions of the Diaspora. There was a touch of Victorian melodrama about the latter volume. For it was originally undertaken by its author to still the doubts of a beloved sister whose bridegroom had employed the honeymoon period to assail her faith by reading her the books of Volney and Baron d'Holbach, and who ended up by yielding his own faith to the infidel texts. It is worth adding the fact that the eminent Strauss himself paid the book a handsome tribute by encouraging the publication of a German translation. That the two books were couched—unlike the earlier deistical polemics—in a spirit of calm judicious enquiry made them all the more appealing to the young girl. And if to all this is added the influence of the poetry of

Robert Burns—whose poems castigated the churches for their failure to fight for the rights of the Scottish Highlands crofters evicted from their lands by a landlordry anxious to convert them into huge sporting pastures, just as George Eliot herself later noted the apathy of the English churches in the face of the displacement of the Lancashire handloom-weavers with the advent of machine-based industrial capitalism, as she described that process in *Silas Marner*—the account of the various sources of her agnosticism is completed.

To move on to the continental positions after all this was a logical step. Her translations of Strauss's *Das Leben Jesu* and Feuerbach's *Das Wesen des Christenthums* carried her to the end of the road. The critical argument of both books completely destroyed the orthodox interpretations. For Strauss, the Christian literature emerges as the expression, in cultural mythology, of the Jewish national experience, both in the homeland and in the tragic exile. Its inner drama centers around the promise of a Messianic salvation offered to the Israelite subject-peoples in the Captivity, just as later the unknown mystic-author of the Book of Revelation prophesies the downfall of the hated Roman imperialism. The salvation did not materialize. But, for Strauss, the beauty of the Gospel ethic, as well as the revolutionary message of the Minor Prophets, remain for all time as historic responses of the oppressed of the ancient world against its cruel Oriental despotisms. For Feuerbach, more radically, the Christian documents, as much in their ideology as in the events they purport to describe, are to be seen as a sort of compensating magic in which men find consolation for the harshness of the social struggles in which they live. The two great truths that emerged from this scholarship—so shattering to the conventional view—were self-evident. First, there was the lesson that the corpus of the literature, both pre-Christian and Christian, could only be understood as elements in the eternal struggle of the wretched of the earth to seek consolation and relief from their bondage; that explains why Renan, in his *History of Israel*, could see in Amos and Hosea, Jeremiah and Isaiah (even though disapprovingly) the forerunners of the socialist parties of the Third Republic after 1871. Secondly, there was the lesson that the critical literature, by insisting, in Strauss's sentence, that the secret of theology is anthropology, made possible the development of the scientific study of comparative religion as a new scholastic discipline. For George Eliot, as for many others, it opened up an entirely new way of looking at the Christian heritage, the existence of which had not before even been suspected.

It was left to Marx, of course, to draw out the fully revolutionary implications of the historico-critical school in terms of its contemporary applications. George Eliot, like most fellow Victorian agnostics, could not go that far. What her reading of the literature achieved was to rob her of a moral serenity she could never fully recapture, and a stern message of duty based on the Christian ethical precepts. Most of her novels, in one way or the other, are concerned with the effort of their leading characters to discover some cosmic principle to fill the void of religious disillusionment. Like the hero of her *Daniel Deronda*, they are not so much militant atheists as devout skeptics who share her own dislike of controversy, her reluctance to cause needless pain to others, her possession, in brief, of a sort of reverent agnosticism. She appreciated, this is to say—as do most persons who have originally been brought up in a family religious background—the varieties of religious experience. "I have too profound a conviction of the efficacy that lies in all sincere faith," she wrote, "and the spiritual blight that comes with no faith, to have any negative propagandism in me."

She never lost, perhaps, a sense of nostalgia for that efficacy. Her chapter in her greatest novel, *Middlemarch*, entitled "On a Variation of Protestantism unknown to Abbé Boussuet," is done with affection, even though she knew that the Midlands provincial Methodism it described had little tolerance for free thought, least of all in women. While, again, Dickens could write of the Nonconformist religious world of hypocritical types like Mr. Chadband and Mr. Stiggins with fierce distaste, she could write of the Anglican world of types like Mr. Gilfil and Mr. Farebrother with critical kindness. She had a real understanding of beliefs other than her own. So, while Francis Newman could be horrified by an ideal of clerical celibacy and monastic self-denial that seemed to him to have twisted the doctrine of otherworldliness into a vast perversion of sexual human nature, she could write with severity and yet also with sympathy—in her *Essay on Dr. Cummings*—on the theme of how the self-righteous character of Calvinistic Puritanism had dried up the springs of social sympathy in its congregations. The truly religious society, for her, like the truly religious person, released the whole best of itself in the service of a larger good. The portrait of the gentleman-scholar Casaubon in *Middlemarch* —which can almost be seen as an anticipatory portraiture of the contemporary card-index research scholar of the university of today—was thus meant as a terrible example of the moral stultification that comes from the excessive cultivation of one faculty or talent in human beings to the exclusion of all others.

She was, all in all, even perhaps more than the younger Mill, the Victorian humanist par excellence. She fought valiantly against bigotry and dogma, from whatever quarter of the religious compass it came. Against the Anglo-Catholic theory of the Romeward movement—which assumed that once mankind was seen as the victim of an innate massive corruption that from the beginning had convulsed the infinite universe, it followed that nothing less than a moral sacrifice, so tremendous that the mind sank crushed before the contemplation of it, could restore the deranged balance —she argued for the sovereignty of the individual intellect and its divine right to make its own choice. Against the ugly sectarianism of the anti-Roman Protestant churches she echoed the noble protest of Coleridge—from whom she had learned so much—that "if any one begins by loving Christianity more than the truth, he will proceed to love his church more than Christianity, and will end by loving his own opinions better than either." That she thus enhanced the moral and intellectual quality of Victorian life is beyond doubt.

[136]

All this, of course, is the history of the battle between science and religion of early and mid-Victorian times. By 1870 or so, the battle had been won, and most of educated England was by that time religiously indifferentist, although it was still socially and politically dangerous to openly avow it. It is worth making a brief comparison with the similar struggle that was proceeding at the same time, although far more bitter, in the France of the Second Empire. For if the Victorian freethinker had to face a conservative state and a moribund church, the English liberal tradition at least made it possible that in the long run both state and church would give way, albeit slowly, to the tradition. By comparison, the French freethinker had to face a ruling class forced into a reactionary panic after 1848, and in control of a state completely ultramontanist, after the fashion of de Maistre's political theory, and of a Catholic church utterly determined to crush the liberalism which it viewed, in horror, as responsible for everything evil in French society. The alliance of Louis Napoleon and the pope meant the control of France for a generation by antisocialist reaction and papal absolutism. Historians like Guizot rehabilitated a Christianity already made obsolete by the spirit of the age; while Taine, later on, could devote the four great volumes of his *History of the French Revolution* to the facile thesis that 1789 was simply a pagan conspiracy that led logically to the Paris Commune of 1871. The control of the Catholic apparatus passed into the hands of princes of the church like Mgr. Dupanloup who could prostitute their real intellectual powers to justify the *Syllabus of Errors* of 1864; while its popular defense passed into the hands of disreputable journalists like Louis Veuillot, whose infamous *Odeurs de Paris* traced every vice of the corrupt regime of the Second Empire, from free thought to prostitution, to the revolution of 1789. The old school of liberal Catholics was swept away, to give way to a group of men who identified religion with the pope, property, and law and order, thus ushering in that civil war between the clericalist and the republican ideologies which gradually drove all of the masters of French thought into anticlericalism.

[137]

For periods of political stagnation are frequently periods of intellectual ferment. Protestant historians like Quinet and Catholic historians like Michelet defended the revolution of 1789 in monumental histories as the true embodiment of French national and democratic patriotism; both wrote books on the Jesuits that saw the Catholic church as the enemy of progress; while if Michelet, as in his *Bible de l'humanité*, argued further for a new universal humanist religion deriving new moral truths from India, Persia, and Greece, Quinet, in his book *Le Génie des religions*, employed the method of comparative religion to argue for a new ethics which would combine the best of the Christian heritage with philosophy, and of which he claimed to see in the Unitarianism of American thinkers like Emerson and Channing a noble example. The great literary critic Saint-Beuve, in turn, gradually progressed from a supporter of the Napoleonic regime to become, even though a member of the Imperial Senate, the protagonist, underneath his style of detached and elegant skepticism, of free thought and science; and his great life-work, *Port-Royal*, remains for all time the classic account of the seventeenth-century struggle between the Jesuits and their quasi-Protestant enemies, the Jansenists, whose doubts drove Pascal into his famous crisis of faith. To all this, finally, was added the contribution, essentially antireligious, of the poets and novelists of the period—Victor Hugo, Mérimée, George Sand, de Vigny, Eugène Sue, Leconte de Lisle— whether it was a romantic humanitarianism, led, incomparably, by Victor Hugo in the years of his self-imposed exile, or a poetry of fine pagan despair, as in Leconte de Lisle. Few of the readers, after all, of Sue's *The Wandering Jew* or Hugo's *Notre Dame de Paris* could have read those books without appreciating that the spirit that informed them was one of an impassioned hatred for the historical excesses of organized Christianity.

Yet there are two accounts of this—that of the Protestant minister Edmond Scherer and that of the Catholic *seminariste* Ernest Renan—that depict with peculiar poignancy the private anguish that it involved. For—typically French—many of the freethinkers of the time were almost born as such, in the Voltairian manner. The difference with Scherer and Renan is that, born and raised earnestly in their respective churches, theirs was a brave struggle to emancipate themselves from an inherited faith. Their careers possess, equally, the dramatic interest of evolution, each of them moving from strictest orthodoxy to complete free thought. Scherer, educated at the University of Strasbourg, moved to the Geneva Oratoire as professor, a school founded to defend orthodox Calvinistic theology against the more liberal teaching of the State Faculty. But growing doubts persuaded him to resign after four years, although it took him another eight long years before he fully renounced his Protestantism. Renan, by contrast, coming from the ultra-Catholic background of Brittany, over which the great events of 1789 seemed to have passed, leaving it still a part of the old feudal society, was educated at the Jesuit seminary of Saint Sulpice which still retained the combination of otherworldliness and brilliant learning which, two centuries earlier, had already made it almost the peer of Port-Royal. It was still strongly tinged, indeed, with Cartesianism; and it was the reading of Malebranche, along with his Hebrew studies, that gradually eroded the faith of the young novitiate, finally persuading him to leave the church in the same year, 1845, that Newman entered it.

It was a life-or-death struggle for both of them. Renan's *Souvenirs* reveal how the passion of intellectual curiousity made him into a rebel against a church that demanded conformity which need not be genuine so long as it was publicly decent. His Hebraic studies, resulting in his great work *Corpus Semiticarium Inscriptionum*, led him to discover that the simple tenets of the New Testament concealed complexities of text and authorship not easily reconcilable with official doctrine. His philosophical studies brought him a lifelong passion for the German romantic literature; while it is worth noting that he should have learned his philology from the forgotten volumes of that Jansenist Archbishop of Lyons, M. de Montaret, who had tried so vainly to fit Cartesian principles into the framework of medieval scholasticism. He told his friends that it was not in the power of institutions to stifle that passion to examine which, however wretched in spirit it will make him, will yet brook no denial, especially the institution of the Catholic church in which, in his phrase, a single error proves that the church is not infallible, and a single weak point proves that a book is not revealed. "Man," he wrote to the Abbé Cognat, "can never be sufficiently sure of himself to swear unwavering fealty to a given system, though at the moment of his vow he hold it true. All he may do is to dedicate himself to truth, whatsoever she be, wheresoever she lead him, no matter what the sacrifice she may demand." He felt on the threshold of a new world, and to read his moving *Lettres Intimes* to his sister Henriette is to see him looking questioningly at the tenacious dogmatism of a church which is fighting a losing battle for an impossible metaphysic and an outmoded interpretation of the Bible. The break, then, was inevitable. Yet, on Renan's part, it was made without bitterness or rancour. The *Souvenirs,* indeed, paint a picture of his affectionate regard for his teachers at Saint Sulpice, for he had none of the anticlerical violence of Lammenais. The main note of the memoir, on the contrary, is a spirit of tolerance which insisted not so much on freedom of enquiry because men have a right to entertain absurdities, but because the scholar has the obligation to be hospitable to all ideas, to congratulate his adversary on his convictions even while trying to detach him from them, even to console him for causing him to abandon them. The end result of all this was Renan's entry into a new life of secular scholarship. "Believe me," he wrote in his later *Avenir de la Science*, "your true philosopher is the philologist, the student of myths, the critic of social constitutions." That combination of spiritual gentleness and rigorous scholarship went into the making of his sympathetic portrait of the Christ-figure in his famous life of Jesus. No man, as one French critic put it, has ever been the worse for reading Renan's *Vie de Jésus*.

For Scherer the experience was far more traumatic. For whereas Renan passed almost immediately from the religious to the secular world, Scherer took twelve agonized years to release himself finally from his beloved Protestantism. For the best part of his life he had been, theologically, so to say, a child of Calvin's Geneva. Yet his reading of the new critical literature—including Bishop Colenso's demolition of the theory of the Mosaic authorship of the Pentateuchal narrative—during his tenure of the professorship of biblical exegesis at the oratoire drove him into the beginnings of serious doubt. As one reads his *Confessions d'un Missionaire* the distress that the process brought is vividly realized. He wrote of men like himself:

> They did not doubt in order to get rid of a doctrine, the holiness of which weighed upon them; they did not deny it because it was their interest so to do; it was in spite of themselves that their faith left them. Far from seeking out objections, they have recognized their weight with reluctance. They yielded to evidence. Their souls, when they saw for the first time the abyss gaping before them, were seized with immense and grievous terror; they cast themselves on their knees, they struggled with tears, they tried all remedies, had recourse to all advisers. Feeling the thoughts that had been their joy and their strength escape from them, realizing the worth of all that was about to fail them, not conceiving that anything could ever fill the vacant place, accustomed to considering dogma as the food of spiritual life and the only safeguard of human virtue, it seemed to them that they were going to fall endlessly into abysmal darkness.

They are led, he ended by saying, to unbelief, then, paradoxically, through their very devotion to religion itself.

His tragedy, as he thus clearly saw, was that he longed for an unchangeable faith in an age of transition. The edifice of the Old World rested on the acceptance by all of unquestioned first principles. Calvinism placed an absolute barrier between truth and error; there was nothing else to query. "Today," Scherer admitted reluctantly, "nothing for us is truth or error; we must find other words. We see everywhere nothing but shades and degrees. We must admit even the identity of contraries. We no longer know religion, but religions; ethics, but customs; principles, but facts. We explain everything, and as it has been said, the intellect approves in the end whatever it is able to explain." Contemplating this tremendous collapse of all the old certitudes, he could only compare it to the general dismay that spread throughout the world when Pantagruel, in Montaigne's great satirical tale, announced the death of the great god Pan. The impact of all this on his spirit was so tremendous that, unlike Renan, he felt incapable of moving on to an alternative philosophic system. His skepticism of all systems was complete; and he ended with a consolatory stoicism learned from Marcus Aurelius.

The Anglo-French comparison becomes even more intriguing if one notes the divergent responses to the crisis in Catholicism of two great sons of the church—the Abbé Loisy in France and Lord Acton in England. They were both part of the generation which, with the promulgation of the formal decree of Papal Infallibility at Vatican Council I (1870), lived through the most vital decline that had ever taken place in the life and power of their church. Both were Catholic historians. Yet while the Frenchman, in response to the crisis, was excommunicated by Rome, the Englishman elected to remain within the system.

Loisy's odyssey is described in his *Mémoires*. The stage had been set for his critical work, of course, by the earlier work of scholars like Keunen and Wellhausen in Germany and Peyrat and Havet in France, as well as by the impact of the new areas of knowledge opened up by Egyptology and Assyriology. His ambition was to restate orthodox dogma and theology in the light of that new learning; for what had perished forever, he urged, was the combined dominion of magic and myth in religion. The church, he argued, must accept the weighty evidence of the discoveries of the century: the proven debt of Christianity to the Roman cult-religions, the gross unreliability of the Gospel accounts, the deliberate construction of a Christ-legend by the later commentators, the relationship of the movement to Judaic nationalism. The historical Jesus, in his books, emerges as a peasant agitator caught up in a vast religious ferment, the meaning of which he misunderstood, but whose Messianic message gave hope to the disinherited multitudes of the ancient world. The Gospel anticipated the end of the world in its own lifetime; it did not seek, accordingly, to institutionalize itself into an established religion, which thus must be seen as dangerous accretion. "What we have to do," he wrote, "is to renovate theology from top to bottom, to substitute the religious spirit for the dogmatic spirit, to seek the soul of theological truth, and to leave reason free under the control of conscience." He clearly saw the difficulties involved:

> Certainly the adoption or toleration of scientific methods by an institution like the Catholic Church is difficult, because great social institutions, particularly religious ones, are governed by routine, and because the Roman Church, in the interests of domination, claims to be unchangeable by principle and even by the will of God; but it is not impossible, because institutions only endure by adapting themselves to the changing conditions of humanity. . . . The Church, composed of men and administered by men, is a human institution and human institutions must be carried forward or be destroyed in the vital evolution of human life.

Yet all this—part of the Catholic modernist movement of the time—was doomed to failure. It is vital to remember that when the young Loisy entered the seminary at Chalons-sur-Marne the victory of the reactionary ultramontanists of 1870 was already four years old. Rome reacted in a mood of panic; the Institut Catholique deprived Loisy of his professorial chair in 1893; and he was finally officially condemned by the Curia for the publication of his book, *L'Evangile et l'église*, in 1907. The documents of his condemnation graphically reveal the temper of the hierarchy. His work, it is alleged, disturbs the belief of the faithful. It destroys the very basis of the faith. It is the sign of an intellectual pride which refuses to accept the lesson that the answer to difficult or obscure text in the sacred literature is the resort to prayer. How uncompromising the official reaction was, indeed, can be gauged from the fact that, in the condemnation of Loisy, Cardinal Parraud of the French church should have felt compelled to quote against him the angry language which two centuries earlier Bossuet had employed against the rationalist investigations of Richard Simon. Loisy, reluctantly, recognized his defeat. He could truly say, in a letter to his friend Miss Petre, that "in reality, the Roman Church is being transformed into a barracks, with intellectual and moral mobilization." He was driven from a home that he had cherished; he could properly remark that he was the victim rather than the agent of the crisis. It was typical of his Christian temper that, once evicted, he did not choose to fight back, but finally moved forward toward an acceptance of the mysticism of his friend Brémond.

Lord Acton's response was, by any standards, far less heroic. His recent biographers, like Gertrude Himmelfarb and Bishop Mathew, have been far too kind to him in discussing his role in the crisis. Like most commentators, they have been too overwhelmed by his reputation as the most erudite historian of his times to dare criticize him. He has been called a "rebel against the Vatican." Yet it would be difficult to imagine a rebel so cautious, so prevaricating, so anxious to minimize the real meaning of the victory of Vaticanism in 1870. It is true that he condemned the new dogmas announced by the council. But he did it in language so insufficiently culpable that Cardinal Manning was unsuccessful in his attempt to have him excommunicated. He indulged, in fact, in a series of intellectual gymnastics involved in straddling the fence between submission and resistance; he even invoked Fenelon's argument that a loyal Catholic could publicly aver his orthodoxy and privately protest the truth of his condemned views, a dubious theisis based, perhaps, on his conviction—clearly heretical in any Catholic—that it was possible to give formal adherence to a decree while reserving private judgment on its meaning and even its legitimacy. That explains why he was dismayed by Gladstone's *Expostulation* of 1874 which argued, correctly, that the Vatican decrees logically demanded that all national congregations, including the

English, owed their primary allegiance to Rome, thus demanding civil disobedience to the state if and when a conflict of loyalties should arise.

But there was even a more fatal flaw in Acton's position. He had made the cardinal principle of his theory of history the stern application of an absolute moral judgment irrespective of historical time and place; yet in arguing that the Vatican decrees should be accepted so that time would soften their ultramontanist implications he was, in effect, employing the quite different thesis of historical relativity. He never reconciled, in fact, his historical science and his Catholic faith. He wrote savage indictments of the history of the popes which at times outmatched the most virulent of rationalist attacks (although, suggestively, the most savage of all were contained in his private correspondence); and he could remain in a church with fellow members like the Jesuits of whom he wrote to Mary Gladstone that "it is this combination of an eager sense of duty, zeal for sacrifice, and love of virtue, with the deadly taint of a conscience perverted by authority, that makes them so odious to touch and so curious to study." It is true that the Jesuits were no longer the powerful order they once had been. But the spirit of Vaticanism was essentially Jesuit; as was also the spirit of the rulers of the church who pushed through the 1870 reaction: the scholar Duchesne who was too obsessed with the dream of a professorial chair in the Institut de France to allow conscience to stand in his way, the prudent trimmer like von Hügel, the perfect ecclesiastical diplomat, who used his contacts to strengthen his position in the hierarchy, the Mgr. Dupanloup of whom few stories are more damning than the pages in Renan's *Souvenirs* in which Renan describes how the future cardinal-archbishop effected the reconciliation of the aging sinner Talleyrand with the church. Yet whereas Acton's great mentor, the German scholar Dollinger, left the church rather than be associated with such men, his disciple elected to remain.

If, then—in Renan's metaphor—the Catholic theologian was a bird with its wings clipped, the Catholic layman like Acton

[145]

was a liberal with his hands tied behind his back. He could write as liberally as anyone on the supremacy of truth, as in his assertion that "a discovery may be made in science which will shake the faith of thousands; yet religion cannot regret it or object to it. The difference in this respect between a true and a false religion is, that one judges all things by the standard of their truth, the other by the touchstone of its own interests." Yet he could not come to the point of recognizing that his own church, by that token, was guilty. The manner of his thought, with its paradoxical subtlety, fatally crippled him from such definitive assertions. He seems to have thought as if he could repeat within his church the role of the leader of a forward-looking wing, which he played, as an intimate ally of Gladstone, in the Liberal party of his time, without realizing that they were two entirely different organizations in spirit. For English liberalism was a secularized politics, Roman Catholicism a religious imperialism. So, while the elder Newman came gradually to realize, after 1838 or so, that his differences with his Anglican church were so profound that only secession could resolve them, Acton remained in a Catholic church despite the fact that his differences with it were no less profound. The last word lay then with Loisy. "Being convinced," he wrote, "that theological orthodoxy could not in the long run prevail against scientific truth, but would be forced to reckon with it and accommodate to it, I did not think that the fact of having lost confidence in the absolute value of traditional dogmas unfitted me for the teaching of exegesis in a Catholic faculty. . . . The great— I might say the only—difficulty, against which I was to be broken, was real, substantial and living; it was the authority, or rather the tyranny, which in Roman Catholicism has supplanted, not only the Scriptures, but even tradition, and which aims at the domination of thought, history and politics."

It may well be that Acton did not write his planned monumental history of liberty because he almost certainly knew that it would have been placed on the *Index*. He was only in fact saved from excommunication because Rome was unlikely to mete out to a communicant who was at once an English peer and a member of the European social aristocracy the treatment that it meted out to the son of a Marne peasant. Acton's failure, indeed—for, after all, he was a staunch free-thinker in his own chosen field of history—becomes all the more emphatic if it is remembered that the only penalty he could have received would have been that of excommunication. Earlier on, it had been different. Spinoza had been persuaded to end a famous chapter of his *Tractatus Theologico-Politicus* in defense of free thought with a declaration of his readiness to submit to the censorship of the rulers of the seventeenth-century Dutch state, while with the memory of Galileo's fate in mind Descartes had relinquished his grand scheme of writing an encyclopedic treatise on the nature of the world in order to preserve peace with the Catholic church; for both knew that the penalty of heresy at that time could mean imprisonment, perhaps even death. Living in the golden afternoon and twilight of liberal Victorian England, Acton faced no such danger. Yet he failed, unlike others, to carry his free thought to its bitter end.

Victorian free thought, by any standard, contributed immensely to the victory of liberalism during the century. It put organized religion on the defensive. It decisively defeated the defenders of religion in the intellectual debates of the time, whether it was Darwin and Huxley on one front, or Bradlaugh and Clifford on another. It helped bring to an end the real terror of divine retribution for sin that haunted the spirit of even educated Victorians. It had, of course, its own defects, for it was never a single, coherent movement so much as an undisciplined congeries of different elements, each often going its own way. Annie Besant went off into the stratosphere of theosophical studies. Samuel Butler used his agnosticism to get sidetracked into a fiction of esoteric satire against the more absurd aspects of the Victorian bourgeois scene. Scientists like Maxwell, who, along with Faraday, established the modern science of electromagnetic technology, still managed to retain powerful elements of mysticism in their nonscientific selves. Many of the antireligious protagonists, again, failed to penetrate behind the appearances of religion, in dogma and theology, to the reality of the social and economic class interests that religion only too frequently defended. Thus, the enormous popularity of Comtean Positivism immeasurably helped the cause of the antireligious movement; but whereas in the hands of the Fabian socialists it became a tool in the collectivist cause, in the hands of Herbert Spencer it became part of an antistate sociological synthesis catering to the most reactionary views of the Victorian business class. Much of the rationalist movement, this is to say, was at once intellectually nonconformist and socially conservative; so, to take another example, Lecky's learned *Rise and Influence of the Spirit of Rationalism in Europe* ended in its last pages with a eulogy of the new capitalist industrial order and pious congratulation on the fact that the English working class had not succumbed to the socialistic attacks upon the rights of property that had disgraced, in Lecky's words, the French democracy. The attack, then, upon that new industrial capitalism had to come, paradoxically, from the social gospel elements within the churches themselves, beginning with the 1848 Christian Socialist movement within the Church of England. Notwithstanding all that, however, the final comment upon the freethought movement must surely be that it achieved the end result of bringing about a new climate of thought in which religion ceased to play a primary role in the general cultural process, and the religious compulsion began to lose much of its original omnipotence.

[Chapter 4]
1848
The Christian Socialist
Contribution

The post-1848 Christian Socialist movement in the Church of England may legitimately be regarded as the pioneer of all those subsequent movements—the social gospel movement in America, Catholic Socialism, the dialogue between Marxist and Christian of the present day—that have attempted to reach a common ground between the secular and the religious world-outlooks. For whereas the rationalist movement sought to undermine the credal and historical foundations of Christianity, the radical churchmen of 1848, led by the remarkable trio of F. D. Maurice, Charles Kingsley, and John Ludlow, sought to renovate its social and economic implications. The literature on the movement has been woefully inadequate. Canon Raven's early book of 1920 suffered from the temptation, simplistically, to see everything in the movement as socialist, which of course it was not, for it contained a large dose of both Tory Democracy and mere social reformism. Torben Christensen's book of 1962, on the other hand, overemphasizes the theological elements of the movement, hardly the most exciting part of the story. Kingsley, because of his flamboyant personality, has been written up by innumerable superficial biographers seeing him as an Anglican eccentric or "Parson Lot," and failing to deal with the serious character of his socialism, as he understood it. A serious analysis of the movement has to look more closely at its literature: the *Tracts on Christian Socialism*, conceived in part as an answer to the socially reactionary *Tracts* of the Oxford movement of Newman; the weekly newspaper, *Politics for the People*; and its successor *The Christian Socialist*.

The leaders of the movement were an impressive group of men. Of the unique quality of Maurice, its acknowledged leader and theological mastermind, there is universal agreement. It is true that no one today, except perhaps the professional theologian, reads his weighty tomes; he attempted, unsuccessfully, to develop a sort of Johannine-Platonist ecumenical theology walking a tightrope between the narrow individualism of the Protestant sectarian type and the authoritarian tradition of the organized churches, while his understanding of the debate between science and religion was so inadequate that, as one of his biographers has put it, he was saved from any real antagonism to the rationalizing movement because he no more understood it than a traveler newly arrived in some distant land understands the purport of its most idiomatic and hurried conversation. His greatness lay, rather, in the moral force of his personality. He was the genuine Christian; possessed, as Ludlow remarked, of a humility so intense that he was afraid of his own greatness. He had the rare ability to awaken in others an awareness of their inadequacies and at the same time a capacity to arouse in them a determination to improve themselves. There was in him, the German observer Brentano noted, a striking union of severe earnestness of purpose with an irresistible kindliness. He thus exercised a magnetic authority over all who knew him, whether in the famous circle of the Cambridge Apostles or in the conferences with the London working-class leaders that formed so important a part of the Christian Socialist effort.

Kingsley, quite differently, was one of those men in English history possessing all the qualities that have gone to make up the *homo anglicanus* at his best: thoroughly argumentative, boisterously aggressive, eager in heart rather than precise in intellect, anxious for ready action, unable to rest in the presence of injustice. It is the type of Pym and George Fox,

Cromwell and Wesley; and it was not for nothing that his heroes in English history were the great sea captains of the Elizabethan era who had defended the new Tudor church and nation against the Counter Reformation. He was certainly no great Anglican scholar, as the treatment that he received at the hands of Cardinal Newman in their famous exchange showed. But he had a robust capacity for fierce indignation in the cause of the downtrodden masses of Victorian industrial society. His contribution to the movement, then, was less the manufacture of a coherent theory than it was the effective popularization, by means of sermons, pamphlets, and novels, of ideas fashioned by others. He possessed—not the most common of gifts in the type of the Anglican clergyman—a genius at mixing with all types of men without the awkward condescension to the poor so typical of the religious type; and that he was able to evoke the admiration and affection of them all—the London factory operative, the agricultural laborer, the Aldershot army officer, the Cambridge undergraduate—was not the least measure of his sincere and compelling personality. Like Conrad Noel after him, he was, as it were—granted all the differences between early Victorian England and twentieth-century Latin America—the Camilo Torres of his time.

Ludlow, different yet again from his Anglican colleagues, belongs to that type of democratic-radical international itinerant who has from time to time dropped into the English radical movements and given them a healthy injection of wider international sympathies and ideas. Born in India and educated as a young man in Paris, he had read widely in the French pre-Marxian socialists and possessed also a wide knowledge from close observation of the Parisian workers' associations that had been thrown up by the revolution of 1848. In addition to that, a brief period in the West Indies left him with a lifelong interest in the problem of slavery. Unlike his colleagues, he had a ready command of the technical and legal problems involved in matters organizational; and it is only necessary to read his evidence as a witness before the parliamentary select committee that sat in

1850 to investigate the need for legislation to set up working-class trade associations to appreciate the value of his talent in that area. He was, in fact, the originator of the movement, for it owed its inception to the letter that he sent to Maurice from Paris in the early spring of 1848, describing the socialism of the French workers as a challenge which Christianity would have to meet or perish. It was only fitting that he should have been a direct descendant of the soldier-radical Major-General Ludlow of Cromwell's New Model army of the revolution of 1640.

Nor were the lesser figures of the movement less attractive. Parish priests like Hansard were models of lives of eloquent witness to the early Christian ideal. Thomas Hughes had the irresistible charm of the Rugby schoolboy type, although his popular idyllic account of public-school life in his *Tom Brown's Schooldays* could hardly be called a revolutionary manifesto. Vansittart Neale gave up two fortunes, at the price of final impoverishment, to help finance the cooperative shop experiments of the movement. In such figures as Lloyd Jones, the disciple of Owen, there was a direct link with the Chartist revolt. Thomas Cooper helped to advertise the cooperative societies through his *Journal*, while aristocrats like Goderich were evidence of the close relationships existing between Christian Socialism and "Young England." Cuthbert Ellison, indeed, was a member of both movements; and we are assured by Ludlow that he was the original of Thackeray's Arthur Pendennis. There were lawyers like Bellenden Ker and clerics like Stanley and Trench. The early death of the promising young chemist Charles Mansfield deprived the movement of a valuable professional person, and it is to his influence that Kingsley owed his interest in the cause of public health and sanitary reform. There was, again, the inevitable French political refugee: Martin Nadaud was a worker friend of Louis Blanc; as well as the French political adventurer like Jules le Chevalier, who later wrote a book irresponsibly exaggerating the importance of his role in the movement. The young Chartist poet Gerald Massey was also a member, rising from obscure poverty to become, after his Christian Socialist phase, the student of Egyptian mythology, although he never lost the democratic touch characteristic of the Victorian worker-poets like Ebenezer Elliott and Robert Nichol. There were, finally, sympathizers like David Masson, the poet Clough, the publishers Daniel and Alexander MacMillan, Arthur Helps, Spedding—the great Victorian editor of Bacon— and the Reverend John Sherren Brewer, the equally great editor of the state papers of Henry VIII. It is of interest to note, too, that the younger Mill himself—who gave valuable aid to the movement in its parliamentary lobbying for the passage of the important Industrial and Provident Societies Act of 1852—was only prevented from joining the movement because of its religious connections. To name all of these is to illustrate the success of the movement in recruiting, in typical English fashion, members from all classes and all walks of life.

The immediate occasion of the movement was the fiasco of the last great public meeting of the Chartist revolt in the summer of 1848. The Christian Socialist leaders shared none of the Chartist aspirations. But they felt deeply that Chartism was a natural response to the grievances of the English worker and peasant. Kingsley's hurried visit to London from his country rectory after that last Chartist defeat was born of his desire to assure their shattered forces that there were still elements in the middle and upper classes that viewed their cause with real sympathy. The immediate outcome of that visit was the decisive meeting with Ludlow and the drafting between them both in a long night of frenzied work of the *Address to the Workmen of England* which Canon Raven has described as "the first manifesto of the Church of England, her first public act of atonement for a half-century of apostasy, of class-prejudice and political sycophancy."

The main energizing thrust of the movement was thus the sense of stricken conscience, a sense of undeserved privilege,

[153]

a conviction that the church had failed in its trust to the poor and the oppressed. Its literature is full of the note of self-indictment and earnest repentance. The church, it felt, possessed little significance for the popular audience. "Our words and phrases," confessed Maurice, "touch no want of which they are conscious, excite in them no fears, kindle in them no hopes." It noted with pain that the typical working-class leader was more at ease in negotiation with the average member of Parliament than in conference with the Anglican minister. "We have told you," Kingsley acknowledged to his working-class readers, "that the Bible preached to you patience, while we have not told you that it promised you freedom." Both of them, in turn, recognized the roots of that failure in the historical fact that the clergy had become, since the Reformation, the handmaiden of the state, the ally of the comfortable and wealthy classes. "The English clergyman who most properly represented the age of George III," their literature wrote of the type, "understood that he was not meant to be a recluse, that he had a work to do in the world, that he was cast among men, and was to understand men; that he had social duties to perform. But unhappily his notion of society was derived from the maxims of the upper classes, in London or the country. Society meant well-behaved people, magistrates, country gentlemen, members of Parliament, members of clubs, all those who give the form and pressure to the age. With these he was to mix. It was good for them, he thought, that he should do so." The movement thus recognized frankly the mockery of merely urging moralistic lessons upon a working class living amidst conditions which exacted immorality almost as the price of survival. "We feel," wrote Maurice again, in introducing the movement, and with reference to the life-style of his middle class, "how its comparative ease and comfort weakens our sympathies; how mean and restless we become through our ambition to climb; how little we understand that the right way is to be abased to abound; how we combine suspicion of the upper classes with servility to them; how little we know the heart of the lower class; how much we regard the living beings who compose it as masses or machines rather than as men. Far be it from me to wish that we should mould the rest of society in our own likeness."

They wanted, then, to begin with, a spiritually reinvigorated and socially conscious church. That meant a number of things. It meant the construction of a renovated theology which, while retaining the beloved patristic language, would address itself meaningfully to the "condition of England" question: "A society," wrote Maurice with rare sarcasm, "which should testify against gladiatorial exhibitions in the nineteenth century, or against cannibalism in Europe, might be entitled to the praise of great prudence, but could scarcely allege any evidence of a divine vocation." It meant searching out the real, as distinct from the artificial congregation of the church, for while it was easy to preach to the fashionable congregations of the London West End it was much more imperative to cultivate the masses who felt, rightly enough, that the churches were their bitterest enemies. It meant, even more, a radical democratization of the church. Ludlow, in particular, impressed by the democratic form of the American churches of the period, argued for an Americanized church, including popular election of ministers, and, too, the active recruitment of staff from all social classes. "To reach the working classes," the movement's press argued, "you must make some other men parsons besides University class-men. We want men who know the ways and can understand the language, and enter into the feelings of workingmen." This made the movement, inevitably, the sharp critic of its rival Tractarian movement and its characteristic features: its exaggerated emphasis on creed and liturgy, its inbred ritualism, its reactionary adoration of the past, and especially its social elitist tone. "They want the living God," Maurice commented on Newman's volume on doctrinal development, "and they fly to the fiction of ecclesiastical authority; they want to be delivered from the burden of self, and they run to the confessor, who will keep them in an eternal round of contrivances to extinguish self by feeding it and thinking of it." In similar vein, Ludlow, in reviewing

[155]

Froude's *Nemesis of Faith*, reminded its author that to portray the worth and greatness of common people, as Dickens did in his novels, was a far greater and more urgent task than the nice, refined analysis, in the Tractarian manner, of the spiritual difficulties of the well-to-do. "While the Tractarians," a recent commentator has summed it up, "saw in the revolutionary forces of the time something to be kept at bay by the building of a wall of supernatural doctrine and other-worldly anti-rationalism, Maurice saw in those forces a set of aspirations to be met by churchmen upon their own level and, if not to be corrected and purged, at least to be spoken to with some appreciation of what they were 'at'."

All this added up, in effect, to two major theses: first, a demand for a radical reorganization of the church, both in membership and machinery, and, secondly, a search for a new radical theology to fit the changing needs of the time. The first thesis was based on the recognition that the old church-state concordat of the sixteenth-century Henrican settlement had become anachronistic. That envisaged a full-scale reshaping of the administrative machinery of the church. "It is now only beginning to be seen," wrote Ludlow, "that the admission of Dissenters, and subsequently of Roman Catholics, to Parliament, entailed of necessity a thorough change in the political constitution of the Church of England. . . . From the moment that by the admission of Dissenters and Roman Catholics Parliament became a mixed body, no longer representing the laity of the church, from that moment it became needful, not only that a Convocation of the clergy should be revived, but that the laity of the church should recover their own due weight and influence, claim their rightful responsibilities of many a neglected duty." That meant, particularly, he went on to argue, the elimination of the gross inequality of size and salary between individual parishes, the suppression of the select vestries, and the investment in each parish of those functions of local government appropriate to it: the operation of savings banks, parochial baths, lending libraries, and social services such as health and prison conditions.

Such reforms implied, logically, a new relationship between church and state, avoiding at once the extreme Erastian position of church subserviency and the extreme Nonconformist position of separation between the two bodies. For the first position assumed a humiliating role for the church, simply doing the bidding of the state, tolerating the genial contempt of the worldly lawyers and politicians of the time. "They have, of course," wrote Maurice of that type, "the greatest possible respect for the clergy. They consider we are well-disposed, useful men; bustling and troublesome now and then, fond of contention, not over wise; yet still, as things go, indispensable, a part of the social machine which could not hastily be removed without putting it very much out of order." The second position, in its own turn, was religious individualism run rampant; it enshrined private judgment, and "private judgment means the judgment of a man who is cut off from his fellows"; it meant, furthermore, leaving the secular state-power to continue as the agent of industrial capitalist and territorial magnate without the ameliorating influence of a church as partner. The Christian Socialists, in brief, following Coleridge and the elder Arnold, wanted a genuinely national church which would put an end to futile religious sectarianism and compel the state to seek social justice. "The state . . . ," wrote Maurice to Ludlow, "cannot be communist; never will be; never ought to be. It is by nature and law conservative of individual rights, individual possessions. To uphold them it may be compelled (it must be) to recognise another principle than that of individual rights and property, but only by accident. . . . But the Church, I hold, is communist in principle; conservative of property and individual rights only by accident; and bound to recognise them, but not as its own special work; nor as the chief object of human society or existence."

The movement, clearly enough, can thus be regarded as a pioneer in at once the movement of ecumenicalism and the movement of a socially radical Christianity. But that required, at the same time, a new theological orientation to give it its intellectual foundations. It is surprising, wrote Proudhon at

[157]

one point, how at the bottom of our politics we always found theology. The remark emphasizes a crucial element of the English endeavor. For they were not simply a "social gospel" group. Its leaders recognized clearly that merely to emphasize the material benefits of Christian social action had the effect of converting the church into a social-service agency; Maurice went even further, insisting that such an emphasis opened up the danger of evangelistic demagogues seeking to reenact for their own selfish ends the role of the original founder of Christianity. The history of the social gospel movements in nineteenth-century America, at least, certainly proved that he was correct in that fear. The Christian apostolate, true enough, meant that a Christian must become a socialist. But socialism did not mean, mechanistically, merely a structural reorganization of society. It meant, equally urgently, the infusion of life, both personal and collective, with the indwelling principle of love and fellowship.

For Maurice, the key to that development lay in the Christian doctrine of the Incarnation. The supreme error of both Catholic and Calvinist theological systems was that, accepting the myth of the fall of man, they predicated his innate degradation. All of the Protestant ideologies, in particular, assumed a bleak estimate of human nature, encouraging the unhappy neurosis of fear and terror that comes from the awareness in the individual believer of his alienation from the divine purpose. In its Quaker-Unitarian form, especially, it rested on sanctions of regulative law rather than of social love, so that its devotees became, as it were, inward circles of a dark self of anguish and doubt. The Quaker "inner light," as Maurice wrote to a member of the Society of Friends, had become secularized because of its neglect of the great truth of the Incarnation; so, although the greatness of Fox's insight into the nature of the religious experience must be conceded, his preoccupation with the pathology of sin destroyed the possibility of peace of conscience. As Bishop Westcott, consciously following the Maurician tradition, remarked later of Fox, he disinherited the Christian society and maimed the Christian man.

As against all this, Christian Socialism insisted, the Christ-figure came not as an alien into an unknown foreign land but as an ally into human lives of which he was already the leading principle. Man was not a guilty creature to be reconciled but an imperfect creature to be illuminated. It is the spirit, altogether, of the great hymn to love of the Johannine Gospel. Its implications for a socialist view of man are obvious, for it is to that gospel, historically, that all of the left-wing movements in the history of the churches, going back to the medieval Franciscan friars, have instinctively turned. "I am obliged," protested Maurice against the Calvinist dogma of the division between the elect and the reprobate which so hurt his sense of the brotherhood of man, "to believe in an abyss of love deeper than the abyss of death."

The main target of the Christian Socialist assault, it followed logically, was the new industrial capitalism of the time and the economic theories of laissez-faire individualism seeking to justify it. "Are we to remain satisfied," asked Maurice, "whilst society is parcelled out into darkness and light, as really as the period of the earth's revolution round her axis, whilst a few privileged classes live as it were in the full day-glare of publicity, or in the mellow twilight of comfort, and the masses on the other hand grope unheeded in almost unbroken night? . . ." "Society," in the words of one of the movement's working-class members, "in the feverish excitement that accompanies the thirst for gain, has neglected those objects for which wealth should chiefly be pursued, till the pursuit has become an absorbing passion, and the ends to which the means should have been consecrated have become totally forgotten or neglected." It is, in brief, a doctrine of unbridled acquisitiveness, the "one deep radical disease" of profit-making, which accounts for everything wrong in the social state. It persuades the workman that he must struggle after prizes of material gain that he is unlikely ever to win. The "freedom of industry" it preaches is, in reality, the "despotism of capital." It makes of society "one huge war" between its different classes. Men are thus invited to fight each other in a competitive struggle for place and privilege, instead of learning that society is an organic whole in which the good of each ought to be the good of all. Nor is it enough, the literature continued, to accept the competitive ethic and merely deplore its "abuses," for it is the ethic itself that is destructive of the true elements of the national commonwealth. It is a theory, as Maurice told Kingsley on the occasion of the publication of the latter's angry pamphlet, *Cheap Clothes and Nasty*, which must be fought with to the death. For it has penetrated so deeply into the national consciousness that even in the life of religion it has produced a commercialized theology full of the phraseology of the money-getting habit. In equating its "laws" of economic behavior with immutable truths it also corrupts the very possibility of change, for it teaches that pauperism, economic rivalry, business success or business failure are the unavoidable results of the process of industrial capitalist civilization.

"A chain of circumstances," wrote Maurice of the Chartist workers, "is binding them in; the attempt to break any link of it is ridiculed as idle and useless." Kingsley, in his *Sanitary and Social Lectures and Essays*, noted further how the resistance of landlord and ratepayer to even the barest minimum of sanitary reform was rationalized by economists on the ground that we must obey "nature," not seek to conquer it, and by clergymen who by force of their financial dependency became the prisoners of middle-class audiences whose prejudices they dared not challenge. All classes, in brief, suffered from the disruptive atomism of the individualistic creed. "The upper classes," wrote Maurice, "become, as may happen, sleekly devout, for the sake of good order, avowedly believing that one must make the best of the world without God; the middle classes try what may be done by keeping themselves in dissent and agitation, to kill the sense of hollowness; the poor, who must have realities of some kind, understanding from their betters that all but houses and lands are abstractions, must make a grasp at them or destroy them."

Much of all this, and especially in Maurice and Kingsley, was an eloquent fury of moralistic denunciation in the Carlylean manner. They fancied, as W. R. Greg remarked in an essay of witty demolition on Carlyle and Kingsley, that the cause consecrated the passion. The Christian Socialist press itself half-acknowledged the comparison when it observed that it welcomed Carlyle's unremitting insistence that the condition of the masses was the most urgent question of the day, and that if he was not a socialist it was only because he had been born an age too soon. But Ludlow was different, and managed to write a professional criticism of economic individualism. As much as his colleague Neale—who, as Hughes asserted in in his later character sketches of the movement in the *Economic Review* of the 1890s, knew the history of every system of socialism that had been tried, both in England and on the continent—he possessed a full mastery of socialist economic doctrine that enabled him to meet the bourgeois economists on their own ground. Martin Nadaud, who was Louis Blanc's emissary to the London group, referred in his book of 1873, *Histoire des classes ouvrières en Angleterre*, to Ludlow's systematic study of French socialist theories during his early Paris period before 1848; and Ludlow was also friendly with Harney, one of the leading Chartist theoreticians and an early friend of Marx. The various tracts and lectures that Ludlow produced on socialist economic theory, then, constituted a vital element in the total Christian Socialist literature.

Even before J. S. Mill's well-known recantation on the matter, Ludlow saw that there was a fatal flaw in the reasoning behind the "iron law of wages" argument. Its chief error, he argued, was to have assumed the static character of market demand. The real problem, on the contrary, was to recognize the vast latent demand present in the mass destitution of the English people and to clothe it with sufficient purchasing power so that it could become an effective pressure upon the powers of production technology. "To meet the over-supply of human labour," he wrote, "there needs but an adequate demand of human wants. There would be no glut of labour in England, but a dearth of it, if the purchasing power of the masses could be made large enough." It was only in a wrongly constituted system, where the balance between production and consumption was insufficiently organized, that machinery came to be seen as the enemy of labor, since the increased volume of commodities made possible by machine technology was not matched by a comparable advance in consuming power. The supply was made valueless because the demand had been destroyed. The various panaceas offered by others were inadequate because they neglected that vital truth. Currency reform proposals were useless because the gross inequality in the distribution of income remained unaltered; money could only facilitate exchange between those who initially possessed it. Suggestions of planned emigration and peasant proprietorship in land, or the Malthusian schemes of population control, were equally inappropriate. Emigration was too uncertain in its results, for different economies required different skills and the need of New South Wales for agricultural laborers could not be adequately satisfied by an influx of English paupers. Peasant proprietorship—the last forlorn program of Chartist leaders like Feargus O'Connor—overlooked the technical problems of planned agricultural development, for there was no guarantee, as the record of the French peasant since 1789 made clear, that the scheme was synonymous with efficient husbandry. The Malthusian prescription, finally, failed because it urged the habit of sexual prudence upon men and women who were either so poverty-stricken that they had naturally lost all incentive to prudence or who would never have dreamed of weighing the possible sufferings of others against their own present enjoyment. What was needed, beyond all these various nostrums, was a national system of organized production and sale in which "consumption may be made to depend entirely on the power of production instead of production depending on consumption."

The argument was continued later by Ludlow in his 1851 lectures on *Christian Socialism and Its Opponents*. The classical economists, he argued, claimed that they were enunciating immutable laws that were in fact "benevolence under the guidance of science." They were in fact "laws" that as frequently ignored as they described the realities of experience. They assumed, for example, that low wages in an industry were evidence of insufficient market demand and that workers in it would automatically move out into more remunerative industries, thereby neglecting to appreciate that the specialization inherent in capitalist technology made such occupational transference a difficult and hazardous enterprise. They assumed, further, an arbitrary quantity of "demand" of capital for labor without seeing that, on the contrary, the demand rested on elements—distribution of customers, the presence of parasitic middlemen in the market, the harsh competitiveness which drove even the humane employer to harsh exactions—that were flexible and were amenable to social legislation. They proclaimed a law of "competition" and then proceeded to transgress it with the Malthusian precept that the worker should seek to escape its consequences by withdrawing new "supplies of labor" from the market by family restriction. To leave, again, the recruitment of personnel in any area to competition was a perilous principle; and Ludlow went on to point out that the nascent public services of the state replaced the principle with a planned effort to apportion their intake of employees to their capacity to employ; a precaution of commonsense, he added, that should be applied to the private sector as well. Such a measure would only be an example of the larger vision that government should take of its responsibilities. It must go even beyond the supervision of the production and distribution of wealth to the science of the total relationships of men in industrial community. Its task was the science of welfare, the care of the Commonwealth so pronounced in the social thought of the great writers of the sixteenth and seventeenth centuries. There must be a leading ethical principle, a larger meaning, to guide the national destinies.

Ludlow, in brief, saw that the bourgeois economic theorists fatally identified the particular laws of capitalist production with general laws of social development. At the same time, he recognized the great tradition of social humanism resident in the older school of political economy. He thus noted, appreciatively, that Ricardo had been able, with a noble frankness, to confess his mistake in presuming, wrongly, that there was no justification for the argument that the introduction of machinery would be detrimental to the working conditions of the artisan, and that it was now only too evident that, granted capitalist conditions, an increase in the net income of a society did not necessarily mean an increase in its gross income. It was only necessary to add to this, Ludlow insisted, the lesson that the beneficent effects of machinery could be retained and its evil effects avoided by the adoption of a system of industrial cooperative enterprise. It had been, again—Ludlow continued—the lesser commentators upon Malthus, and not Malthus himself, who had employed his famous theory of voluntary restriction upon birth—which he himself did not even admit to the rank of a fourth fundamental axiom—as a weapon against the interests of the working class. Malthus himself had urged—despite his pessimism about the future happiness of mankind —that one of the best means whereby the condition of the working class might be improved was by the "extension of luxury" as against the economic theory of Paley, whose moral philosophy he generally shared, of "a laborious frugal people ministering to the demands of an opulent luxurious nation"; and Ludlow approvingly quoted the passage in the *Essay on Population* to that effect. Malthus, again, like Adam Smith, Ludlow reminds his readers, had been prevented by a natural sympathy of spirit from fashioning out of his economic insights a theory to be used solely in the interest of trader and capitalist; and Ludlow quoted his assertion that "to wish to better the condition of the poor, by enabling them to command a greater quantity of the necessaries and comforts of life, and then to complain of high wages, is the act of a silly boy, who gives away his cake and then cries for it." The younger Mill was likewise quoted as possessing sufficient manliness to confess to the very real contribution that the trade union had made to the improvement of the lot of the worker. To that quotation Ludlow added the well-known passage in the *Principles of Political Economy* in which Mill, while declaring himself for social improvement through extending the private property principle, at the same time paid his generous tribute to the socialist theoreticians and concluded that the supporters of the existing order had much to learn from their ideas.

All in all, Ludlow did not so much completely reject the orthodox economists as to go back to the larger view of the political economy of their first leading figures. It was a lucrative quarry to mine. There was Smith's preoccupation with a larger social good in his seminal book. There was, both in him and Ricardo, the lesson that labor is the source of value which, on its radical side, gave birth to the school of Ricardian socialists. There was the sense of history and historical processes in Malthus which deterred him from completely embracing the arguments in favor of laissez-faire. There was, finally, the feeling of fine disgust for the actual working of the new industrialism that was ultimately to persuade J. S. Mill, in his posthumously published essays, into the socialist camp. When Ludlow wrote that "I am happy and proud to acknowledge that all of our great economists, Adam Smith, Malthus, Ricardo, Mill, have been and are men full of the deepest and most genuine interest in the condition of our toiling and suffering masses," he was resuscitating an older humanistic tradition betrayed by the popularizing writers, like Harriet Martineau, who converted economic theory into a vulgar apologetic for the brutal capitalism of the bleak age. As Bonar aptly put it in his book on *Malthus and His Work* (1885), "orthodox economy became most abstract when on the death of Ricardo in 1823 its doctrines passed into the hands of the Minor Prophets." The Christian Socialists sought to reverse that process, to go back to an older tradition that saw political economy not as simply the science of the productive process but as the study of the total relations of man, society, and nature within the framework of a common welfare and a common good.

This line of argument led, logically, to a Christian Socialist theory of property. For—as Godwin wrote—"the subject of property is the keystone that completes the fabric of social justice." There were, in fact, two elements of property theory within the 1848 movement. The first element was avowedly socialist—the organization of cooperative workshops after the French fashion, based, as Ludlow argued, on two principles: one, that the remedy for competitive capitalism lay in a planned system of joint work, with shared or common profits; and, two, that a system of interassociational cooperation would, by means of exchange of products between the individual cooperatives, open up a vast and almost new home-market for their commodities. There was an element of guild socialism in this, for Ludlow traced the experiment to the trading guilds of the medieval period. It was true, as he told his English readers, that in their modern French form their gradual decline into petty trading aristocracies had led to their suppression in the eighteenth century. Yet their ideal still lived on; nor ought it to be overlooked that their suppression had simply meant for the French workman merely an exchange of masters: "Industrial feudalism in the hands of the capitalist might be at least as grinding and extortionate as the antiquated tyranny of those bodies from which Turgot's edict had freed them three-quarters of a century before." It was now time to revive them as genuinely socialist entities. They would provide social as well as economic benefits. Like the French associations, they would become benefit societies looking after the sick and the aged, the widow and the child. They might even take over the functions of the model lodging-house, the mechanics' institute, and the school. Property, this is to say, must become more and more corporate in its character. In the economic sphere, that meant—speaking now of the land problem—farmworkers' cooperative enterprises under the guidance and control of a national board of agriculture staffed by socialist ministers of state. In the religious sphere, it meant seeing that, notwithstanding the very real evils in the Victorian administration of both crown and church lands, they exemplified the

[166]

principle of collective ownership as against uncontrolled private disposition. What we have to remember, Maurice warned, is that "what we call the property of the Church is its least important accident, and to make us ask ourselves whether we have not been inclined to regard it as the very substance."

The second element, then, of the movement's theory of property was that of the fiduciary trusteeship of all property. Property, as the patristic theory of the early church fathers had insisted, must be viewed as being held in trust for the common good, thus reiterating the Aquinan elaboration of the Aristotelian dictum that possessions, although private in ownership, should be public in use. In our own day, Maurice added, thinkers like Proudhon had been right to recall the medieval teaching that property was a social and not a natural right. Property was less a right than, at best, a concession to the imperfections of the social condition. The evil of economic liberalism was that it treated labor as a saleable commodity in whose final product the worker had no possessive share. It forgot that property was a social expedient, that, as one of the later Anglican socialists put it, there was a vital distinction between the rights of property and the absolute rights of property. "Questions of property," the Christian Socialist literature summed up, "are those which disturb, more than most others, the peace and order of a community."

These twin elements—of socialist ownership proper and the concept of trusteeship—help to explain much of the ideological confusion of the 1848 movement. For the first element led logically to approval of collectivist state action, while the second, so much akin to Tory Democracy, led logically to an appeal, hardly socialist in any way, to the English ruling class to willingly reform itself and thus inferentially preclude state interventionism. The ultimate failure of the movement can be traced in large part to this fatal ambiguity about tactical strategy, what body should constitute, that is to say, the agent of the new society it wanted.

Concerning state action, while the Christian Socialists—

unlike the German socialists of the chair or the later English Fabians—did not put their main emphasis on a state-managed socialism, at the same time they championed the idea of the positive state. There was, they urged, a larger view of politics and freedom than that of the utilitarian school. There did not exist, as the utilitarians argued, a necessary hostility between liberty and power. On the contrary, liberty included and needed power. "It is increase of power," they wrote in *Politics for the People*, "to do that which man seeks to do, and to obtain that which he seeks to obtain; that is the real end of society, as of every other partnership." When even Chalmers, the most outstanding of the socially-minded Scottish religious leaders of the period, could insist, in Benthamite fashion, that "the world is so constituted that if we are morally right we should be physically happy," they fully saw, as they quoted the remark in the *Christian Socialist*, that it justified both social inequality and state inactivity. The real function of government, on the contrary, must be positive. "The worst error, perhaps, in politics," wrote the editors of *Politics for the People*, "is that which considers government as a mere force of repression, as a mere check upon the movements of the nation. Not only has government no business to slacken the national impulse when it is driving on the right tack, and there are no dangers ahead, but it is bound by every possible means to promote such an impulse."

That meant, inferentially, a number of things. It meant, as Kingsley put it, "the science of organizing politics," so that active citizenship could emerge out of positive social planning. It meant a political leadership that led rather than merely followed public opinion. The leaders of the day deserving of applause were men like Lord Shaftesbury even though his boldness in social reform might only be half-conscious in its sources. Mere political reform was not enough; it had to be followed by social and economic reform. "The Reform Bill," observed Ludlow presciently, "is not a more decisive era in the history of the nineteenth century in England than the Ten Hours Bill; if, indeed, the latter be not greatly the more important of the two." In industrial relations, Ludlow went on to say, there was much to be said for the use of the machinery of compulsory arbitration for the settlement of industrial disputes. He could even go so far as to refuse to support the campaign of men like Collett against the "taxes on knowledge" because he considered its propaganda pandered too much to the antistate prejudice of the laissez-faire philosophy. This meant, in turn, support for reform measures in the machinery of government itself. The Christian Socialist literature severely criticized the corruption and gross inefficiency of that machinery; its remarks, for example, on the War Office contracting system clearly anticipated the breakdown of the entire army regime that was to occur a few years later in the Crimean War. But the lesson they drew from their criticism was not for less government, but for more efficient government.

It was the same with their argument about parliamentary government. They shared with all early Victorian reformers a deep contempt for the House of Commons which, like town council and parish vestry at the local level, was dominated by the spirit of landowner and businessman combined. This required, as Kingsley wrote in his *Sermons on National Subjects*, a larger representation in Parliament of educated and intelligent men who knew something, by scientific induction, of social problems, and a thorough reform of local government which placed parish, borough, and county under the guidance of an enlightened central body. "Few bodies in England," wrote Kingsley, "now express the opinions of educated men less than does the present House of Commons. It is not chosen by educated men, any more than it is by *proletaires*." To remedy that defect the Christian Socialist papers advocated, variously, the replacement of property qualifications with educational qualifications, paid parliamentary service, an annual withdrawal of a certain proportion of members in order to guarantee a sufficient identity of feeling between Parliament and public opinion without inviting the convulsions of a general election, the plural vote, and a system of voting which permitted the organization of electoral unions between minority groups in different constituencies. It is true that the 1848 movement was against universal suffrage. But the rejection was based on the plausible argument that universal suffrage could too easily lead to the dictatorship of a popular demagogue; the outcome of universal suffrage in France in the form of the pseudo-Caesarism of the Second Empire was never far from the mind of the Victorian liberal. Nor is it insignificant that when some years later Maurice wrote his *The Workman and the Franchise* he supported the alternative scheme of functional representation in which groups such as trade unions and cooperative societies would be enabled to elect parliamentary members; a thesis based philosophically on the argument that rights were not personal but social. The rights of others sprang from our duties, not as properties in them but as obligations within ourselves. The machinery of government should reflect that collectivist view. It is an argument that has always been implicit in socialist theory; and the Webbs revived it some seventy years later in their book of 1920, *A Constitution for the Socialist Commonwealth of Great Britain*.

The Christian Socialists themselves were ready enough to push their theory of the positive state—despite Maurice's frequent misgivings—to its logical conclusion. That can be seen, to take a single example, in their discussions on the matter of public health. No thinker of the period was more insistent than Kingsley that that matter should not be left to the hazards of the profit motive. There was a direct relationship, he told the readers of *Politics for the People*, between cholera and consumption on the one hand and the working conditions of the London tailor, the Sheffield knife-grinder, and the Manchester cotton-spinner on the other. Victorian social work, he added, attacked the symptoms, not the causes. What was required, quite simply, was a concerted drive by government and public opinion alike against those physical conditions, both in town and countryside. The Public Health Act of 1848 had shown the way. But more was needed. "The true wealth of a nation," he wrote, "is the health of her masses." He envisaged an imaginative national campaign in which, in the countryside, the insights of science would help conduct a sweeping revolution in the methods of husbandry and, in the towns, the medical professional would become, as he put it, the ally of the social reformer rather than the appendage of the clergyman. Alongside that would go a national building program which should have as its purpose a "complete interpenetration" of city and countryside, a "complete fusion of their different modes of life," to the mutual advantage of both. The program would include construction of dwellings around the urban areas rather than in them, and the replacement of present ugly, ill-built rows of undrained houses with large blocks of apartment buildings replete with restaurants, baths, and reading rooms. Further articles in the *Christian Socialist* added to all this perceptive criticisms of the architectural profession, noting particularly how the competitive ethic had helped destroy the pride of workmanship in architect and workman alike. It would be no exaggeration to claim Kingsley, in this field, as one of the early Victorian pioneers in town and country planning. His friendship with men like Dr. Southwood Smith, Ernest Chadwick, Sir John Simon, and Sir Arthur Helps was a link that binds him, in the long run, to the town and country planning aspects of the modern English welfare state. As much as Engels, this is to say, the 1848 reformers were aghast at the foul ugliness of the new industrialism. Lloyd Jones thus reminded the readers of the *Christian Socialist* in 1851 that of all children born in Manchester one-half died before reaching the age of five; that one-half of its adult working population was untaught and illiterate; and that whereas the life-expectancy on the national level was forty years, for the Manchester workman it was no more than seventeen. He went on to quote Sidney Herbert's remark that the prime cause of the national distress was that the nation had too much wealth and too many people, and added himself that the more ultimate reason was that the wealth was not properly distributed.

All this, then, was a socialism of state action. Yet the other principle of Tory Democracy was also an integral part of the Christian Socialist ideology. It was, of course, an empty fiction. Yet it was still plausible enough in the middle of the century to believe that the English gentleman-class, with all its distaste for trade and commerce, might challenge the capitalist ideology. "Let the upper classes," wrote Kingsley, "learn . . . that the just and wise method of strengthening their political power is to labour after that social power, which comes only by virtue and usefulness." "The real battle of the times," he wrote again, this time to Hughes, "is, if England is to be saved from anarchy and unbelief, and utter exhaustion caused by the competitive enslavement of the masses, not Radical or Whig against Peelite or Tory, but the Church, the gentleman and the workman against the shopkeepers and the Manchester school." The note of romantic obsession with the continuity of English history, where the Saxon ploughs his field and the Norman defends his manor-castle, is unmistakable. Ludlow, in turn, could describe the type of old-fashioned Tory squire as a gentleman whose natural sense of equality enabled him to see a man in every beggar.

This general thesis led the Christian Socialists, at times, into curious paths. Maurice angrily refused to publish a pamphlet by Lord Goderich on the necessity for popular democracy; Kingsley could believe that the absence of the hereditary principle in the political institutions of the United States would lead to the certain demoralization of the American character; Maurice wrote a curious defense, similarly, of the House of Lords; and, certainly, none of them would have accepted Robert Owen's thesis—which Owen himself outlined in a long letter to the *Christian Socialist*—that the proposed Owenite system of education would do more for human happiness in one generation than had been attained during all past ages, or that "the religions of the world are the stumbling block to all mental improvement." There was, indeed, a distinct note of "muscular Christianity" in the movement. Thus Kingsley could write a letter to Sir Henry Taylor criticizing the "effeminacy" of a middle class unused to the Spartan hardiness known to every public-schoolboy, while Hughes wrote an essay on "The Manliness of Christ" almost as if Jesus had been head prefect at Dr. Arnold's Rugby. The aristocracy, in brief, was to be recalled to its historic task of active concern for all other classes placed within its responsibility. In this sense, the 1848 movement, as a later critic observed, was a demand for a restoration and not a reformation of society. In this sense, too, it looked backwards to an older, rural, traditional England, in the manner of a Tory radical like Cobbett or Oastler. It was altogether fitting, then, that of all the early Victorian novelists it was Mrs. Gaskell who chose to contribute to the pages of the *Christian Socialist*; for if there is any portrait of the idyllic life of the English village that was so close to the heart of the ideal Tory Democracy it is contained in the delightful pages of her novel *Cranford*.

Yet despite these weaknesses of its general dialectic the movement wanted and argued for a new social order. It wanted a new social contract based on a sense of the organic whole of society. "In offering this machinery to others," wrote Ludlow and Sully in defending their cooperative schemes, "we are bound to protest against that idolatry of social mechanism which imagines society as a mere assemblage of wheels and springs, and not as a partnership of living men; which takes account of the form only, and not of the spirit which animates it; but we have also to protest with scarcely less of earnestness against that idolatry of individual will, which scorns all regular means of action, looks for all social improvements to the mere genius of some mighty leader in whose way it would place obstacles, like hurdles, for him to leap over, rather than smooth the way for the feebler crowd." There is, this is to say, no preestablished harmony of individual interests. There is only a social commonwealth composed of the welter of rich relationships that exist between man, nature, and society.

Some of the concomitants of that new social order have already been noted. But there were others no less urgent. The numerous articles and letters in the movement's literature on law reform, for example, graphically reveal how urgent this question was felt to be by ordinary men and women in Victorian society. They touched on a number of points: that the system of fines did not deter the rich offender, while for the poor offender the choice between fine and imprisonment was really a mockery on words; that the magistracy belonged in its personnel to the well-to-do class, usually being composed of legal talent not sufficiently able to become great judges; that, as Ludlow put it, the present system prevented the rise of any large and living school of jurisprudence. Ludlow noted further the difficulties faced by the new cooperative enterprises because they were not covered by the principle of limited liability, difficulties that could only have been resolved by resort to a suit in Chancery; the modern reader of those remarks is tempted to wonder what would have happened to the cooperatives if they had been caught in the evil legal web of *Bleak House*.

The Christian Socialists, here, even though they could not accept the Benthamite theory of a science of morals and politics divorced from religious presuppositions, at the same time wrote their appreciation of how a creed that had meant for Hume the "comfort of the refined classes" had become transmuted, with Bentham, into the "greatest happiness of the greatest number." The Benthamite argument, Maurice clearly recognized, had exposed the legalistic Blackstonian defense of governmental inertia. "The *Fragment on Government*," he wrote appreciatively, "exhibits the transition of the Oxford Tory into the modern Utilitarian Radical Reformer, just as Paley's philosophy exhibits the formation of the modern Utilitarian Whig out of the old Cambridge Whig of 1688." It had put the old legal-political system on the defensive: "When Bentham proceeded to show, in the case of his class especially, how much 'sinister interest' had interfered with the public convenience, it was far easier to resort to such phrases as *stare super antiquas vias* or *quiete non movere*, than to invoke principles which Betham cast aside in words, and which were habitually denied in act." It was now time, the Christian Socialists concluded, to push on with the work thus begun by Bentham.

Of all the Victorian legal abuses the movement especially singled out as a target the infamous game laws. For it did not allow its ingredient of Tory Democracy to blind it to the realities of rural English life. Laborer, yeoman, and tenant farmer all had to suffer from the lust of game preserving, a lust which quickened the accumulation of land into the hands of an ever decreasing number of large owners. This, wrote Kingsley, was the "worst economic curse" of rural England. It produced, even worse, the degradation that converted the villager into the poacher and, through the harsh cruelty of the game laws, a wall of distrust and ill-will between squirearchy and peasantry. The *Christian Socialist,* in one of its reports from the agricultural districts, quoted Henry Mayhew's reference to the villager who said to him "We don't live, we only breathes." Kingsley's novel *Yeast* made plain the meaning of the remark, for some of its passages describing game poaching painted a picture of what was almost a state of civil war between the poacher and the gamekeeper. It was an indictment all the more creditable to its author since he himself did not escape in his own day the charge of embodying in his own person the figure of the fox-hunting clergyman out of the pages of Fielding and Smollett.

There was, again, a theory of citizenship which the movement was anxious to propagate. It was lukewarm toward national parliamentary reform, especially the idea of national universal suffrage, because it believed that the municipal and parochial franchise was far more important. The "habitual exercise of the subordinate functions of government" was a far better training in self-government than the "occasional exercise of the right to elect a member of Parliament." That required, the literature urged, a reform of local government so that its machinery ceased to be dominated by "an hereditary working aristocracy of landlords," and would permit the active participation of ordinary people. This would foment a "free circulation of political life" at every level. The argument recognized that the key to freedom is the exercise of small authority in "every living branch and function of the social body." "Let every man," Ludlow summed it up, "learn to govern himself, not in solitude, but in fellowship with others, and from fellowship to fellowship, from circle to circle, the privilege of the few ever widening to admit the many, the collective self-government of English Democracy is achieved." A really functional citizenship must thus come not from the top but the bottom—the church vestry, the cooperative shop, the local government committee, the mechanics' institute.

Yet it was in the sphere of educational reform in which this note of functional citizenship was sounded the most emphatically. The 1848 group, although mostly themselves products of the Oxford-Cambridge system, attacked it root and branch. Scholastically, its writers argued, the system was far behind that of the Scottish universities, its colleges being little more than intellectually inept retreats for the sons of the rich. The *Christian Socialist* paper severely criticized their defects: "that they do not prepare men for the earnest fight of life, that they do not show how the studies of the closet are connected with the work of the world, that a great part of the teaching which was provided in the old times through the professors is neglected, that the collegiate discipline which was meant to be of a more domestic and personal kind, has lost that character." Their teaching was reactionary, for they did little to relate ancient philosophy and politics to contemporary problems, and, indeed, as one Christian Socialist writer observed, their study of the classics actually became a means whereby Plato and Thucydides were converted into apologists for Charles I and Louis XVI. Kingsley's other novel, *Alton Locke*, was in part a forceful plea for a return to the original principle of the collegial foundations of the nation, so that they might again become schools for the talented of all social classes. The portrait its author drew of his working-class hero walking through the King's Parade at Cambridge with the bitter knowledge that because of his class stigma he was forever barred from its colleges anticipated the tragedy of *Jude the Obscure*. "Does not the increased civilisation and education of the working classes," Kingsley demanded, "call on the Universities to consider whether they may now not try to become, what certainly they were meant to be, places of teaching and training for genius of every rank, and not merely for that of young gentlemen?" Maurice in turn asked for a revolution in curriculum. This, he urged, should go far beyond Hume's philosophical skepticism which sought to rehabilitate the old Stuart cause against the Puritanism he so heartily disliked, or Macaulay's Whiggism which led to the distortion of character evident in that historian's portraits of George III and the Duke of Marlborough, and should rather teach something of the social and cultural life of the common people, so that it would constitute a genuine people's history.

The major premise of all this was recognition of the truth that the working class was cut off from the rich cultural heritage of English life. A Christian nation must remedy that, must in effect provide the good life, in its fullest sense, to all of its members. There was a rich interplay of politics, art, culture, and daily life that must be encouraged by the state. "The rights of a man in the eyes of the law," commented Kingsley, "and his functions, if any, in the business of government, are not the only questions of politics. . . . The rate of his wages, and the state of his dwelling, and the cut of his coat, and the print he stops to look at, and the books he reads, and the talk he has with his neighbours, are all political matters." Thus, to take another example, the worker-poet Gerald Massey wrote pieces of literary criticism in the *Christian Socialist* in which he applauded the wholesome democratic truths of Tennyson's poetry, and emphasized the general principle that the reading of poetry ought to be a daily part of the workingman's life; while Ludlow, in turn, praised Dickens for "having done in respect of common men what Wordsworth had done in respect of common things—brought out their worth, their poetry, their greatness." Ludlow again—who knew his continent—wanted a national program of popular recreation and entertainment, so that the English workman could emulate the French workman who regularly attended the great botanical gardens of

Paris and the German workman who patronized his Tivoli gardens. Kingsley envisaged the British Museum and the National Gallery as potential centers for such a program; while Maurice defended the popular theater, and in doing so reminded its Victorian Sabbatarian enemies that the Christian religion had been able to make its way in the Roman Empire despite all the Roman popular entertainments that had gratified at once every intellectual and every brutal taste.

The Christian Socialists, in brief, saw clearly that socialism must mean the mental and cultural elevation of the masses or mean nothing at all. They saw clearly, too, that such an aim must have as its prerequisite the economic emancipation of the masses. Thus, Kingsley argued correctly that the notorious drunkenness of the period could only be solved once the worker was not obliged to run to the gin shop or the public house as a desperate escape from a wretched home. That habit, he urged, was an effect, not a cause; and he aptly pointed out that if during the last century the same habit had noticeably declined among the upper classes it was because the alternatives of travel, art, and cultural interests had become more accessible to them, and it was the task of the present age to do the same for the worker and his family. Some of the most absorbing pages of the *Christian Socialist*, again, were those in which Lloyd Jones traced, with bitterness, the record of grim poverty, shameful beggary, cheap commercial exploitation, and futile chapel revivalism, that had finally driven him into the Chartist ranks and, after the Chartist collapse, into a Christian Socialism having as its final purpose, in his words, the resuscitation of "the poor man's Church, till there are no poor."

There are two further points to be made about this aspect of the 1848 movement. First, in the early Victorian England of the "two nations" it made a serious effort to bridge the gulf between them. Its leaders confessed that in 1848 they

[178]

had not known a single working-class man as a personal acquaintance. "I suspect," wrote Maurice, "that there is a whole world of thoughts in the minds of our working population of which gentlemen in London have no notion." "By looking," he added, "at the uneasy, turbulent members of a class, you may often ascertain what the whole class is in need of, whereas the satisfaction of the calmer members might mislead us." The outcome of this was a dialogue between the movement's leaders and the working-class rank and file which flowered into many lifelong friendships; thus the French scholar Louis Cazamian was able, later on, to devote a whole book to documenting the immense debt that Kingsley owed to the friendship of the Chartist lecturer Thomas Cooper, and showing how the story of *Alton Locke* was in all of its major episodes based on the actual life history of that remarkable self-educated working-class agitator. This fraternal identification with the laboring class was all the more impressive when the general Victorian bourgeois fear of the masses is remembered; when, as Hughes put it in a Christian Socialist tract, it was a new thing even for a minister of state to toast the working men of the nation.

Secondly, this meant an equal emphasis on the social responsibility of the intellectual. That concern was stated in Maurice's book *Moral and Metaphysical Philosophy*, the purpose of which, he said, was to "show how the great social movements of the world have affected, have been affected by, the studies of the closet." Political and moral philosophies were thus not to be seen as verbal substitutes for the phenomena they described, but as efforts to relate the meaning of experience. It is true that the Johnsonian ponderosity of style of that book, as well as of Maurice's other books—*The Kingdom of Christ* and *Social Morality*, for example—make him difficult to read. But all of them carried as their main note the demand that ideas must have contemporary relevance to the social question or remain sterile academic exercises. The history of ancient Jewish nationalism must thus be seen, for instance, as holding a modern meaning, so that the seventeenth-century Scottish Covenanters were right in insisting that the divine government of the ancient Jews was identical with the divine government of modern peoples, despite their error in converting a deity of love into a captious Jehovah. The great Catholic scholarship of Bossuet on Jewish history, on the other hand, was defective because that ecclesiastic historian ended his work by seeking to elevate Louis XIV into the king of kings. Spinoza's demand on the Dutch state of his time, to take a further example, for freedom of thought and speech was a demand for a tiny intellectual elite only, and in so limiting the idea of permissible state action anticipated that liberal theory of the state which now, two centuries later, has become one of the chief targets of Christian Socialism itself.

Other thinkers were taken equally to task: Fénelon, because dreams of good government in the age of Ulysses seemed in his mind to have no relationship to the life of contemporary France; Butler, because he drew up a doctrine of conscience which only the rich could satisfactorily observe; and Burke, because he wept over the fate of the Queen of France when he should have wept over the evils of the *ancien régime* that precipitated it. The social responsibility of the intellectual, in turn, logically inferred his freedom to pursue truth to its fullest conclusion. Maurice thus defended that freedom in his *Philosophy* volume, in which, although no freethinker himself, he defended all schools of free enquiry in the history of Western thought, from Islamic scholars like El-Farabi to more modern writers like Reimarus, Vico, Gibbon, and Voltaire. The right of the sceptic to free speech was paramount for him, an attitude summed up in his sympathetic and approving quotation of the admonition of Mendelssohn writing to Jacobi in the previous century: "Your course of argument is quite in the spirit of your religion, which imposes upon you the duty of crushing doubt by faith." Maurice, in brief, was far from being the merely theological antiquary he has been pictured as being in the standard accounts of the history of Anglican doctrine.

These twin ideas—of interclass solidarity and the social awareness of intellectual endeavor—flowered in the establishment by the movement in 1854 of the Workingmen's College as a pioneer effort in Victorian adult education. The young men who followed their leaders in that effort, as faculty members, were in themselves a remarkable group. There was the artist Lowes Dickinson, father of a more famous son. There was the young scholar F. J. Furnivall, who was later to bring to his work in the publications of the Early English Text Society, which he helped to found in 1864, a democratic passion for the documents as expressions of the virile life of an earlier England. There was the George Tansley, of whom Canon Raven remarked that he possessed "that peculiar *ethos*, that nameless but quite tangible quality, which Oxford and Cambridge in their arrogance have sometimes claimed as the heritage of their sons alone." Finally, there was Ruskin himself; and it was fitting that at the opening meeting of the college, Furnivall distributed to the membership the two chapters of Ruskin's *Modern Painters* on "The Nature of Gothic" and "The True Functions of the Workman in Art" which later on helped teach William Morris his socialism. The purpose of the college was eminently democratic. It would help, observed Maurice, to counteract the exclusiveness of literary men, and undermine the notion that the patronage of rank or wealth was necessary to the mental elevation of the workingman. In addition to this, Maurice was instrumental in the founding in 1848 of Queen's College in London which was to become one of the leading schools in the serious education of the Victorian woman. It is worth recalling that when Maurice, as professor of divinity at King's College, was under fire at the time by the more reactionary elements of his church—an episode that evoked from Carlyle the gibe that the Church of England believed in no damnation except ruin at the bankers—his colleague Professor Trench congratulated him on having been the driving force in securing from the Crown the first charter for female education. Some of the leading Victorian feminists—Sophia Jex-Blake, Octavia Hill, Gertrude Bell—came out of these foundations. To read Kingsley's correspondence with J. S. Mill on the question of women's rights is enough in itself to appreciate the Christian Socialist concern with the subjection of the Victorian woman.

The final important element of the 1848 movement was its strong internationalist sense. It can be seen, indeed, as the last episode in an older cosmopolitanism before the alliance of democracy with nationalism persuaded Victorian England to turn its back on Europe and cultivate that temper of self-righteous parochialism that astonished almost every European visitor for the next hundred years. The theological premise of that cosmopolitanism was the conviction of a universal society of which both nation and family were only subsidiary components. The nation-state, of course, was a given fact, and that is why the Christian Socialists could applaud the national liberationist wars of their time. But it was pregnant at the same time with the concept of a universalist ethic, so that the history of the English people could only be properly understood as part of world history; which explains Maurice's favorite analogy of the history of modern England as comparable to the history of ancient Jewry. His Hebraic studies, indeed, taught Maurice the supreme lesson that all world history belongs to socialism. So, while Jowett's translation of Plato, for example, converted the Platonic Socrates into an educated Victorian gentleman-teacher dispensing a narrow code of conduct to the young men destined to become rulers of the British Empire, the Christian Socialists emphasized rather the ultraradical tradition of the Greco-Roman intellectual world, including the Platonic critique of property and property relations. As against the reactionary theology of Augustine, who directed his arguments against the North African rural and town proletariats of the fourth century, they emphasized the arguments of the other Christian fathers —Justin, Clement, Origen, Ambrose, Gregory Nazianzen— in favor of economic communism. Maurice had the kind of mind for which things lived not within a framework of historical time or place but within a framework of continuity and

[182]

universality. For the Christian Socialists, then, the whole world was their parish.

More particularly, this was reflected in the extensive attention given to the various European socialist theories in the movement's literature. Neale's series of articles on those systems concluded that the English movement was anxious to combine something of all of them into its philosophy, while Ludlow further stressed the point by saying that they sought to take over the best of what they found in the utopian socialism of thinkers like St. Simon and Cabet on the one hand and the practical socialism of thinkers like Owen and Fourier on the other. Neale's observation that "to pass from the picturesque and exciting world of Fourier to the New Moral World of Owen was like passing from a brilliant ballroom to the quiet of a cloister," showed how much they appreciated the difference between the French and the English way of looking at things. There were articles, again, on the Continental cooperative societies; on the world-wide application of the radical Christian idea from the American Nauvoo community to the cooperative groups of Dijon and Bordeaux; and the movement's New York correspondent, writing on the difficulties of proselytizing the American workingman, reported that "there's no desire for justice among them yet, all they want is to get on." Maurice, in turn, could write appreciatively of both St. Simon and Robert Owen, for, in his view, the Frenchman's maxim, *chacun selon sa capacité*, and the Englishman's theory of environmental determinism, in that both dismissed as insignificant all peculiarities of race and language and national custom, apprehended the thrust toward a world society. The internationalist awareness was there, again, in Maurice's laudatory notice of the fact, in his lecture on Milton as a schoolmaster, that that great European scholar had made it a condition of his acceptance of the secretaryship under Cromwell that correspondence with foreign powers should be conducted in Latin as the common language of international intercourse. It was there, too, in Lloyd Jones's remark to his working-class readers that he did not oppose those who sought to abolish wars between nations, but that until justice had been done between individuals and classes within each nation it would be in vain to pursue such an ideal.

How lasting was this internationalist principle can be seen in the later life-work of men like Kingsley and Ludlow, long after the 1848 movement proper had disappeared. Ludlow's later lectures on the American democracy given at the Workingmen's College thus emphasized the international implications of the Civil War. "The principles put forth by the South in defense of its slave-system," he observed, "are such as threaten the freedom of the working classes throughout the world." His later book, *President Lincoln, Self-Portrayed*, taught the lesson that with Lincoln's assassination the cause of international democracy had lost its best champion; while his 1867 book, *Progress of the Working Class*, noted with pride the fact that even in the midst of his own grievances the English worker of the Chartist period had never forgotten the issue of slavery. Ludlow clearly saw the interconnection between the domestic and the international social struggle. "You cannot do justice to India," he wrote, "without striking a blow at the fetters of the American slave; you cannot free the latter without giving an enormous impetus to the development of India." For him, it was a first principle, as he put it, "that the over-taxation of India and the exactions of London slop-sellers, the massacres of Ceylon or Cephalonia and the beating to death of parish-apprentices at home, are but pustules of the same plague."

Kingsley's later work showed the same thing. A later writer on the 1848 movement remarked suggestively on the comparison between the English Anglican and the French Catholic Lammenais; for if the one learned his radical bent from witnessing the Bristol riots of 1831 as a young boy, the other traced his *haine éloquente* to a boyhood memory of the proscribed Mass being surreptitiously performed in his father's St. Malo house by a disguised priest in 1793. That sense of being part of a larger movement, extending beyond England, remained with Kingsley to the end. His American tour helped him to see immediately the challenge of the New World, that it embodied new principles of social organization of tremendous importance for the future; although, admittedly, Mormonism was too much for him. He appreciated immediately, then, the importance of establishing on a firm basis the academic study of the American democracy in the English universities, and it only showed how far ahead he was of English academic opinion that his proposal of 1866 to set up a chair of American history at Cambridge, on the invitation of Harvard College, was rejected by a purblind and reactionary university senate. We should not judge America, in his words, by the Ku Klux Klan any more than England should be judged by the Newgate Calendar. Yet the result of his failure on this score was that even educated Englishmen continued well into the twentieth century to judge America in those ignorant terms.

But it is Kingsley's account of his West Indian tour, *At Last: A Christmas in the West Indies* (1869), that reveals most clearly the lasting impact of his socialist period. Not only, in that volume, did he make handsome amends for his unfortunate support of Governor Eyre in the 1865 episode stemming out of that colonial governor's brutal repression of the Jamaican "rebellion" of that year, but, even more, he showed a sympathetic insight into the whole problem of race, empire, and race relations rare indeed for its time. He defended the postemancipation West Indian peasant and worker in the same spirit with which earlier he had defended the Chartist workman. On every issue of mid-Victorian West Indian colonial society—the need for higher education, the need to break down the evil legacy of sugar and the sugar plantation economy, the advance of self-government, the continuing moral responsibility of Britain toward the colonial peoples—he came down on the right side. He demanded, almost a century before it became reality, a federal university for all the islands. He urged the thesis, supported by all subsequent scholarship, that it was the old white plantocracy and not the act of slavery abolition that was responsible for the decline of the sugar system. He recognized that the co-

[185]

lonial economy now needed not the *grande culture* of the sugar estate but a planned *petite culture* to make of the ex-slave a successful peasant proprietor on his own land. Above all, he frankly admitted the right of Negro revolt:

> We white people bullied these black people quite enough for three hundred years, to be able to allow them to play (for it is no more) at bullying us. As long as the Negroes are decently loyal and peaceable, and do not murder their magistrates and drink their brains mixed with rum, nor send delegates to the President of Hayti to ask if he will assist them, in case of a general rising, to exterminate the whites—tricks which the harmless Negroes of Trinidad, to do them justice, never have played, or had a thought of playing—we must remember that we are very seriously in debt to the Negro, and must allow him to take out instalments of his debt, now and then, in his own fashion. After all, we brought him here, and we have no right to complain of our own work. If, like Frankenstein, we have tried to make a man, and made him badly, we must, like Frankenstein, pay the penalty.

It was a rare Victorian indeed, however liberal, who managed to perceive so clearly the real nature of the race issue.

The movement failed, of course, in its two major undertakings: the industrial workshop experiment and its effort to revolutionize the relationship of its church to the state. The workshops failed because they were organized in the old craft trades untouched by the use of machinery—tailors, shoemakers, builders, printers, smiths, and bakers—and whose members evinced a typical independency of spirit fatal to the cooperative habit. They were isolated, that is to say, from the new type of factory labor-army being developed by the economic revolution unleashed by steam power. To read the various reports published in the movement's literature is to be made aware of the problems that stemmed out of that fact: shortage of able managerial talent, too many middle-class philanthropic types knowing nothing of financial or organizational systems, failure to arrive at a reasonable compromise between managerial authority and workers' participation, the tendency of the shops to set up a new aristocracy of labor, the fatal absence of a central administrative body able to eliminate the hostile rivalries between the different associations. More important, the human material used was that of the broken forces of Chartism; and there is no worse material with which to build a new society than the embittered victims of a defeated revolutionary movement. That point was seen clearly by Harney at the time; it was impossible to see, he wrote, how thousands of poorly paid and half-starved laborers could ever accumulate the capital needed to launch successful cooperative shops, and in any case it was obvious that escape from their wage-slavery could only come about through a mass revolutionary movement, based on class-conscious militancy, and seeking full political power. The leaders of the movement, being mainly middle-class, could not thus appreciate the thesis—advanced earlier on in books like Thomas Hodgkin's *Labour Defended against the Claims of Capital* (1825) and William Thompson's *Labour Rewarded* (1827)—that only the trade union could become the proper mechanism for such a revolutionary movement.

This general failure to recognize where the real heart and center of the labor-capital struggle lay is all the more interesting in the light of the fact that at least one of the Christian Socialist leaders—A. J. Scott in the series of articles he wrote for *Politics for the People* on "The Development of the Principle of Socialism in France"—fully recognized that truth. Social suffering, Scott wrote, was age-old. But the enormous increase of manufactures has now brought men into a new world. Vast numbers of men, with habits and interests in common, are related to their employers by a monetary arrangement only, and have been drawn into the new factory system. Their work conditions have helped destroy the native intelligence and zest for education that characterized their fathers. The uncertainties of the system, based now on a precarious world market, have converted life for its victims into "an exciting and anxious lottery." The evils of the system have given rise to socialism; socialism, in fact, is "the growth of the modern manufacturing system."

But because the main thrust of the 1848 movement did not follow this analysis its industrial experiment failed. Likewise, in the sphere of church-state relations, it was equally utopian. Its literature dreamed of the church as partner to the state. It thus romanticized the original concordat of the Henrican Reformation, which from the beginning made the church the creature of the state. It even quoted Cardinal Wolsey's famous lament that he had served his king more ardently than his God; but it failed to see that such subserviency was no accident but logically inherent in the relationship, so that the Christian Socialist of 1848 stood no better chance of converting the church to social radicalism than did the cardinal, three centuries earlier, of saving Henry Tudor from those corruptions of power to which he himself had finally succumbed. The entire relationship was Erastian in character. "The nation," as Cardinal Newman rightly put it, "drags down its church to its own level." "That Church," wrote another critic, "was established by the State; it received its colour and character from the State; so long as it remains a National Church it must admit to the control and regulation of the State." Parliamentary enactments, court decisions, and administrative regulations throughout the nineteenth century illustrated the truth of those observations, all of them demonstrating that the church was little more than a department of state, dependent upon parliamentary whim for changes in both its machinery of government and creed, and beholden to a system of ministerial jurisdiction in its top executive appointments; the object, that is to say, of the direct will of a popular assembly and of the spasmodic action of irresponsible royal or parliamentary commissions.

Faced with such a humiliating situation, the Christian Socialists could not accept the logical conclusion that real freedom for the church meant, at the least, complete independence from the state. They did not see that religious toleration itself, since 1689, had only been made possible by the agnosticism of the state. Nor did they see that so long as they accepted the church-state relationship in a secularist age they would continue, like their church itself, to be subject to what Figgis has termed the concession theory of corporate power. The result was that, after the 1860s, it was the Nonconformist chapel rather than the Anglican rectory that became the ally of the working-class movement.

Yet, in the last analysis, the movement must be seen in positive terms. It showed that religion need not be simply the opiate of the masses. It agitated against the idea that nothing could be done to alter social conditions. It fought against liberal complacency; and it is worth recalling the story —which Kingsley was fond of telling—of how Emerson, on his English visit, had so irritated Carlyle with his transcendentalist optimism that the English seer had attempted to shatter the American's outlook by taking him to the darkest spots of London and then to a sitting of the House of Commons, but with Emerson remaining undisturbed by either terrible spectacle. It helped facilitate the welfare state; as the *Christian Socialist* editors pointed out, if the state could concern itself actively with the health of recruits into the army and navy there was no reason why it should not look after the health of the populace as a whole. It vigorously fought against reaction in both church and state; for, as Ludlow remarked in his later reminiscences, "all parties in Church and State treated us alike as dangerous madmen." It sought to marry theology and social protest. Its ideas, indeed, in those two fields complemented each other, and a biographer of Maurice has properly noted how those ideas hung together in "a common revolutionary system . . . Maurice's social reform advocated the rising of the poor against their masters, while at the same time his theological eccentricities removed the only guarantee of the morality of the poor which is provided by the fear of the hereafter."

A later critic has observed that the movement challenged the affirmations of John Stuart Mill with the proclamations of the Book of Deuteronomy. But that is to miss entirely the import of the movement. For all of the modern socialist and communist systems have been as much a moral critique of the grotesque immorality of capitalist society as they have been a rational critique of its economic limitations. It is in that sense that Maurice belongs with Blake and Carlyle and Marx himself. For they all shared a deep rage of indignation against the new industrial society, a consuming hatred of its bourgeois philistinism, a prophetic vision of its ultimate collapse. They saw the bourgeois order in large historical perspective. So, just as Marx used medieval German legends, Shakespeare, and Jewish and Indian religion to provide him with the satiric, savage imagery of *Capital*, Maurice drew on the Judeo-Christian tradition to reinforce his socialism. The Davidic Psalms, for him, castigate the mammonism of contemporary England as much as that of the ancient Jewish commonwealth. The arrogance of the young advisers in the court of Rehoboam anticipates the contemporary European conservatives who defend with equal insolence a privileged social order. The assault of Amos and Hosea against the corruptions that the old Jewish nobility had learned from the Oriental despotisms of the time, and the denunciations of Ezra and Isaiah of the massive cruelties that the monarchico-theocratic temper of those despotisms had encouraged in the powerful Assyrian and Babylonian kings: these are openly invoked as warnings to the ruling classes of nineteenth-century Europe itself. The evil corruptions of Babylon, similarly, are transformed into the plutocratic evils of early Victorian London; and in his *Lectures on the Apocalypse*, where the analogy is used, Maurice almost rises to the cadences of fear and hate of the Roman Empire which the unknown mystic-author of the Book of Revelation poured into his apocalyptic vision.

The power of apocalyptic vision, then, is not a weakness of revolutionary movements. It is, in fact, their strength: the conviction that a new heaven and a new earth are possible, that the Messiah is at the door, that at any moment the world might renew itself. All of the great modern revolutions have possessed it: England in 1640, France in 1789 and 1848, Russia in 1917, China in 1949, Cuba in 1959. The lasting contribution of the English Christian Socialists is that they shared the vision. "I believe," wrote Maurice, "that the trumpet of the Archangel has been sounding in every century of the modern world, that it is sounding now, and will sound more clearly before the end comes." In believing that, he perceived the corroding disease that lay at the heart of the emerging bourgeois civilization of his time. He saw the fatal flaw in the doctrine of progress. "In sociology," a recent commentator on the movement has observed, "it was too often assumed that the Logos doctrine sanctioned the Victorian ideas of progress in a Christian guise; and Mr. Reckitt has described how even a mind as prophetic as Scott-Holland's could think of the 1914 war as an isolated interruption of our civilization and not as the irruption of a disease which lay deep within its life." It is safe to say that Maurice would have understood the Nazi holocaust of the World War II period, with its deep satanic roots; it is equally safe to say that John Stuart Mill would not have understood it. Any socialist who does not learn that lesson does not understand the nature of the world in which he lives.

[Chapter 5]

1871
The Influence of the Paris Commune

With the disappearance of Chartism and Christian Socialism the Victorian bourgeois civilization moved on into
its golden afternoon and Indian summer, ending finally in
1914. Both ruling and working class generally accepted the
individualistic philosophy summed up in the sociological
theories of Herbert Spencer, at least until 1889 or so, when
the publication of the *Fabian Essays* heralded the coming
victory of collectivist ideas. England as the workshop of
the world; the growth of empire; the rise of a labor aristocracy accepting middle-class leadership and ideas: all
contributed to a national temper of confident optimism
which discouraged any rigorous examination of the first
principles of the social order. That explains why Marx
could live out his life in London as a neglected exile, why
Queen Victoria could regard a politician as mildly liberal
as John Bright as almost a sedition-monger, why a pioneer
in factory legislation like Lord Shaftesbury could look with
disdain on the efforts of men like Joseph Arch to organize
the agricultural workers of the period, and why even a great
novelist as socially conscious as Dickens could write, in
Hard Times, a novel of outright hostility to trade unions and
trade-union leaders. It was a period, in brief, of almost
complete bourgeois complacency. Radicalism, in any form,
was rendered null and void by the genius of a ruling class
which bought over the agitator by absorbing him into the
system. "There is no doubt," wrote a perceptive writer at the
end of the period, "that if the secret history of the past forty

years could be written in the frank fashion of the *Greville Memoirs*, it would be found that in many instances a judicious course of Whig hospitality during the months of autumn had subdued the wild fervour of the hitherto intractable and irreconcilable democrat."

Yet there were occasional cataclysmic episodes that intruded into this era of social conservatism and helped, in part, to shatter its composure. One such episode was the American Civil War. Another was the Paris Commune of 1871. Both revealed a modern society torn asunder by a Hobbesian war of bitter class conflict. Their impact on English political and public opinion at the time was real and deeply felt. Yet neither, from the viewpoint of its English implications, has received adequate attention. Of the Commune especially, the literature in the English language, as distinct from the prolific work done in French and Russian, has been woefully inadequate. W. J. Linton, an American radical pamphleteer long since forgotten, published an account of the event, from New York, in 1871, the same year in which Marx published his brilliant essay. The English socialist Belfort Bax wrote an interesting but superficial pamphlet on the topic in 1886, while a year later his colleague Henry Hyndman—of whom Shaw said that he looked like God in Blake's illustrations of Job—wrote his own account, *A Commune for London*. Thomas March, again, published a book in 1896 which, while a better treatment because of its extensive use of original documents, was marred by an obvious failure to understand the deep social roots of the revolt. Later in the twentieth century an American academician, Edward Mason, produced a book in 1930 which in its own turn was marred by its anxiety to prove that, whatever the Commune was, it was not a socialist experiment, by which its author imagined that he had answered Marx's essay penned in the stirring days of the revolt itself. In 1937 the Left Book Club issued Frank Jellinek's book. But that was essentially a history only, with its main emphasis on the street fighting, the leading personalities involved, and the tortuous negotiations with the reactionary assembly at Versailles, so fatal ultimately to the Communards. The centennial anniversary naturally attracted more attention, marked by the publication, notably, of Stewart Edwards' *The Paris Commune 1871* and Royden Harrison's edited volume of selected defenses of the Commune in the literature of the period, *The English Defense of the Commune*. Mention, too, must be made of Alistair Horne's *The Fall of Paris*, published a few years earlier.

Yet all of these titles, with the exception of the Harrison volume, do not say much of the Commune's influence on English opinion, especially the favorable radical opinion. It is important to emphasize that influence, if only because there has grown up a myth that English socialism, and its embodiment in the Fabian Society and the Labour party, have been uniquely and peculiarly English, homegrown responses to the English situation. Edward Pease, in his early book of 1916, *The History of the Fabian Society*, sought to play down the Marxist influence on the early Fabians, which was very real, while later academic writers such as Pelling and Poirier have portrayed the Labour party in much the same light.

Yet this interpretation, patently, is reformist mythmaking. The influence of the Commune in the 1870s and 1880s is perhaps the most striking example of how much the small socialist groups that proliferated during that period felt the internationalist impact. There was, of course, first and foremost, the figures of the Communard exiles themselves who fled to London, as others did to Brussels and Geneva. There were writers like Desmoulins, Andrieu, Bergeret, and others, who wrote extensively on their experiences in the London magazines. There was Prosper Lissagaray, who composed his well-known history of the event during the first five years of his exile, and which was later (1886) translated into English by Eleanor Marx; a task that was in part corrected by Marx himself. It was typical of the tragedy of many of the exiles that after a series of unsuccessful business enterprises, Lissagaray ended incongruously, making a living by means of the operation of a casino in the Channel Islands. There were skilled engineers like Langevin and Delahaye. There was Hector France, who wrote lively sketches of the London workers and unemployed of the period. There were exiled Commune generals like Wroblewski, who continued in London his campaign for Polish national freedom. Johannard lived in Manchester, Camélinat in Birmingham, Meillet in Glasgow. Bergeret worked as a photographer, Chatelaine as a chemist. Rochefort continued to publish *La Lanterne* from his London home. Thiesz, chief of the postal service of the Commune, operated a laundry; Richard, a grocery shop; Serrailler, a shoe-repairing business. For many of them, living initially in communal quarters, it was a life of grinding poverty equal to that of Marx. The climate was inhospitable; they had little taste for English beer; and they suffered generally from the typical English hostility to "bloody foreigners."

Yet they made a real, and at times a flamboyant, contribution to English life. There was Paschal Grousset, the fiery little Corsican who had been the Beau Brummel of the Commune, who wrote in the London newspapers, translated Stevenson's *Treasure Island,* and who on his later return to Paris, after the amnesty, became some sort of authority on English literature. There was Elie Reclus, the anthropologist who had been appointed Keeper of the National Library and the Louvre during the Commune, and to whose foresight and hard work Paris owed the preservation of the treasures of those institutions as they were threatened by the Versaillese bombardment. There was the artist Montbard, as well as Camile Barère and the caricaturist Emile Barère, both of the latter being direct descendants of the celebrated Bertrand Barère, member of the convention and of the Committee of Public Safety during the 1793-1794 period of the French Revolution. Eugene Vermesch published various ephemeral journals, and there are glimpses of him in the correspondence of the poet Verlaine giving lectures on Blanquism in London public houses. Others obtained academic appointments through London friends. Dalou became a professor of sculpture at the Victoria and Albert Museum. Vaillant was given a lectureship at London University; both France and Gausseron, army officers of the Commune, obtained teaching posts; while Charles Longuet, who married one of the Marx daughters, became professor of French at King's College. Antoine Brunel, a graduate of the famous Saumur cavalry school, offered courses in French literature at the Royal Naval College; it is ironic that there he taught the Prince of Wales who, later as Edward VII, was to become the close friend of the Marquis de Gallifet, the infamous Versaillese commander who was responsible for the brutal and senseless murder of thousands of prisoners after the Commune defeat. Emile Eudes, after setting up as a secondhand bookseller in Edinburgh, taught at the same institution. It is amusing to think of that superb profligate, whose sexual adventures stirred even the heart of the Paris of the debauched Second Empire, instructing the future officers of the British navy. There was, not least of all, the romantic figure of Louise Michel, full of an incurable revolutionary romanticism which helped to persuade her that she was the Charlotte Corday of the Commune but who is revealed at the same time in her *Memoirs* as a warmhearted woman who befriended the London poor: "It was impossible for me," she wrote, "to incite the wretched poor of Whitechapel to revolution, yet I could not let them die of starvation."

The various memoirs and books of the refugees themselves and of English writers testify to the sort of life they led, helping to impregnate the English radical groups with continental ideologies. Many of the Communards settled down in the traditional area of refugees, the dingy London streets between Soho and Leicester Square, the old political quarter, that is to say, of Victorian London. There were annual commemorations of the uprising; places like Audinett's Restaurant and the old Rose Court Club in Soho became favorite meeting spots; Louise Michel set up a refugee club along with Malatesta, Charles Malato, and Kropotkin himself (who lived briefly in London in 1881-1882), and in which they presented theatrical shows; there was much fraternization with the *Arbeiter Bildungs Verein*, headquarters of the older German socialist and communist refugees, and with English groups like the Social Democratic Federation and the Universal Republican League; and a whole series of radical clubs welcomed the continental newcomers. Many of the refugees, of course, left in 1880 after the amnesty granted by the Third Republic. But many stayed on, and Belfort Bax remembered seeing some of them, now an aging old guard, as late as 1899. It was, of course, a difficult life for most of them: a struggle against harsh poverty, homesickness, police surveillance, not least of all, the oppressive atmosphere of Victorian puritanism. Many of them, indeed—men like Grousset and Vermesch, for example, who had graduated as young revolutionaries in the hothouse atmosphere of the Second Empire—must have come to feel, as Kropotkin said, that a prison in France would be better than the grave of London. Yet, despite all this, they managed to compensate with an oftentimes gay, continental social life. Merely to read a book like Malato's *Les Joyeusetes de l'éxil*, describing that life, is to feel how vigorous political debate in homes and public houses, river expeditions on the Thames, and picnics on Hampstead Heath made life tolerable for the colony.

There already exists a whole literature by English authors that constitutes a mine of information on the period: Raymond Postgate's books, *Out of the Past* and *The Workers' International* (1920), Joseph Clayton's *The Rise and Decline of Socialism, 1884-1924* (1926), William Stephen Sanders' *Early Socialist Days* (1927), *Social Democracy in Britain: Fifty Years of the Socialist Movement*, by H. W. Lee and E. Archbold (1935), James Jeffreys' edited volumes on *Labour's Formative Years* (1948), and others. All of them help to illustrate how the Commune, and the debate unleashed by it, helped convert many to the socialist cause. They show earnest lecturers addressing small and ragged meetings in the obscure conventicles of the radical clubs and movements of the period.

They show, too, many eminent names drawn into the movement. William Morris wrote a poem, "The Pilgrims of Hope," depicting the story of an English worker and his wife who travel over to Paris in order to fight with the Communards on the Montmartre heights. Hyndman, with his journalistic instinct, sought out Marx and talked with him (something the Fabians never did with Engels), a fact that redeems many of his other, less attractive qualities. His friend Bax described in his autobiography how he himself, in turn, came to socialism because the martyrs of the Commune appealed to him in a way no record of Christian martyrology had been able to do. The record of the social mixing in the clubs of the myriad radical and socialist sects elicits other names. There were, among others, Dr. G. B. Clark (later to become a Fabian), the journalist William Harrison Riley, the elegant socialist adventurer Cunninghame Graham, the young John Burns, Edward Aveling whose Byronic irresponsibility later drove Eleanor Marx to suicide, not to mention the exotic exhibitionism of that aristocratic dabbler in radical movements, Lady Warwick. There were, in addition, men like Henry Champion, an artillery officer who retired from the army because he objected to the colonialist Afghanistan war and was later instrumental in founding the Independent Labour party, the Eton master J. L. Joynes, who horrified the officialdom of that august school by being arrested at one time by the Irish constabulary as a dangerous anarchist, the self-educated workman Harry Quelch whose knowledge of languages made him an important link between the English and the Continental movements, and, finally, the quixotic Adolph Smith who gave a series of London lectures on the Commune as early as 1871 and whose chapter on "Political Refugees" that he wrote for Walter Besant's *London in the Nineteenth Century* throws valuable light on the life of the Communard exiles.

The first task and obligation of all of these was, of course, the defense of the Commune against, one, the peculiar belief of the British public generally that it was the deserved fate of a France given over to atheism and materialism and, two

—more importantly—the massive vilification of the Commune as a barbaric and bestial revolt put out by the European prostituted press, with the French leading. They were joined in that defense by a handful of English intellectuals and writers who, while not themselves necessarily socialist, clearly saw the meaning of the event—John Morley, Professor Beesly, A. J. Mundella, Fox Bourne, Frederic Harrison, J. R. Green, and others. For liberal England, as much as the socialist elements, was in fact horrified by the savage butchery of the repression. The remarkable despatches to the *Times* from its Paris correspondent, in describing that repression, did much to discourage any enthusiasm for Thiers and his bourgeois "restoration of order." The Gladstone government, to its lasting credit, refused to yield to the efforts of Paris to have the refugees extradited. Its stand was supported by the General Council of the International Workingmen's Association, whose English secretary John Hales wrote a strong letter to the *Times* describing how the French government had stooped to the worst sort of calumny in order to intimidate the European chancelleries—an attitude that was accompanied by the council's manifestos on the Franco-German war that had precipitated the Commune, with their eloquent plea for the recognition of the Republic in France and their warning of the dangers for working-class internationalism inherent in Bonapartist nationalism. And, to speak of efforts pressed on behalf of individual prisoners, it was a group of English scientists who finally persuaded Paris to release Elie Réclus into exile. More generally, the editors of the journal *The Examiner* pointed to the clemency shown to the American South after 1865 by the Lincoln administration as a model that ought to be followed by all victorious sides in a civil war. Unfortunately for the validity of that thesis, Thiers was no Lincoln.

The English defenders of the Commune, of course, had to answer all of the popular English national prejudices against the French that appeared at the time in the press. Earl Russell argued that nothing better could be expected of a society whose intelligentsia had accepted the Voltairian hatred of religion; Humphrey Sandwith replied, in an article in the *Fortnightly Review*, that the record of Christian Europe when it came to religious wars or international conflicts was hardly a better model to admire. Or there was the canard that the Commune leadership had been full of dangerous communists. That charge was sufficiently answered by the exiled writers who wrote for the English magazines. Thus Jules Andrieu, writing on the theory and history of the Commune in the same *Fortnightly Review*, reminded his English readers that most of the leadership, in fact, was at best vaguely radical. "Radical," he wrote, "is by no means the same as professional revolutionist, instinctive conspirator, born demolisher. An innovator, with the sense of the true radical, takes his starting point from the conditions of the present, and is conservative as well as revolutionary; he demolishes, but he replaces." A similar rejoinder was made by Vésinier in his book which was translated into English in 1872 by J. V. Weber as *History of the Commune of Paris*. The immense majority of the Assembly, Vésinier noted, were not revolutionary communists but individualist socialists who only under the pressure of the gathering élan of the revolution voted for the radical decrees of the Commune. There was, again, the popular English view of Frenchmen as being psychologically prone to successive revolutions, as if they suffered from some peculiar restlessness that only violence could assuage. It was an ironic charge, because only a brief generation earlier the English image of the French had been quite the reverse, that they were—as is to be seen in the view presented in Thackeray's novels—nothing much more than a race of amusing and foppish dancing masters.

The answer to that last charge was taken up by a number of the English defenders. The Commune, they argued, was no such romantic mystery. It was, rather, an expression of the Paris workers against all of the forces of reaction that, since 1789, had stifled the possibilities of profound social change. It had its social roots in the very history of France itself. The Positivist Frederic Harrison saw that clearly in his articles in the *Fortnightly Review*, based as they were on a study of the Parisian journals and conversations with eyewitnesses, both French and English. "They who think," he wrote, "that such a story as that of the Commune of Paris is explicable on the 'miscreant' theory are unfit to discuss political questions." "The claim of capital to amass wealth by what means it chooses, and to spend it how and when it pleases, is so vile, the claim of the workman to have his part in the social result is so unanswerable, that in the end the issue is not doubtful." He saw clearly that what really enraged the respectability of Europe was the very pretension of the Paris workers that they were able to govern themselves, thus reflecting that paranoid fear of the masses that went back to 1789. "To those," he continued, "who watch with anxiety the future, there is something appalling in the spirit with which the movement of the Commune has been judged. It is true that it was something new in political experience; but at most its ideal was that of government by and for the working classes. An ideal one-sided and extravagant it might be; but when we reflect for how many centuries, and in how many societies, all power has been wielded by the rich or the great in their own exclusive interests, it is an ideal not so entirely preposterous." Vésinier put the same point in more particular French terms. He told his English readers:

Versailles and Paris were in every sense two opposite powers, each repelling the other. Versailles, or the majority of the Assembly, represented feudalism, the middle ages, the old royalist and Catholic society, with all its prejudices and antiquated privileges, anti-revolutionists for whom the years 1789, 1793, 1830, 1848, 1870, 1871, and the whole nineteenth century, had no existence; Paris, or the Commune, personified the aspirations and hopes of the *travailleurs-prolétaires* for a new and better world by the complete transformation of society; it was the negation, the destruction, the absolute overthrow of present institutions, and the radical abolition of all exploitation. This was how the question stood from the first sitting of the Commune.

There were other English voices in the defense too. The

International Democratic Association, with the support of the British section of the International, held a mass meeting in Hyde Park the resolutions of which were printed in the Commune's *Official Journal*. The book written by the English eyewitness, the Methodist minister William Gibson— *Paris During the Commune*—although not a radical piece of work, by the very honesty of its reporting helped its English readers to see what the repression actually meant. The former Paris correspondent of the *Daily Telegraph*, Robert Reid, whose experiences had made him sympathetic to the uprising and who had been disgusted at its dishonest treatment in the British press, undertook on his return a series of lectures throughout the country under the auspices of the General Council of the International. J. R. Green, the historian, wrote in correspondence to his friends about the significance of the Commune, as he saw it, as a conscious return to the independent spirit of the medieval city-states. The thesis was as historically dubious as the other thesis that the event was to be seen merely as a revolt engendered by the patriotic, nationalist revulsion of the Parisians against the treachery involved in surrendering France to the Prussian enemy. Yet at the same time it was a gesture of enthusiastic support on the part of men like Green.

Yet again, there was the intriguing figure of the Nottingham worker Thomas Smith, about whom too little, unfortunately, is known, who both in his pamphlet *Letters on the Commune* and in his articles in the *International Herald* vigorously advanced his own special line of defense. An embryonic Marxist, he saw the French bourgeoisie as the class enemy, the "vampire class" thrown up by modern capitalism. But he added to that an older, eighteenth-century note identifying in addition the French Catholic church and the aristocracy as "twins in crime" who added their own special evil forces to the reactionary cause: "If the Assembly conquers Paris," he wrote, "all liberty of speech and press will be gone, and France will fall back on the old system of repression, based on an ignorant peasantry and the priesthood." It was an ominous prophecy, for the subsequent history of the Third Republic demonstrated its truth. There was, finally, of course, the noble voice of Ruskin. He had begun to publish his *Fors Clavigera* at the very time when the siege of Paris was still going on. In it he advanced unequivocally the argument that the Commune was simply the grand inauguration of the real war between capitalism and socialism. In a passage of impassioned generosity and indignation that recalls passages in Marx's pamphlet, he linked the Commune with the whole heroic tradition of French national history. "*Ouvrier* and *pétroleuse*," he wrote, "they are gone their way—to their death. But for these . . . great Charles shall rouse his Roland, and bid him put a ghostly trump to lip and breathe a point of war; and the helmed Pucelle shall answer with a woodnote of Domremy; yes, and for these the holy Louis they mocked, like his master, shall raise his holy hands and pray God's peace."

The English version of Lissagaray's great history deserves a separate note, if only because it constituted for a whole generation of English socialists after 1886 the definitive account of the Commune. A brilliant journalist in his own right, and a soldier of the Commune, he did not allow his revolutionary spirit to blind him to the truth of the event, or to the weaknesses of its architects. His purpose, as he said, was to tell the complete story, its failures as well as its successes, for he who tells the people revolutionary legends, in his phrase, is as criminal as the geographer who draws up false charts for navigators. The book thus constitutes a remarkably honest account of the uprising from beginning to end.

The Commune, of course, was a heroic failure; and Lissagaray's book shows why with painful clarity. The leadership never knew really where it was going or what it ought to do. Authority was fatally divided between the different bodies of the council, the Central Committee, and the Committee of Public Safety. The leaders themselves, in their personalities, were a mixed lot, few of whom were able to grasp, as did Marx from his London vantage point, the earthshaking implications of what they were doing. They grossly misread the temper of their enemies, whom they persisted in seeing as simply mistaken fellow Frenchmen; and that misconception led to the futile and time-wasting negotiations with Versailles. There was the failure, in turn, to organize a centralized command of the defense, hampered by the localist loyalties which persuaded the individual Communard soldier to fight only for his own quarter once the end was in sight; and that failure was compounded by the romantic obsession with the idea of the street barricade, made utterly obsolete in terms of modern war technology by 1870, a fact that Blanqui had foreseen before the event and which Engels further emphasized in his introduction of 1895 to Marx's *Class Struggles in France*. Personal ambition, doctrinal rivalry, incapacity to make rapid decisions, all added fuel to the disaster. There were the inveterate talkers and scurrilous journalists like Pyat, the inflexible bureaucrats like Jourde, the cowards like Tirard. There were the older revolutionaries trying to reenact 1793 or 1848, and Frankel's taunt to his Girondist colleagues—you go to bed at night and get up in the morning with the *Moniteur* of 1793 —was justified. The habit of parliamentary rhetoric, so dear to the republican tradition and which persuaded too many elected representatives to see themselves romantically as the tribunes of the people, frustrated decisive action at every point; every room, noted Lissagaray angrily, had its government, its orators. There were the vain, inefficient generals like Rossel or the delegate of war like Cluseret (who later wrote maliciously hostile articles against his Commune colleagues in *Fraser's Magazine* during his London exile) whom the General Council never learned how to manage; indeed, the Commune in one way collapsed because of its failure to solve the problem of military-civilian relationships. All of these factors help to explain the fatal errors of the Commune: the failure to take the military offensive against the demoralized Versaillese troops at the very beginning, the failure to dismiss incompetent military leaders, the failure to seize the gold reserves of the Bank of France, the failure to control the intractable provincialism of both the rural townships and the separate Paris *arrondissements* which Lissagaray correctly termed the cancer that devours France. In annotating all of this the book acted as a powerful antidote against the temptation to romanticize the Commune, a process that started immediately once the movement had been suppressed.

There are two points of especial importance in the account. In the first place, Lissagaray saw the significance of the superb revolutionary spirit of the Parisian proletariat, and especially of its women. Revolutions, as Marx said, are the locomotives of history. They produce, almost overnight under the pressure of the dialectic of revolutionary development, a new awareness in the masses of their historical destiny as the only class that can inaugurate and develop a socialist society. Lissagaray's description of the popular clubs, the local, committees, and the upsurge of a new popular street press, fully document that important truth. It was evident to him in all the daily scenes of sacrifice and devotion that he witnessed and recorded. This, he remarked, is the drama of the revolution, simple and gigantic as a drama of Aeschylus. His chapter on "Paris on the Eve of Death" still moves the modern reader with its eloquent testimonial to the accelerated class consciousness of the ordinary people of the Commune. Lissagaray noted, furthermore, how this spirit was reflected in the rich outburst of popular theater, revolutionary song, vivacious and satirical poster art, and newspaper satiric cartoon, despite the fact that much of it was couched in the grandiloquent, romantic manner of Victor Hugo's *Les Châtiments*. Paris rediscovered Mozart, Meyerbeer, Rossini; the great works of art, in Lissagaray's phrase, have driven away the musical obscenities of the empire. All this, in brief, was the cultural expression of the nascent socialist society, still retaining much of the presocialist ideologies of the sansculotterie of 1793 but also imbued with a new conviction, as against neo-Jacobinical utopianism, that the new society could only come about through the mechanism of the armed class struggle.

The second point to note is Lissagaray's full recognition, equal to that of Marx, that the Commune finally proved the international character of the class struggle and, indeed, the grim character of the struggle itself. Every revolution, to be successful, must be able to recognize who and what are its enemies. Once the Marxist precept of an international civil war is accepted, it follows that the enemies are both internal and external: the bourgeois order, that is to say, in both its national and international aspects. For the local French class enemy, Lissagaray could say nothing positive, and indeed reserved some of his most bitter passages for the old republican left personalities—Louis Blanc, Gambetta, Schoelcher, Adam—who connived at the victory of reaction by their refusal to intervene. Even the aged Mizzini, who could find little, as a republican nationalist, to sympathize with in the revolt, was shocked by that treason, and in his essay of 1872 on "M. Renan and France" he described how the leading intellects of France, including Renan himself, had abdicated their humanism and social sense by the act of their silence during the Commune and its aftermath. For the old republican revolutionary it seemed, surely correctly, a proof of the moral decay of French life. He might indeed have added that elsewhere Renan had written with prescience on the general theme that democracy, along American lines, was advancing in Europe and was certain ultimately to replace the old social order, but that when faced with that democracy in concrete form, as with the Commune, he sacrificed the prescience to irrational hostility. Victor Hugo had been the great singer of the June days of 1848. By contrast, all of the literati of the Third Republic—Daudet, Dumas *fils*, George Sand, even Anatole France—combined to portray the Commune as an act of murderous imbecility. It was necessary for them, in Lissagaray's phrase, to abandon the Commune in order to save the republic; which meant, bluntly, that the middle-class republic was erected on the grave of working-class hopes. That betrayal, of course, was only surpassed by the insane savagery with which the victorious bourgeoisie destroyed the Commune survivors, testifying as it did to the truly bestial depths to which a ruling class on the defensive will descend under the stimulus of class fear. Lissagaray's volume thus fittingly ended with a description of the tropical hell of the penal colony of New Caledonia to which the French courts condemned so many of the Communard prisoners.

There was, after that, the international enemy of the movement. The Commune was crushed by the unholy alliance of Thiers and Bismarck; for the French bourgeoisie feared the internal class enemy more than they feared the external national enemy. Class interest, in other words, was stronger than patriotic sentiment. It was only a logical step, after that, to 1940 and the betrayal of the republic itself. It was logical, too, that in 1871 the French bourgeoisie was prepared to physically destroy Paris itself, with all of its wealth of civilization, in order to destroy its working-class enemy, whereas, by contrast, it was willing in 1940 to hand over the city, without resistance, to the Nazi enemy. All this, in turn, was related to the imperialist phase of modern capitalism, the gathering imperialist expansion, that is to say, of the capitalist order against the native peoples of the world. It was no accident that, in America, the response to the Commune was summed up in the editorial observation of the *Chicago Tribune* that the Paris Communards were "worse than Comanche Indians," for all of the new imperialisms of the period, notwithstanding their nationalistic elements, were agreed on the principle that the growth of capitalism, both at home and abroad, required the genocidal destruction of any group—revolutionary working class in Paris or Indian tribes on the Great Plains—that stood in its way. Nor was it any accident that the leading French military officers who massacred the Communards, like those who massacred the 1848 fighters, had been formed and trained in the French colonial wars against Algeria, thus illustrating how the authoritarian habits learned in the colonial adventures become deployed by the ruling class in the home struggle against its domestic class enemies. It is true that Lissagaray himself did not elaborate all of this in his book. But he accurately perceived its implications in his remark that after every victory over Parisian workmen the bourgeoisie has preferred throwing its victims to the antipodes to fecundating Algeria with them. It was, this is to say, Algeria for the white *colons*, Noumea, New Caledonia, and Cayenne for the class enemies who were regarded as the scum of the earth. The only answer to this bogus internationalization of the bourgeois world lay in the real internationalization of the working-class movement.

In the long run, of course, the influence of the Commune on this embryonic period of English socialism—the two decades of the seventies and the eighties—lay in the area of socialist theory: the nature of socialism itself, the character of the state, the theory and practice of revolution. The Commune—which Eleanor Marx in her preface to the Lissagaray volume correctly called the greatest socialist movement of the century—became the touchstone upon which the validity of competing theories—Marxist, Proudhonist, Blanquist, and Bakunist—were to be tested. It is therefore difficult to separate the immediate impact of the Commune from the intellectual impact of Marx and his system. Both Marx's household and, after his death, that of Engels became social centers in which the English radicals of the period mixed with the continental friends and visitors. It is also urgent to remember that the post mortem on the Commune was conducted by all of the competing factions, of which Marxism was only one, and not necessarily always the most correct analysis. For although it was the Marxist analysis that finally came to be accepted, through the mechanism of the later powerful European communist parties, during the early period his was only one voice among many, and in fact regarded with hostility by many of his rival analysts: it was not for nothing that he was known, in Paul Brousse's hostile phrase, as "the Pope in London." The social and political thought of the Commune itself had been divided between Proudhonist mutualism, authoritarian Jacobinism, Girondist federalism, the Blanquists who wanted insurrections arising from closed conspiracies, the old-fashioned republicans who dreamed of the great Commune of 1793, and, lastly, a small handful at best of Marx's own disciples. It was to this rich mixture of revolutionary thought, summing up nearly a whole century of European utopian, socialist, and communist idea systems, that the English radical groups were exposed. To read their literature today is to be made aware of the intellectually emancipating character of that exposure, and of its influence upon them.

In part, as already noted, this process was facilitated by the personal interchange between Communard refugee and English radical: as early as September 1871 prominent refugees such as Johannard, Longuet, Martin, Vaillant, Frankel, Rochat and Wroblewski had been elected to the General Council of the International in London. In part, it was the influence of groups like the Socialist League and the Social Democratic Federation, not to mention smaller groupings such as the International Club, the Labour Emancipation League, the Chelsea Labour Association, and others. Their influence has tended to be summarily dismissed by orthodox English historians, who have seen them as little more than argumentative sectarian cliques wasting their time in internecine and fratricidal intramural struggles. Yet it is sufficient to quote from two observers of the period, one a famous Russian refugee and the other an upper-class English politician, to appreciate how wide of the mark is that attitude of amused contempt. Kropotkin, in his *Memoirs of a Revolutionist*, described the ferment of radical ideas that he found during his visits of the 1880s, involving both workmen and middle-class people. In his turn, Mr. Arthur Balfour, later to become Conservative prime minister, delivered a remarkable testimony to Marx himself at the Industrial Remuneration Conference held in 1885. "To compare," he marked, "the work of such men as Mr. Henry George with that of such men, for instance, as Karl Marx, either in respect of its intellectual force, its consistency, its command of reasoning in general or of its economic reasoning in particular, seems to me absurd." It would be difficult to imagine any later British prime minister, however progressively minded, a Welsh agrarian radical like Lloyd George, for example, or a Labour party socialist like Ramsay MacDonald, paying such a tribute. Clearly, all sorts of revolutionary ideas, including the Marxist variant, were "in the air" during this period. Even the Fabians, with all their intellectual disdain for romantic utopia-mongering, were not immune; and it is only necessary to read the contributions of Sidney Webb and Bernard Shaw to the *Fabian Essays* to see how much they owed to the analysis of the process of capital accumulation described in the historical chapters of *Capital*.

An analysis, then, of the theoretical positions taken by the English defense of 1871 reveals a number of points. First, it identified the bourgeois class as the main instrument of reaction. The point had been made, early on, in the English version of Vésinier's book. "The victorious bourgeoisie," he wrote, "showed neither pity nor mercy. It had sworn to annihilate the revolutionary and socialist proletariat for ever— to drown it in its own blood. Never had a better occasion presented itself; and it profited by it with ferocious joy. To destroy its enemies was its highest enjoyment." William Morris took up the theme, writing within the context of the event: "I have never underrated," he wrote, "the power of the middle classes, whom, in spite of their individual good nature and banality, I look upon as a most terrible and implacable force." Professor Bridges likewise emphasized the truth, in the *Beehive*, that it was Thiers and his class, and not the Communards, who were responsible for the death of the Archbishop of Paris and other hostages shot during the last days of the event, since that act was the act of a small group maddened by the mass executions of their captured comrades perpetrated even before the fighting had ceased. Other commentators noted the more general fact—in answering the legend of the Commune as organized terror—that the Reign of Terror of 1792-1793 was far less bloody than the *semaine sanglante* of 1871.

It followed from this, in the second place, that socialism would have to come from the efforts of the working class itself, thus abjuring reliance upon middle-class movements.

The lesson was underlined in the statement of various of the London clubs put out in 1883, *A Manifesto to the World,* which noted the reactionary climate of opinion prevailing throughout Europe since the suppression of the Commune and declared that groups such as themselves would continue the work of the International. The same lesson was emphasized by the manifesto of the Socialist League issued in the following year, noting the necessary hostility between the two classes of capital and labor, and emphasizing the truth that all of the prevailing political systems—absolutism, republicanism, constitutional liberalism—had failed to deal with the real evils of society. Marx and his ideas, it added, had saved the English movement from two dangers: that of embracing a purely philistine and mechanical conception of politics, and that of depending upon the continuing advance of the capitalist industrial system for future progress. For us, it went on to say, there are no nations. Real change of any socialist character "can never happen in any one country without the help of the workers of all civilizations." The main note struck here is that of the need to recognize the existence of the international civil war between capitalist and worker. The Commune itself had openly welcomed the foreigners who joined it, and to read the names of the governing council during the revolt is to realize its international character. Hyndman, responding to this, reminded his English readers that Robert Owen had had a lengthy correspondence with the French socialists of 1848, and that it was an example always to be followed.

Caution, of course, must be exercised in reading all of this. This, after all, was a period of embryonic socialism. The very term "socialism" meant different things to different people. It is true that the intercourse with the Communard refugees sharpened the class consciousness of all those who came into contact with them. But at the same time the Communard influence also tended to add to the eloquent confusion as to what exactly "socialism" meant. "The term 'Socialist,' " Champion remarked at the time, "is made to cover every sort of politics, and to include proposed changes in our industrial system varying from compulsory state life-insurance to the establishment of free federated communes." The Communard exiles inevitably added to this confusion because they belonged, all of them, to different schools of thought. It was that ideological separatism, after all, that led to the breakup of the International in 1872. For socialists like William Morris, the Commune reinforced his antiparliamentary feelings, feelings based less on grounds of principle and more on the idea that parliamentarianism seemed such a slow and cumbrous method of reaching a result that could be attained much more swiftly through revolution: the Bakuninist influence is obvious. For many of the members of groups like the Socialist League, quite differently, the lesson of the Commune lay in its idea of federalist communalism. "The idea implicit in not a few of those who belonged to the Socialist League," wrote a later commentator, "was more or less that of a federation of socialist societies throughout the country, bearing some sort of analogy to the federated Jacobin clubs of the French Revolution, which should educate and organize public opinion, especially of the working classes, so that when the cataclysm to which the capitalist system was leading should supervene, these societies might be in a position to give direction to the revolutionary movement": the mixture of Blanquist and Proudhonist ideas is obvious. For others, yet again, the Commune was important because it was essentially an anarchist negation of the state. In part, that was the Proudhonist thesis of a socialism for peasants and "rurals" who had been dominated for too long by the centralizing tyranny of vain and luxurious Paris, the argument, that is to say, of Proudhon's famous essay on the *Principe Fédératif* which went back for its inspiration to the impassioned argument of Rousseau's *Lettres de la Montagne* in favor of a pastoral social egalitarianism pitted against the massive corruptions of city life.

In part, it was the argument, with a somewhat different emphasis, that the Commune was a genuinely revolutionary act on the part of the proletariat, but that it had been subverted by obsession with state power. That particular argument was spelled out by anarchist Communards like Arnould in his book *Histoire populaire et parlementaire de la Commune de Paris* (Brussels, 1878), and Lefrançais in his book *Etude sur le mouvement communaliste à Paris en 1871* (Neufchatel, 1871), for the European audience, and later by Kropotkin in his pamphlet of 1896 for the English audience. The English socialist movement, Arnould argued, had gone astray by accepting the method of the *état administratif* as against mass popular agitation against the state. "By proclaiming the free commune," Kropotkin argued in turn, "the people of Paris proclaimed an essential anarchist principle, which was the breakdown of the State, but as the idea of Anarchism had then but faintly dawned upon men's minds, it was checked halfway, and in the midst of the Commune the ancient principle of authority cropped up." There was, finally, of course, the Marxist interpretation of the Commune as a revolutionary act replacing the machinery of the bourgeois state, albeit imperfectly, with that of the new socialist state. How these various interpretations were frequently taken over by the English groups, mixing them up in contradictory fashion, is evident enough, to take a single example only, in Morris' utopian novel *News from Nowhere*, where a revolutionary uprising, commencing in Trafalgar Square, and patently modeled on the Commune events, ends in an idyllic account of a pastoral socialism set in the Thames Valley countryside.

A perennial theme running through all of this confused debate was, of course, the problem of the methodology of change—which constitutes in effect the third component element of the total impact of the Commune. It is well known that in the long run the English movement accepted the path of orderly industrial trade-union agitation and constitutional-electoral politics. But the more overtly revolutionary theories popularized by the Commune had their brief day of prestige before that path was finally accepted. Much of the literature of the Social Democratic Federation repeated those theories, much to the consternation of the ruling class at the time. "Mr. Hyndman's repeated prophecies of a revolution," wrote Henry S. Salt with some amusement, "were none the less disturbing because they were always unfulfilled, Mr. Burns was dreaded as a demagogue who had been imprisoned owing to his defiance of law and order, Mr. Champion as a retired army officer who might possibly turn his military knowledge to deadly account." Even the Fabians in their early period were not immune to this temper of revolutionary optimism. "We were for a year or two," wrote Bernard Shaw in an early Fabian pamphlet, "just as insurrectionary as the Social Democratic Federation and just as anarchistic as the Socialist League . . . the object of our campaign was to bring about a tremendous smash up of existing societies to be succeeded by complete socialism." But this, at best, was revolutionary play-acting, at worst exaggerated fear drummed up by the cheap yellow press of the period. Champion himself, indeed, far from being a military adventurer plotting a coup d'état in the Bakunist fashion, was a sober man who had written articles on the Commune pointing out, correctly, the obsolescence of the technique of the barricades and the fact that the Communards had been the last practitioners of the technique. The English defenders of the Commune, in their final estimation, came to emphasize its lasting significance as an expression of class conflict within capitalist society rather than romanticize its violent character. "Armed revolt or civil war," wrote Bax, "may be an incident of the struggle, and in some form or another probably will be, especially in the latter phases of the revolution; but in no case could it supplant . . . change in popular feeling, and it must, at all events, follow rather than precede it." "As a political and violent remedy of profound social disorders," Harrison wrote in his turn, "the revolution of the Commune is abortive and must fail. But their great political programme is effectively founded in France; is sufficiently suggested to Europe; and the bloody vengeance of the Monarchists will not blot it out from the memory of the future."

The truth of the matter is, of course, that the England of 1870 was not the France of 1870. Political liberty and constitutional government were firmly established and universally accepted by all Englishmen; the Reform Act of 1867 had extended the franchise to the more educated sectors of the working class; and the habit of social-class deference was endemic in the national psychology. Those who defended the Commune, then, had to accommodate its lessons to the English setting. It was the difference—although they did not put it in those terms—between an English bourgeoisie that was secure and a French bourgeoisie that was insecure, beset by powerful enemies both on the left and the right. The Communard exiles, after all, were no more than a minuscule group (although no smaller, it is fair to add, than the Fabians themselves a decade or so later). They lived in a society in which the trade unions, as Bronterre O'Brien had prophesied earlier, had become a conservative labor aristocracy concerned with their own narrow privileges within the system. The French writer Taine—whose book on the history of France, incidentally, was one long polemic on the thesis that the Commune was the penance France had to pay for the sin of 1789—saw that clearly in his visit to England in 1874. "As a consequence of aristocratic institutions," he noted, "every class in society sees one which it regards as superior, keeps the boundary line clearly drawn, and never mixes with that below it. Thackeray has sharply depicted this caprice; it was that of the Court when Louis XIV was king." Such a society was hardly likely to accept the dream of violent revolution promulgated by men like Hyndman, who was even prepared to believe that the emergence of the Knights of Labor and the scandals at the time of the Standard Oil Corporation presaged imminent revolution even in the American republic. Nor was it likely to accept the philosophical atheism of men like Bax, for the Church of England, after all, with all its faults, was not the ultramontanist French Catholic church. The defeat of the Commune, more generally speaking, meant that the day of the centralized international association was over, and henceforth the socialist movement would be compelled to turn to nationalist organizations accepting the framework of the individual nation-state.

What this involved, then, was a theoretical analysis emphasizing two theses: (1) that the Commune must be accepted as an element in the continuing international class struggle based on international working-class solidarity, but (2) that it must not be erected—because of the peculiarly French conditions of its outburst—into a model to be slavishly accepted by other national movements of the struggle. The two points were ably argued in a pamphlet written by an anonymous English author in 1894, entitled *The Commune of Paris*. He had obviously read the histories of Vèsinier, Arnauld, Lissagaray, and Rossel, and also talked extensively with the exiles. Noting, to start with, that the English idea of the event has been a biased one propagated by the bourgeois press and that even many socialists spoke apologetically of it, he insists that it is time to look beneath the surface of things and recognize the great central fact that the movement had justice and even a sort of historical necessity behind it. Although an English constitutionalist at heart, he defends the burning of the Tuileries and the destruction of the Vendome column, not as acts of vandalism, but as the justified elimination of monuments that symbolized at once, with reference to the first, the decadent life of the *ancien régime* and, with reference to the second, the nationalist Caesarism of the Napoleonic period. Even hostile historians, he adds, admit that that jingoistic column was in questionable taste. He recognizes, in turn, the peculiar savagery of civil war, quoting English newspaper correspondents who declared that the fighting between the defenders and the Versaillese troops was more deadly and desperate than anything they had witnessed in the campaign with the Germans. As an Englishman, again, he could not entirely approve of the anticlerical edicts of the Commune, the spirit of which was summed up in Rochefort's charge, which the author quoted, that "our eternal belief is that Jesus having been born in a stable, the only treasure that Notre Dame ought to possess is a bundle of straw." Yet at the same time he admitted that the Church of France deserved the attack.

As for the ultimate meaning of the event, the author took the attitude of friendly critic. There is a difference, he wrote, between a revolt and a revolution. Revolts abolish slavery or emancipate serfs or destroy a dynasty. But revolutions, to last, take ages to accomplish; they cannot change the basic structure of society overnight. In England itself, he noted, serfdom began to break down at the time of the Wars of the Roses, but until the middle of the eighteenth century Newcastle colliers were sold along with the mines in which they worked and vassalage in Scotland survived up until the same period. Lincoln freed the slaves, and Alexander II the serfs; but the American ex-slave and the Russian peasant still lived in conditions only slightly different from slavery and serfdom. The lesson was obvious: a change to socialism requires patience, perseverance, knowledge, long-term organization, persistent propaganda to change the whole climate of public opinion. Revolts leave behind them unreason and violence. The idea in the head is worth everything, the bullet in the rifle is worth nothing. At the same time, the argument terminates, this is not to be construed as an exercise in English complacency. The Commune achieved much. It asserted the theory of local communal control of the means of production subject to federal control for national purposes. Above all, it demonstrated the power of secular altruism in the common people. Men like Dombrowski and Delescluze showed how they could die for an ideal of human brotherhood, without hope of heaven and without fear of hell. The pamphlet ended on a fine note:

No great cause can afford to forget its martyrs; and we have reason to remember and be thankful for ours. Just because they greatly hoped and gloriously erred and fought and died in those early spring days so many years ago it is the easier for us to be brave in the altered conditions amid which our work has now to be done. Where they were strong we can be stronger for the example they set; for the capabilities of human daring and enduring are made up of all suffering and tradition of heroism that went before. Chastened by their failure as if it had been our own, yet devoid of the combatant's rancour of defeat, we may learn to be wise where they were wilful, to be patient and unflagging in our efforts whether in partial success or in temporary failure.

Nothing illustrated better the truth of this than the fact that the French exiles themselves came reluctantly to see it. They saw that Europe was entering the period of Bismarckian "blood and iron," that England, by contrast, was entering a period of expanding social-welfare collectivism. The anarchist tradition of "war to the knife" against bourgeois society, summed up in the statement of the seceding Blanquist faction at the 1872 Hague Congress that "weakness, like legality, kills revolution," was, they came to appreciate, comically inappropriate to English conditions. As refugees, they appreciated the English climate of opinion, the readiness of its government to honor the law of political asylum. Even a Communard as fiery as Louise Michel noted the difference of behavior between the Paris and the London police, was impressed by the fairness of English criminal procedure, and freely acknowledged that the London aristocracy with which she sometimes mixed listened to her courteously although they found her beliefs incomprehensible. Lissagaray, in turn, noted in the very last pages of his account how Irish public opinion had rallied to the defense of the prisoners and their families of the Fenian insurrection, while in comparison the French subscriptions for the families of the condemned of the Commune were disgracefully small. Class hatred poisoned French public opinion; English public opinion, by contrast, exhibited a characteristic generosity to the losing side. The influence of the Commune in England was clearly a two-way street.

The really lasting impact of 1871, then, must be looked for in the slow maturation among the English groups of the Continental socialist theories. That can be seen most clearly in the various books written by men like Bax, Morris, Hyndman, and others. The Commune was, as it were, the trigger that set off that ideological penetration. Hyndman's book, *The Historical Basis of Socialism in England* (1883), was a lengthy analysis of English history since the fifteenth century based, as the author acknowledged, on the Marxist methodology. Its tone was avowedly internationalist. The English working class, it argued, had been in the vanguard of that movement; witness the tremendous welcome given to Garibaldi in 1863 by the London workingmen. The Commune, unfortunately, was not the Marxist revolution but a Proudhonist uprising, which gave a fresh impetus to anarchism; and it is difficult, wrote Hyndman, for an Englishman not to suspect that the anarchist is in reality only a reactionist in disguise. Nothing of improvement could be expected of present-day society, for, despite the liberalism of the English ruling class, English capitalism was still subject to the general laws of capitalist development and decay. Parliamentary government has proved an utter failure. At the same time, serious structural change could only come about in England by a slow and peaceful transition; there would be compromise in order to avoid bloodshed. Nor was this prognosis a betrayal of Marxism, for Marx himself had admitted that socialism could possibly come about in England by constitutionalist means. Much the same lessons were drawn by Bax and Morris in their book, published at much the same time, on *Socialism: Its Growth and Outcome*. The chapter on Marx elaborated the concept of surplus value as well as that of the historical process based on the class struggle. At the same time, the argument emphasized the evolutionary as distinct from the revolutionary thesis. It envisaged the gradual decentralization of state powers to municipal bodies and trade organizations, so that ultimately that power would be replaced by a federation of local and industrial organizations. It is true that both books tended to reduce their Marxism at times to nothing much more than municipal socialism, almost as if the formation in the 1880s of district and parish councils could be viewed as the first step toward the ideal socialist society. Yet they were an earnest attempt to transcend the intellectual parochialism of the time; they recognized what ought to be the proper relationship between the intellectual and the working class; and they accelerated what Bax and Morris termed "the growing instinct towards socialism." At a time when most Englishmen regarded Marx, if they had heard of him at all, as some sort of angry prophet denouncing evil, like Carlyle, they instinctively recognized him as perhaps the greatest sociologist of the century. And at a time when the French intelligentsia, like Flaubert, Goncourt, Renan and Taine, blamed education as one of the causes of the Commune—as Lidsky's French study, *Les Écrivains contre la Commune de Paris*, has shown—they saw radical political education as the salvation of the working class.

Looked at from a somewhat different angle, what the English champions of the Commune were doing was to help resuscitate the memory of an earlier English social radicalism that had been forgotten after the Chartist defeat of 1848. Whereas an old fighter like Mazzini, for example, writing for the English audience, could dismiss the Commune as, in his phrase, the necessary consequence of an abnormal incident in the development of the republican enterprise, they saw it as the highest expression, in French terms, of an older revolutionary tradition in England itself. That tradition had been all but obliterated by the revisionist work of the Whig historians. Gardiner's lectures, for example, on Cromwell had converted the great republican Puritan into a sort of liberal Victorian statesman fighting the "impractical" schemes of the Diggers and the Levellers of the Civil War interregnum. Jowett's edition of Plato had converted the advocate of an ancient-world communism into a sort of Oxford philosopher-don. The transformation of the figure of Milton, again, is a well-known story, so that whereas in the early part of the century a popular reading public, including Chartists and Christian Socialists, had seen him properly as the great radical-republican defending the republic against European reaction, by the latter part of the century a new academic scholarship, as in the work of Walter Raleigh, had put him through the narrowing prism of an "art for art's sake" theory to emerge as nothing more than the "sublime poet" of the English literary tradition. All of this had resulted in obscuring the neosocialist origins of both English democracy and radicalism.

The discussion on the Commune must therefore be seen as part of a radical reaction against that tendency of the orthodox literary world to reduce everything revolutionary to respectable terms, almost as if the old English revolutionary tradition had never existed. It was there in J. R. Green's pioneering *Short History of the English People*, with its refreshing emphasis upon the social experience of the common people. It was there in John Stuart Mill's three essays on socialism, published posthumously, in which he finally and fully identified himself with the socialist ideology. It was there in rationalist writers like Joseph McCabe and Francis Newman who during this period wrote books attempting to remind the English audience of the great contribution that the earlier English radical and humanitarian movements had made to the antislavery campaign, a contribution by that time long forgotten. It was there in Hyndman's republication in 1882 of Thomas Spence's well-known lecture on land nationalization. It was there in the new recognition of the older school of Ricardian socialists contained in Professor Foxwell's introduction of 1899 to Dr. Menger's book, *The Right to the Whole Produce of Labour*. And finally, it was there in the various books published during this period by the remarkable scholar J. Morrison Davidson, including *Home Rule for Scotland, Politics for the People, The Gospel of the Poor,* and *The Annals of Toil*. The last book especially was significant, for it consciously went back to the early radical origins of modern socialism in the class struggles of sixteenth- and seventeenth-century England. Its author looked at the Digger and Leveller movements; reminded his readers how bourgeois writers had conspired to suppress all mention of the revolutionary element in Cromwellian republicanism; and quoted extensively from books like Whitelocke's *Memorials of English Affairs* and Clement Walker's *History of Independency* to prove his point. He went on to point out how the principle of land nationalization, popularized in Henry George's economics, went back much further to Spence and Ogilvie (from whose *Essay on the Right of Property in Land* [1782] he quoted extensively), and to Patrick Edward Dove's volume of the 1840s on *The Theory of Human Progression*. He went on, in turn, to note how the Commune of 1871 had been unjustly turned to account in order to discredit the English republican movement then enjoying a brief popularity, and ended with the warning that the whole monopolistic system of land, capital, monarchy, and aristocracy could only be brought to an end by replacing parliamentary government with direct, popular democratic government.

This movement of return to the old radical roots, of course, was in its own turn forgotten as Fabian administrative state socialism took over and dominated the later Victorian and twentieth-century debate. The English labor and trade-union movements became inward-turned, parochial organizations hardly interested in any serious way in the outside world. One consequence of that—or perhaps even cause—was that, as A. L. Morton has described in his fascinating book, *The English Utopia*, of 1952, the great English tradition of the literary utopia, from More's *Utopia* up to Morris' *News from Nowhere*, with all of its brave optimism and faith in the possibility of a new world, was replaced with a new, reactionary anti-utopia literature, starting perhaps with Lord Lytton's *The Coming Race* (allegedly influenced by his own reaction to the episode of the Commune) and going on through Wells, Shaw, Aldous Huxley, and George Orwell. The dark pessimism of those anti-utopias, in which the old radical dream is changed and prostituted into an ugly totalitarian world of corruption, insecurity, thought control, the social engineering of people as robots, and the utter degradation of human nature, in reality reflects the growing crisis of Western capitalism and the gradual collapse of the old temper of bourgeois optimism and self-confidence. The ardent conviction of the Communards that the working classs could storm the heights of heaven thus became corrupted into the legend that such action, whether in France or Germany or England or Russia (with a cavalier disregard for different historical traditions and circumstances existing between one society and another) would surely lead mankind down into a nameless hell. Morton, indeed, might have gone further and noted the historical irony of that transformation. For the notion of an

Edenic society, so central to the utopic literature, was the work, from the sixteenth to the eighteenth centuries, of, so to speak, the literary left wing of the European emerging bourgeoisie, using the device as a means of criticizing all of the constrictions of the old feudal world against which that bourgeoisie was struggling. But, once its victory was completed in the nineteenth century, the device was no longer necessary; and, even more, it became necessary to denigrate it lest it be employed by other, more radical social forces for antibourgeois purposes. A literary idea in the service of an emerging bourgeoisie, this is to say, could not be allowed to become an idea in the service of an emerging proletariat. The treatment of the Commune by bourgeois historical science can only be fully understood in terms of that process.

There is one final point to make about the Commune. As both Marx and Engels insisted, a variety of theoretical interpretations of the event was possible because of the rich variety of revolutionary ideologies that were embodied in its leadership and in its rank and file. No one single ideology, it followed, could claim the Commune as its own; it belonged to them all. It is suggestive that the original Marx-Engels accounts accepted that truth. Marx's pamphlet emphasized the popular, democratic character of the revolt and the fact that the collective leadership was based on, and accountable to, the spontaneous revolutionary spirit of the people organized in the committees of the different arrondissements. Engels, in turn, in his 1891 introduction to the pamphlet, paid generous tribute to the Blanquists and the Proudhonists who composed the majority of the leadership, although noting at the same time that both of them had had to adjust their respective ideologies to the pressure of the popular democracy. In both cases, there was a noticeable absence of any argument in favor of a centralized, revolutionary cadre imposing its policies upon the elected bodies of the Commune.

It was, then, Lenin, in the passages on the Commune contained in his *State and Revolution* pamphlet over forty years later, who wrote a new gloss on the Marx-Engels interpretation. That gloss became the official doctrine of the European Communist parties, including the British Communist Party after 1920. It traced the weaknesses of the Commune to the lack of a ruthless, disciplined cadre of leaders who had the eye to see and the will to act against the class enemy. It thus distorted the reality of the event, for it injected a theory of antidemocratic elitism that did injustice to the multitudinous groupings of the movement and converted the Commune, as it were, into a sort of dress rehearsal for the October Revolution. It surely would have surprised most of the Communard leaders to have been told that they had been fighting for a reincarnation, in the style of Stalinist Russia, of that autocratic tradition, both Bourbonese and Napoleonic, that they all hated so much. It is the chief irony, indeed, of the official Communist thesis on the Commune that its finest heroes, whose portraits Lissagaray painted so lovingly in his history—Vermorel, Delescluze, Dombrowski, Maroteau, Varlin—were the sort of old-style European revolutionaries whose Russian counterparts of the old guard were among the earliest victims of the Stalinist dictatorship that set in after Lenin's death in 1924.

The Commune, clearly enough, has to be seen in terms of its own contemporary reality, its own contemporary expectations. "For the first time in modern Europe," wrote an English observer, "the workmen of the chief city of the Continent have organized a regular government in the name of a new social order." "If the nations," wrote a Communard exile, "do not open their doors to the working classes, the working classes will turn to the International. There exists in society a numerous and laborious class, powerful because able to act in masses, to whom your laws of property, family and inheritance do not apply. Either you must modify your laws, or this class will obstinately persist in attempting to create a society of its own, in which there will be neither family, inheritance nor property." On that radical question of social organization all the factions of the Commune were agreed. It is on the basis of that cardinal truth that they have to be written about, interpreted, and ultimately remembered in the pantheon of socialist history.

[Chapter 6]
Fabian Socialism:
The Collectivist Contribution

Of all the various factions that contributed to the ferment of ideas of the 1870s and 1880s—the Socialist League, the Social Democratic Federation, the republicans, the Communard exiles, the second Christian Socialist movement, the small band of Marxist disciples, and others—the Fabians were destined to have the most profound and lasting impact upon the development of English society. They helped shape, more than .any others, the philosophy of the Labour party. They laid the foundations, starting with their pioneer work in the study of national insurance against sickness and unemployment, of the modern welfare state. In their famous series of pamphlets, that dealt literally with every topic of national and social matters, from municipal socialism, the eight-hour day and local taxation, on to school clinics, the state purchase of railways, the endowment of motherhood, the legal minimum wage and workmen's compensation, they built up a veritable library of socialist propaganda based on a careful analysis of fact. They were, in a way, the progenitors of modern British sociology. The digging up of facts, to be later used as the basis of advisory briefs to be presented to civil servants and politicians, was far more congenial to them than the easy art of metaphysical generalization. Mrs. Webb learned the art from her master, Herbert Spencer, and then employed it to demolish the assumptions of Spencer's economic individualism. The London School of Economics and Political Science became a monument to that new methodology of social investigation. And to all that has to be added all of the qualities that came to be recognized as the trademark of Fabian effort: accessibility to new ideas, open-minded criticism, an immense learning that escaped from being mere academic pedantry, a sense of compromise, the distrust of mere rhetoric, an intense conviction of social service as the only real standard of personal life, an irreverence for established wisdom and a genius in demolishing its unexamined premises. The labor and trade-union movements of today, some ninety or so years later, with all their defects and virtues owe a large debt to those qualities.

Its main driving force, of course, was the remarkable intellectual partnership of Sidney and Beatrice Webb, aided by others like Bernard Shaw, Olivier, Bland, and, in a different way, H. G. Wells. But it was the Webbs who set the characteristic tone of the movement. Their work, over forty years or more, made them a force as powerful as that of Bentham a century earlier. Only to look at their series of books is to realize that truth. Their history of trade unionism—started, with that characteristic Fabian note of sacrifice of personal pleasure to public service, by using their honeymoon to delve into dusty trade-union records in provincial towns—established the study of economic history from the viewpoint of the ordinary trade-union member. Their *English Local Government* recovered for a field which had been rendered barren by the genealogist and the antiquarian a sense of how parliamentary institutions, throughout English history, had in a way only been made possible by the dedicated, obscure work of nameless ordinary men and women in the committee rooms of the vestry, the parish council, and the county council. Their *Socialist Constitution* showed, step by step, what the transition to a socialist society would mean in terms of institutional arrangements. Their *Decay of Capitalist Civilisation*, like Tawney's *Acquisitive Society*, was a powerful indictment of the erosion of moral principles that takes place in profit-oriented capitalism and indeed revealed a capacity for moral indignation which elsewhere was only too frequently hidden under the Fabian temper of dispassionate clinical analysis. It is not too much to say that, despite the hostility of the

[227]

orthodox academic world, this groundwork of research and writing prepared the way for the later work of the Hammonds, Cole, Postgate, and others. It even helped, slowly, to change the character of the universities themselves; a change summed up in Mrs. Webb's description of how, when seeking lecturers for the faculty of the new London school, candidates from the ancient universities were sharply disabused of their assumption that political science simply meant a formal study of ideas from Plato to de Tocqueville and were scandalized to discover that they would be expected to give courses on municipal taxation or electoral methods or housing legislation. The Webbs, in brief, revolutionized the study of English institutions from a socialist angle. They thus made possible an analytical understanding of institutions and institutional processes comparable to what Maine had done for ancient law and what Maitland had done for the medieval common law.

It is vital to appreciate the intellectual foundations of Fabianism. They were immensely diverse. There was something of Comteian sociology, something of Emersonian moral transcendentalism. There was something of the great movement of German thought, going back through the medium of Coleridge, which thought of the state organically and of society as composed of corporate persons and not simply the self-contained individual persons of the utilitarian creed. This element flowered in the new teaching of Bradley, Bosanquet, and T. H. Green in the Oxford quadrangles, in which the state came to be seen as the embodiment of the general will of society, and its function to at once remove the hindrances from and to provide the conditions for the good life of all of its citizens. There was, again, something of John Stuart Mill in his later socialist phase, despite the fact that, as Shaw at one point noted, it was the earlier Mill of the individualistic *Essay on Liberty* who was most influential at this time, so that an ardent Millite disciple like Henry Sidgwick could denounce Shaw's proposal for land nationalization as "a criminal proposal." But the Fabians, by contrast, learned more readily from the Mill of the later, and more radical, editions of the *Principles of Political Economy*. There was added to that influence the new marginal economics of Jevons as it was transmitted to the Fabians through theoreticians like Wicksteed, and the elaboration of the Ricardian theory of rent that had been worked out by Henry George. Something more, again, was contributed, as Olivier's contribution to the original *Fabian Essays* made clear, by that simple passion for social justice which, starting with the Lake Poets, passed through the Christian Socialists to culminate in the teachings of Matthew Arnold, Ruskin, and William Morris. To all that, finally, there must be added, as Mrs. Webb later noted, the sense of stricken conscience which the graphic revelations of Booth on continuing mass poverty in the London of the period engendered in members of the Victorian middle class. The influence of many of these varied strands of collectivist or neocollectivist thought can be seen, to take a single example only, in Sidney Webb's observation in his own contribution to the *Fabian Essays* that "the perfect and fitting development of each individual is not necessarily the utmost and highest cultivation of his own personality but the filling, in the best possible way, of his humble function in the great social machine."

Altogether, Fabian thought was a perceptive selection from the myriad ideas being propagated at the time. It did not claim originality in that field. It conceived of itself, in Bland's phrase, as merely giving intelligent direction to a thought-wave of terrific potency. The new ingredient it added, of course, was socialist; that is to say, it gave a consciously socialist dimension to ideas which, as with Green, for example, were those of a teacher who was merely a liberal in politics or, as with Bradley and Bosanquet, were those of mystic neo-Hegelians who thought of the state as some sort of higher consciousness unrelated to the social and economic structure of things. Looked at in this way, this is to say, the Fabians poured, as it were, new wine into old bottles. Thus it is misleading—as an American writer, Stanley Pierson in his book of 1973, *Marxism and the Origins of British Socialism*, has attempted to do—to interpret all of those pre-Fabian intellectual movements as in themselves socialist. All they did was to provide vastly different ideas which the Fabians then proceeded to adapt to their own ends. They encouraged and accelerated, in that way, an intellectual development toward collectivism which Bagehot had earlier prophesied with apprehension and which later Dicey regretfully catalogued.

Out of all this the Fabians, for a period that lasted into the twentieth century up to the period of World War II, created a movement of political education the impact and ramifications of which were no less remarkable because it was conducted without rhetorical fanfare or revolutionary posturing. It was imbued with an English sense of intense practicality. Merely to read the titles of the pamphlet literature put out by the movement over that time-period is to be made aware of the enormous range of questions—social, political, economic, administrative—with which the Fabian contributors were concerned. It had a passion for the assiduous collection of verifiable data, which constitutes the very essence of the modern social-sciences methodology, and its early historian, Edward Pease, has recorded how in 1905 the society undertook among its own membership the first reliable statistical enquiry into the voluntary restriction of pregnancy and birth in middle-class families. It was eager for workers' education, and did much to encourage the birth and growth of bodies like the Workers' Educational Association. Nor was the movement merely concerned, in the academic fashion, to collect knowledge. It knew that knowledge, to be fruitful, must be used as ammunition in a politically activist campaign to change society. With the Webbs, of course, that led to their doctrine of "permeation" and their lifelong campaign to educate the more intelligent sector of the English governing and ruling classes. In that campaign they were masters of the art. To be patient and accurate in their command of a topic; to persuade by careful argumentation the doubtful minister or the cautious civil servant; to wait for the moment when the time has come for the direct offensive; to be careful that the parliamentary troops in their favor have been fully briefed: these, after all, are the qualities essential to the art of political statesmanship. The Webbs themselves, in their personal qualities, were ideally fitted for the task. Sidney had the civil servant's capacity to organize a succinct brief, Beatrice the genius for informed and forceful conversation which would bring over the timid listener. The tactics frequently worked; and it is a well-known story how the modern Labour Exchanges system was born when Sidney persuaded the young Winston Churchill, then a liberal president of the Board of Trade in the Liberal 1906 government, to take William Beveridge, trained in Jowett's Balliol, out of the social settlement program of Toynbee Hall in East London and bring him to the Board of Trade. The Webbs, in brief, can be regarded as the founders of modern parliamentary socialism as we know it today.

In this capacity for hard work and no play the Webbs, indeed, were, ironically enough, eminent Victorians. They had all of the virtues of the Puritan ethic. They had the moral enthusiasm, the deep sense of duty, the awareness of the proper relationship between ends and means, of the Victorian mentality. In religious terms, it is true, they were agnostic. But it is only necessary to read Beatrice's published diaries to see that, in the manner of George Eliot, she had spiritual yearnings that had to find expression in some sort of secularized ethics, which for her became socialism. In that search there was no room for nonessentials. Their married life was probably sexless. Margaret Cole has described, in her memoir of Beatrice, what a visit to their London house or their weekend country retreat meant. Woe betide the unfortunate young man or woman who preferred to play tennis or billiards, or arrange a party, or read a novel, to joining in earnest conversation, or undertaking a piece of serious research, or becoming, generally, an undergraduate in the Webb academy. One had to be up and doing in the cause. Shaw has described, in his own turn, how, in the early beginnings of the society, its members eschewed the London gay life to read assiduously in the British Museum and then use the knowledge gained to attend every lecture available, held by whatever group, in order to bombard, sometimes metaphorically destroy, the speaker with deadly Fabian questions. It is easy enough to laugh at much of all this. But these are the qualities that any socialist movement must possess if it takes itself seriously. The observer of the contemporary English welfare state, especially in its "permissive society" phase of the 1960s and 1970s, with all of its hedonistic pursuit of pleasure, may perhaps be forgiven if he wonders whether the socialist movement does not require a revival of those virtues.

It is true that much of this was a quality of philistinism, which Shaw noted in another of his pamphlets. There is little evidence that the Webbs, and those who became their disciples, were interested much in art or literature. Novelists like Proust or Henry James would have seemed to them—if they had read them—to be wasting their creative genius in the nice, delicate analysis of the psychological springs of behavior in the members of the privileged upper classes. The visionary society of Morris' *News from Nowhere*, in which men have been released from the more onerous forms of work in order to enjoy leisure, must have seemed to them to constitute a life of terrible boredom. Nor must Chesterton's pungent and lively sense of religious faith as the popular culture of a new Merrie England—summed up in his characteristic assertion that "if by vulgarity we mean coarseness of speech, rowdiness of behaviour, gossip, horseplay, and some heavy drinking, vulgarity there always was wherever there was joy, wherever there was faith in the gods"—have seemed to them any more persuasive or attractive. They were, in brief, Puritans in Babylon; a judgment summed up in Wells', *The New Machiavelli*.

Yet there is a defense to be made even on this score. The Fabians, after all, were not living in the Merrie England of the utopia-makers but in the England of vast poverty, unemployment, malnutrition, and terrible slum housing conditions unveiled by the Booth investigation and further described, a generation later, in the angry indictment of C. F. G. Masterman's *Condition of England* book (1909), a volume

[232]

all the more remarkable because it was written by a Fabian sympathizer who had found, as junior minister in the reforming Asquith government, that the Fabian strategy of reform by means of the statute book could only manage to make a small dent in the massive social illnesses of Edwardian England. If, then, the Webbs felt impatient with the poetic fire of Morris, the mordant wit and verbal extravaganzas of Shaw, the passion for verbal perfection of Logan Pearsall Smith, the satire, at once half-gentle and half-savage, of Max Beerbohm, and the preoccupation of Clive Bell with the higher aesthetic forms of civilization, it was because they felt that these were private intellectual and artistic indulgences, fiddling, as it were, while Rome burned, and that as such they did little to contribute to the social reorganization that the Fabians wanted. In some of those individual cases, admittedly, they were wrong; they failed, for example, to see that underneath the teasing banter of Shaw, which almost made him into the licensed court jester of English literature, there lay a fierce anger with the same social injustices with which they themselves were concerned.

At the same time, their distrust of the habit of intellectual individualism was surely justified. They did not allow themselves to be sidetracked by individual campaigns against religion or in favor of vegetarianism or antivivisection. They knew that they had to have organized institutional allies, whether they were the Liberal party or the Trades Union Congress or the Labour Representation Committee. They were frequently impatient of the type of trade union leader, but they knew that he had to be worked with. They thereby ensured that Fabianism would not simply be an elegant intellectual coterie but a dynamic social force working within the mainstream of the national life. That explains why they did not degenerate into the kind of group that was the so-called Bloomsbury circle, with all of its ridiculous pretensions and private obsessions, notwithstanding the fact that many middle-class Fabians were intimately connected with that curious phenomenon of the London literary scene. The typical Fabian, as a result, never declined into being the type of well-meaning progressive who desperately wants to improve things but is convinced that improvement must follow his own pet prescriptions: a fault patently and glaringly evident in the figure of H. G. Wells. Nothing, perhaps, illustrates this Fabian temper better than the contrast between Mrs. Webb and Margot Asquith, as a reading of their respective diaries will make readily evident. Mrs. Asquith was the liberal society hostess in whom an undoubtedly genuine social-mindedness was subordinated to the intense enjoyment of Mayfair drawing-room politics and conversation. Mrs. Webb, on the contrary, was always the earnest social reformer bored and at times disgusted with the empty frivolity of that life-style, with its malicious gossip, its mannerisms, and its general tone of high society. The Fabians, in sum, knew that a meaningful social philosophy had to be founded upon the experience of those compelled to work for their living and that all private pursuits that frustrated its development and application had to be ruthlessly discouraged. Like the utilitarians before them, they were not interested in the "pursuit of happiness." They were interested in the "greatest good of the greatest number."

Their indictment of capitalism was, in essence, that through its very nature, and its property-relations, it frustrated the fulfillment of that end. The *Decay of Capitalist Civilisation* volume set the indictment in openly moral terms. Capitalist institutions are condemned as much because they degrade character and intellect as that they result in cyclical mass unemployment and the wastage of social and economic resources. As Plato noted, the division between rich and poor breeds the habit of arrogance on the one side and of servility on the other. The modern formulation of the division, the Webbs argued, produces a life of unconscious theft on the part of the wealthy and a spirit of vulgar respectability on the part of the poor. "The worst circumstance of capitalism," they wrote, "is . . . neither the poverty of the wage-earner nor the luxury of the property-owner, but . . . the glaring inequality in personal freedom between the property-less man and the member of the class that 'lives by owning.' " "The resulting servility, on the one hand," they continued, "and on the other the envy, or even the simple-minded admiration for a life' which is essentially contrary to all principles of morality, is as demoralizing to the poor as it is to the rich." Only the complete abolition of the "dictatorship of the capitalist," to be replaced by the socialist commonwealth based on intelligent national planning, could put an end to that condition.

It was perhaps the chief virtue of the founders of the movement that, in seeking that general purpose, they adjusted their ends and means to the special qualities of the national life and the national character. For good or ill, they made the labor movement that came in part out of their influence into a uniquely English thing. They avoided the spirit of antibourgeois bohemianism that was so typically continental, and that did so much to lay waste the genius of contemporary radicals like Oscar Wilde. The problem, as they saw it, was not to import alien methods and ideologies but the discovery of ways and means that were congenial to the English temperament, with the end result of building a planned society which safeguarded the habit of freedom by providing room for the individuality each British citizen, in his own unique way, tried to exercise. That meant two things. It meant, in the first place, an emphatic acceptance of the constitutionalist path, so that they would be accepted by the vast mass of ordinary, commonsense Englishmen as a group with their feet firmly fixed in the English habit of doing things. Revolutionary phrase-mongering, as they saw it, could only do immense damage by frightening the ordinary voter. It had to be replaced with organization, practical sagacity, well-informed educational agitation. "There is some truth," wrote Mrs. Webb, "in Keir Hardie's remark that we were the worst enemies of the social revolution. No great transformation is possible in a free democratic state like England unless you alter the opinions of all classes of the community—and, even if it were possible, it would not be desirable."

In the second place, this meant a determined effort to abjure anything approaching ideological rigidity. "There has never been a Fabian orthodoxy," wrote Pease, "because no one was in a position to assert what the true faith was. They applied the method of social engineering to questions hitherto left to the realm of sentiment." Fabianism, as a result, did not become an ideological tradition nor, indeed, a systematic world-outlook based on fixed principle. It thus avoided that equation of intellectual dissent with moral turpitude which was one of the least attractive aspects of Marx. It made it possible, in a very English sense, for people to be political enemies and social friends at one and the same time. It made it possible—through the loose affiliation of the Fabian Society with the Labour party—for the intellectual to enter into the mainstream of socialist politics, with the result that men like Tawney, Cole, Cripps, Laski, have been able to play a vital, active role within the party while, by contrast, their American counterparts have been denied such a role within the major American parties due to the powerful strain of anti-intellectualism in the American democracy. The Fabian slogan of the alliance of "worker by hand and worker by brain" thus became a reality, despite the natural strains and stresses between the intellectual wing and the trade-union wing of the party. It helped to break down the ivory tower character of the universities, as the work of Lindsay as master of Balliol showed; it helped to bring the university graduate nearer to working-class life, as the work of the young Clem Attlee in Toynbee Hall before World War I showed; and it helped, in turn, to bring the young working-class boy or girl to the university, as the work of Ruskin College demonstrated. That achievement in itself, apart from all of the others, would have justified the existence of Fabianism.

All this adds up to the credit side of Fabianism. Yet there is a debit side that has to be looked at, if only because, in retrospect, it has become so obvious to students of the movement in its various phases. It is true that whole new areas of the public sector of the national life have been largely the outcome of Fabian research, the great Minority Report of the Poor Law Commission of 1909, for example, or the recommendations of the Webbs in their book of 1920, *A Constitution for the Socialist Commonwealth of Great Britain*, on which the organization of the nationalized industries after 1945 was basically modeled. "We set ourselves two definite tasks," wrote Shaw in 1908, with that sense of supreme assurance which was itself one of their characteristic qualities, "first, to provide a parliamentary programme for a Prime Minister converted to Socialism as Peel had been converted to Free Trade; and second, to make it as easy and matter-of-course for the ordinary respectable Englishman to be a Socialist as to be a Liberal or a Conservative." They undoubtedly achieved both of those tasks with tremendous success.

The real problem concerns itself, however, with two major queries. First, there is the problem of means, summed up in the Webbs' doctrine of "permeation," as well as their other doctrine of the "inevitability of gradualness." Secondly, there is the problem of ends: what exactly did the Fabians mean by "socialism"? It is seriously open to question as to whether, with reference to both of those problems, they chose the right answers.

With reference to the first question, both the doctrines of "permeation" and of the "inevitability of gradualness" were founded on the grand assumption that the goodwill of the English ruling class, profoundly liberal, would permit, even actively facilitate, the quiet erosion of capitalism. Reasonable members of that class, it was argued, like Lord Rosebery or Mr. Chamberlain, would listen to the message courteously, would even be persuaded to believe and accept it, if its protagonists did not frighten them with wild revolutionary talk or impossibly impractical programs. The difficulty with that thesis was that, on the evidence, it appealed to only a small segment at best of the English ruling class. Mrs. Webb, as her diaries again show, was brought up in the closed, intimate circle of enlightened capitalists and liberal politicians of the period, while Sidney Webb was brought up in the equally closed circle of the middle and upper echelons

[237]

of the Whitehall civil service. Neither of them knew intimately —as did Wells, for example, who came from a different social background—the stolid conservatism of the English lower-middle classes. They tended, therefore, to mistake the response of those closed circles as a genuine conversion to socialism when, in reality, it was nothing much more than the compassion of the gentleman for the misery he sees around him: a far different thing than being a consciously intellectual adaptation to a world in which he accepts the validity and necessity of far-reaching change. With men, for example, like the younger Churchill, the response was merely the expression of the romantic paternalism of his father which went back, through Disraeli, to the old Tory Democracy of the earlier part of the century. With men like Lloyd George, it was primarily a Nonconformist revolt against aristocratic privilege. With men like Haldane, again, it was a passion for German efficiency in science and education picked up in his undergraduate continental experience. In all of them, progressivism of a neo-Fabian character was a partial response to limited problems, not a vision of the complete reconstruction of society along clearly defined institutive principles. And it is arguable that in fact they did not constitute a fully representative sample of the ruling class. That class was more characteristically seen in the type of the commercial adventurer like Wells's Ponderovo, or the munitions king like Shaw's Undershaft, or the hard-headed man of property like Galsworthy's Soames Forsythe. There was, if truth be told, not a little of patrician snobbishness in the Fabian outlook, which received an extreme statement in the curious observation of Ramsay MacDonald in his book of 1913, *The Social Unrest,* that the emergence of types like the Jewish financier, the American millionaire, and the Rand magnate had tended to destroy the "sentiment of respect" which corresponds to "real instincts in the human mind." It took the Fabians a long time, indeed, to realize that during the very same period in which their creed was maturing the intrinsic character of the ruling class and the Tory party was changing, with control passing from the mannered gentleman of the old school to the close-fisted, ruthless business tycoon of the new.

If that development increasingly made the strategy of "permeation" more and more unrealistic, it likewise increasingly invalidated the theory of the "inevitability of gradualness." That theory underestimated the importance of the time element in human affairs; most men, after all, are not prepared to wait for the slow evolution of remedial processes that will finally, at some undetermined point in the future, release them from their chains. It anticipated the quiet erosion of capitalism. That expectation, as R. H. Tawney has remarked, was not the statement of a preference but a sensible recognition of the facts of a world where life is lived in time. That may well be so. But it was a pragmatism that assumed the unbroken continuity of the social process. It was, thus, essentially Victorian, for it accepted the central premises of the Victorian civilization—the facile belief in progress, the concept of rationality, the power of informed argument alone to engineer social change. Like Green, the Fabians believed in the forward march of objective intelligence. Granted goodwill, they assumed that history made itself automatically, and that if given a little intelligent push it would work beneficent results. They thought of their movement, resultantly, as a remedy for ills which existed within rather than because of the major institutions of Victorian society.

The assumptions, of course, were the assumptions of the time, of a mental climate dominated by the ideology, in one way or another, of social Darwinism. With Hobhouse, it took the form of a principle of harmony which conceived the final end of state action to be the balanced coordination of the legitimate interests within society. With MacDonald, an erstwhile Fabian, it became an evolutionary collectivism in which socialism emerges as the outcome of the movement from one set of vital conditions in the social organism to another. With the Webbs themselves, it became the assurance that socialism was inevitable and that therefore its opponents had no alternative but to accept it as the wave of the future. All of these outlooks shared in common a Victorian atmosphere of marvellous optimism. H. G. Wells, writing later of the period, noted its implications. "Life as we knew it," he wrote, "was a leisurely game of consequences. It is difficult now, even for those of us who were already living in those days, to recall the entire absence of urgency that prevailed. We were carried along by habit and that false sense of security which the absence of fundamental crisis engenders."

The hallmark of the original Fabian ideology was its reluctance to think in terms of crisis, even to consider seriously the possibility of crisis. It believed in the sovereignty of reason. It did not sufficiently perceive that reason is a phenomenon related to social environment and that in times of acute social crisis it becomes a luxury that even educated men may be tempted to discard. It is significant that the irruption of World War I did not produce in the Webbs a recognition of the collapse of liberal values that Shaw noted in his savage introduction to *Heartbreak House,* or that the general world-wide crisis of capitalism after 1929 did not generate in them, with any of the profound perception of Wells, an awareness of the terrible power of destructive brutality that lay underneath the thin veneer of civilized habit. Mrs. Webb, on her own admission, did not read *Mein Kampf* until 1939. Obdurately English in their Puritanism, neither she nor her husband came to appreciate what Freud had to say about the nonrational springs of human behavior, a subject that Graham Wallas had always been fascinated with. Primarily utilitarians in their psychology, they underestimated the power of human nature in politics. That was why—to take examples at random—it was left to thinkers like A. D. Lindsay to illuminate the religious sources of English radicalism, why the Fabians never really understood the truth of Figgis' pregnant observation that political liberty has been, historically, the residuary legatee of ecclesiastical animosities, and why, finally, their outlook could not hope to generate the vigorous enthusiasm of the popular socialism of men like Robert Blatchford and the early *Clarion* days.

The Fabian strategy of means, then, was elitist. They sought, from the beginning, to work through the Whitehall civil servant, the liberal member of Parliament, the Fleet Street editor. It was a politics of the committee room, the London club, the country-house weekend meeting, the private assiduous lobbying of strategically located people within the machinery of government. Its basic defect was that, as a strategy, it could only have limited returns. For no ruling class, however liberal, will willingly surrender its real power and privilege. It may yield up the outer defenses; but it will not let go the inner citadels. There is a story of Mrs. Webb trying to persuade Balfour, the future Conservative prime minister, during a walk on the Thames Embankment, to read Shaw's *Three Unpleasant Plays*, and being rebuffed with the brusque answer that he never read unpleasant things; and the story illustrates the limits of the Fabian strategy. The ruling class was prepared to conciliate any challenge to its dominion so long as the continuing expansion of its economic system allowed concessions to be made. But once British capitalism began to contract—as it did after 1918 and increasingly after 1929—conciliation was changed into hostility; and the record of the hostility was contained in the history of the General Strike of 1926, the economic crisis of 1929, the Depression of the 1930s, the growth of the policy of "appeasement" toward Fascism, and, at home, grave violations of constitutional convention on the part of successive Conservative governments which even so cautious an authority as Sir Arthur Berriedale Keith condemned.

Yet it was even more than that. Capitalism, in its imperialist stage, produces war, as in 1914 and 1939. Wars, in their turn, break the cake of social custom; help unwittingly to democratize interclass relationships; create greater expectations in the masses as they come to see that if it is possible to plan for war it is also possible to plan for peace. There is much evidence, then, to substantiate the case that after 1914 it was the devastating social impact of war rather than the Fabian "inevitability of gradualness" that accelerated the chemical processes of change in the English social body.

[241]

Looked at from this angle, the war of 1914–1918 generated the transformation of mass political opinion that led to the decline of the old Liberal party and its replacement by the Labour party; similarly, the war of 1939-1945, by means of a similar transformation, led to the Labour governments after 1945. For the Fabians, those outbreaks of international violence were irrational aberrations from the main line of the evolutionary processes of industrial society. Had they read their Lenin or their Rosa Luxemburg, they would have been able to see them as logically inevitable consequences of that society.

Yet it is to the credit of many of the Fabians, including the Webbs, that they came to recognize, at least partially, their tactical and theoretical errors. That change can be seen in the Fabian work after 1918. They came to see that they would have to work through the organized Labour party if they wanted to get anywhere. They became, at the same time, less optimistic about the possibilities of peaceful change through constitutional democracy, because of the decline in the liberal temper of the ruling class. "We thought, perhaps wrongly," the Webbs wrote in 1923, "that this characteristic British acquiescence on the part of a limited governing class in the rising claims of those who had found themselves excluded from both enjoyment and control, would continue and be extended, willingly or reluctantly, still further from the political into the industrial sphere; and that whilst progress might be slow, there would at least be no reaction." By 1931, with the constitutional crisis of that year, the suspicion had become a conviction—outlined in Sidney Webb's important article in the *Political Quarterly* at the time—that the will and ability of Conservative forces to sabotage change were more powerful than they had imagined. By 1938 that conviction had become, with Beatrice at least, a remarkable apology to Marx. "Where we went hopelessly wrong," she wrote, "was in ignoring Karl Marx's forecast of the eventual breakdown of the capitalist system as the one and only way of maximising the wealth of the nation." They had assumed from the beginning the gradualist march toward a modified capitalism that would transform itself into socialism. They now recognized that there existed a fatal contradiction between capitalism and political democracy. "The rule of the capitalist and the landlord," they wrote, "has proved to be hopelessly inconsistent with political democracy. There can be no permanence of social peace in a situation in which we abandon production to a tiny proportion of the population, who own the means of production, and yet give the workers the political power to enforce demands on the national income which capitalism has neither the ability nor the incentive to supply." It has yet to be shown, a generation later, whether British capitalism, however modified it has become, can ultimately solve that contradiction.

There remains to be discussed the problem of what exactly the movement meant by "socialism." The Fabians tended to evade that question by insisting that theirs was a pragmatic outlook, based on what was possible rather than desirable. But even the most "practical" of outlooks is based on certain inarticulate assumptions; and it is not difficult to identify them in the case of Fabianism and its final achievement in the actuality of the contemporary British welfare state.

There can be little doubt, after reading the literature, that what the Fabians wanted was essentially a socialism of professional and technocratic expertise. They envisaged intelligent government by trained officials. When the Webbs wrote of the British system, as they saw it, that "the great mass of government today is the work of an able and honest but secretive bureaucracy, tempered by the ever-present apprehension of the revolt of powerful sectional interests, and mitigated by the spasmodic interventions of imperfectly comprehending ministers," they were expressing less the facts of the system than the principles of their ideal society in which the politician would defer to the knowledge of the professional permanent official. That antipolitical bias led logically to the particular items of the general Fabian scheme of institutional reform. They were strangely mechanistic in their character. The House of Commons was seen as an administrative institution only. The Cabinet, in turn, was viewed in similar terms, so that the Haldane committee report of 1918 on the machinery of government, with its Fabian inspiration, emphasized the planning and the administrative functions of the Cabinet, with an almost complete oversight of its political functions; an oversight only made possible if the Fabian separation of the machinery of government from the life of politics is accepted. A low estimate of the politician was implicit in that attitude; and the Shavian contempt for the parliamentary process itself was in one way only a logical extension of the hope of the Webbs that a socialist society would witness the replacement of political parties with numerous propagandist groups and the transformation of the traditional type of politician into a vocational representative of special groups. The Fabian proposals for parliamentary reform followed along similar lines. They included a scheme for a dual Parliament, with a political chamber and an industrial chamber, along with the idea that the practice of unified ministerial responsibility would gradually give way to a new type of committee government. They were proposals that were founded on extremely dubious postulates: that the separation of authority between two parliamentary bodies would produce greater legislative efficiency, and that separate categories of public policy can be insulated into different watertight compartments. The experience of the modern democratic state, whether in America or Europe, strongly suggests, on the contrary, that political and industrial problems are inextricably enmeshed one with the other. The experience, even more, of all modern societies, whether socialist or capitalist, suggests that so far no satisfactory mechanism has been found outside of the organized political party that will give the most adequate expression to the general will of those societies.

The Fabian predilection for a socialism of administrative bureaucracy can thus only be explained by the civil-service character of the Fabian outlook. The Webbs were not fascinated by the game of politics. It seemed to them a deplorable waste of powers. As Mrs. Webb said of themselves, they were not leaders of men, but initiators of policies. This led them to found an entire theory of public administration upon the perennial emergence of the first-class career service officer, after the manner of Sir Robert Morant or Sir Warren Fisher. It made them incapable of appreciating the meaning of Gladstone's remark that of all human animals the most difficult to understand is the politician. It persuaded them, at the same time, to exaggerate the character of the expert in government. For the history of the British civil service during the twentieth century, especially its strategic upper ranks, has been one that, generally speaking, has belied the Fabian great expectations. Its members possessed all of their well-known virtues: tact, devotion to duty, loyalty, incorruptibility. But they also had their well-known defects: excessive caution, obsession with routine, the temptation to marshal arguments for letting things alone on the assumption that if left alone things would look after themselves, the assumption, further, that their main task was to prevent the smooth course of departmental routine from being disturbed by ministerial error or parliamentary questioning. Recruited from a narrow social layer, their mental habits, on the whole, whether in finance or economics or social policy, were orthodox. Within his own narrow expertise, then, the average civil servant used his knowledge to resist innovation which, on principle, he regarded as dangerous; outside that expertise, he was the epitome of gross ignorance. Reform, then, when it did come, came from the outside: energetic ministers, members of parliament who were experts in their chosen fields, various sectors of public opinion, and, of course, radically minded political groupings. In a state bureaucracy of that character, in brief, obedience to rule was viewed as the hallmark of the successful official, mental eccentricity as the worst offense. The technique of administration—in a phrase used by critics of Sir Robert Morant—was his passion.

The contemporary welfare-state capitalism of the modern period was achieved, then, by other forces. But because its energizing spirit throughout has been Fabian it has taken on the Fabian bias in favor of centralized administration by experts. The bureaucracy of the private sector of British capitalism has been matched by the bureaucracy of the public sector. The organization of the nationalized industries has failed dismally to bring the worker or the union into the area of the decision-making process. The idea of localist democracy, along with the idea of workers' control—ideas so much at the heart of the short-lived guild socialism movement of the earlier period—has yet to receive any real institutionalized expression in the running of the state. Socialism as complete equality of income, which Shaw championed so vigorously, is still a dream only, as studies of the social background of recruitment in middle-class professions like law and medicine and the civil service itself, as well as the inequality of reward between their salary levels and the wage levels of the working class, adequately demonstrate. Both the public and private sectors of the national economic life are still conducted by what Max Weber, speaking generally, termed "the secret sessions of bureaucratic power."

It is important, of course, not to overemphasize this, if only because the Fabians have only too often been inaccurately portrayed by their critics as inhuman machines more interested in collectivism than in democracy. That note has been emphatic in the half-baked work of the reactionary neoclassical laissez-faire economists of the Simon-Hayek-von Mises school, with their equation of the welfare state and statist authoritarianism. This is to do a grave injustice to the Fabians, and certainly to the Webbs. The Webbs themselves were fully aware of the limitations of the civil service, as it stood in their time. They always emphasized the importance of a general enlightened civic sense and of outside experts which, together, could at once assist and criticize the formal service bodies. They believed passionately in the traditional civil liberties; they placed so much importance, indeed, on constructive parliamentary criticism that they were critical of the device of the quasi-governmental body because it weakened ministerial accountability to Parliament. The ultimate authority in public policy, they believed, should be the verifiable data of social science, which would be the best antidote against bureaucratic *amour-propre*. And not even on that point were they blind to the dangers; and the last chapter of their book on *Methods of Social Study* constituted, as indeed it still constitutes, an eloquent warning against the arrogant presumptions of the social scientist.

The real and rather different criticism to be made is that the Fabian outlook was perhaps too institutionalist. In its reaction against economic individualism it tended to lose that respect for human oddity which the younger Mill, for example, never forgot. What distressed it was less the spectacle of injustice than the waste and inefficiency in the capitalist system. As Chesterton said of Shaw, modern society annoyed the Fabians not so much because it was an unrighteous kingdom but because it was an untidy room. Their real heroes were the great administrators rather than political leaders or trade-union agitators. An interesting example of that preference is to be seen in G. M. Young's well-known *Victorian England: Portrait of an Age*, in which much space is devoted to the disinterested intelligence of the Victorian administrative reformers and little, by comparison, to the human comedy of the life of the masses. Namier, from a different viewpoint, introduced much the same sort of bias into his study of eighteenth-century politics, with its emphasis on political intrigue and connection, while playing down the influence of ideas. The Fabian genius, in brief, was generally practical rather than speculative; too much, so to say, of Bentham, too little of Rousseau. The limitation was aptly summed up at one point in an observation made by Professor Zimmerman. "The Webbs," he wrote, "are interested in town councils; Graham Wallas is interested in town councillors."

There were two consequences flowing from this selective character of the movement that ought to be noted. The first relates to its practical outcome in the post-1945 welfare state. The worst evils of late Victorian and Edwardian England have, admittedly, disappeared. But the society still remains an incongruous mixture of aristocratic remnants, plutocratic influence, and democratic political institutions, with a class structure which, although less rigid than before, still remains a class structure. The new ingredient, which may be regarded as the outcome of Fabianism, is the fresh group, within that structure, of the new meritocracy, selectively recruited by an educational system in which the group of a privileged few rise from the social lower ranks to be absorbed into the echelons of the Establishment: civil service, universities, business, commerce, and the mass media. Looked at, indeed, from a sociological viewpoint, what Fabianism did was in fact little more than facilitate that process of social mobility for the educated working-class and lower middle-class boy, leaving the vast mass of his peers still as the prisoners of an educational system not changed in any fundamental sense by the Education Act of 1944. The "old school tie" network of influence and jobbery has in fact been replicated by a new network whereby the new, rising meritocrats use the traditional ways and means of social status—the public school, London clubland, Hampstead, the city board of directors, the university senior common room—to consolidate their newly found position as an administrative echelon within the ruling class. It is a world described in detail in the saga of the C. P. Snow novels, the leading principle of which is the search for, and the exercise of, power within the same old closed world of English politics and government. No one can read that record without a growing suspicion that the poet's insight which led William Morris to argue that only open revolution can change fundamentally the English class society, with all of its pervasive arrogance and snobbishness, may have been a more perceptive understanding of the realities of the situation than that of his early Fabian critics.

The second consequence of Fabian selectivity, related to the first, concerns itself with the ideas of what might be called its more intellectually adventuresome protagonists. Both Shaw and Wells had their quarrels with the Webbs. Yet both of them exhibited in their own idiosyncratic way the ultimate implications of Fabian elitism. Both of them became caught up in the pseudo-science of eugenics made so popular at the time by the various vulgarized versions of Darwinism. With Shaw, it became a frank appeal for cultural segregation in the Fabian educating task, because only the educated man could lead society into socialism. Rational genetic planning would produce a new world of supermen, while rational sexual mating would produce the counterforce of the feminine life-force. Political democracy was dead, since the most it could do was to produce political leaders, like Boanerges in *The Apple Cart*, who were controlled by invisible business forces beyond the reach of social control. The only way out was a romantic hero-worship in which the strong man would deliver society from its evils. With Wells, this became the foundation for the vision, expressed in so many utopian neoscientific novels, of the Platonic rule of an intellectual race of Samurai who would lead the world into the sterilized and hygienic society of the future. In both cases, there is a marked fear of independent proletarian revolutionary activity: the new society is to be brought about, in some mysterious manner never fully explained, by brilliant philosophers or scientists who will persuade the ruling class to abdicate its power and privilege as it is made aware of the overwhelming inevitability of the laws of social evolution.

Much of all this, admittedly, was uncongenial to the pragmatic Fabian outlook. It would be simply unimaginable to think of Sidney Webb being persuaded by Wells, after having read, say, the latest report by the medical officer of health at Cardiff on the incidence of pneumoconiosis among South Wales miners, that the only solution to the problem was a nocturnal landing by Martian spaceships on Putney Common as a stopover on their superimperialist conquest of the universe. Yet at the same time it all fitted into the Fabian major principle that social ills stemmed from the neglect of applied intelligence and that such intelligence, if given a chance, can confer freedom upon those willing to receive it.

All of the various strands in the Fabian thread, in one way or another, accepted that outlook. Even a younger group of Fabians, in writing their pamphlet of 1930, *A Social Philosophy for Fabians*, despite their plea for institutional reforms such as decentralization and consultation in the processes of government, reiterated it. "Fabian writers," they noted approvingly, "have preferred the argument of fact rather than the consequences of inspiration, and they have often been content to leave latent the socialist position beneath the factual arguments. It is interesting to speculate to what extent this Fabian bias for facts was instrumental in freeing English socialist thought from a subjection to Communist fundamentalism." That temper of smug self-satisfaction helps as much as anything else to explain the Fabian failure. For it fails to see, as men like William Morris saw, that every movement needs its millenarian element; that socialism, like every other mass movement in history, needs faith, as well as reason; and that men, in the final resort, are moved not by what is rationally persuasive but by what is spiritually satisfying. Socialism, like every creed, needs its other component, in part moral imperative, in part crusading zeal, which persuades its devotees that it is not merely something to live for but, if the ultimate sacrifice is called for, to die for. It is enough to read Lady Scott's biography of A. D. Lindsay or R. Terrill's biography of R. H. Tawney to see that those great figures in the labor movement of the time were amply possessed of that component. But both of them were only marginally related to the Fabians and never part of the inner circle. The Fabian constituency was educated England; by contrast, both Lindsay and Tawney, in their common concern with adult education, addressed their socialism to the academically excluded of working men and women in the English social hinterlands. The socialism of the Fabians, in sum, was a sort of educated middle-class social hygiene. That there existed, outside of that world, a vast subterranean working-class culture, with its own history and its own values, was, at best, a phenomenon known intellectually but rarely experienced in any real sense. The Hammonds saw something of it in their histories of the Victorian town and village laborer; Arnold Bennett saw something of it in his novels of the Black Country; even the Webbs themselves saw something of it in their history of trade unionism. But on the whole it was a truth not in any way sympathetically comprehended by the Fabian outlook.

In terms of political theory the Fabians had no satisfactory theory of power because they had no satisfactory theory of the state. Philosophical enquiry, as such, had little appeal for them. They were content to accept the state, as they knew it, as the natural vehicle for their program. They implicitly accepted the viewpoint of Green that classic individualism lacked a sense of political obligation. Correspondingly, they were one with those critics of Mill's mid-Victorian essay who urged that its emphasis on individual freedom neglected to take into account the problem of social community. But they never elaborated a coherent theoretical statement of their position. The state, for them, seems to have presented itself as nothing more than a neutral mechanism largely controlled by administrative expertise. That it could become an engine of class rule they seemed to have rejected on the assumption that the economic types would increasingly become subordinate to the administrative type.

Not only did they thereby, as already noted, exaggerate the possibilities of fundamental change in the civil-service mind. They neglected, in addition, to face up squarely to what Wells aptly termed the "problem of the competent receiver." Their doctrine of "permeation" selected the liberal sector of the ruling class as the appropriate agency of change; after that, it became the leadership of the Labour party. It was supposed that the existing administrative structure, once subdued to the Fabian guiding hand, would be sufficient as a means of applying the Fabian remedies. Evolution, not revolution, was their motto. They consequently were unsympathetic to all of the methods—strike action, mass agitation, the boycott—which the more militant elements of the British working class, like the miners, used in the struggle against capitalism.

The Fabians were concerned, thus, less with the theory of the state than with its rehabilitation. Like Locke before them, they were not interested in its origins. Marx was uncongenial to them, just as Hobbes was to Locke, because he dug into the foundations of the state while they regarded such enquiry as unimportant. They were satisfied that the state was there and they welcomed it as the symbol of the public welfare. The practical problems with which they were concerned seemed to them to be capable of solution only by its increased activity. The problems raised by the nature of its authority over individuals or lesser associations—the central preoccupation of contemporary thinkers like Figgis—they did not broach. They did, of course, envisage a pluralist society in which trade-union, cooperative society, and professional association would play new and enlarged roles. But they always assumed an almost automatic harmony, rather than the possibility of conflict, between such groups and the sovereignty of the state; they had no answer to the problem of competing claims. Their entire outlook, in this field, arose out of their preoccupation with some type of administrative effort. It was an accident of their concern for public administration rather than an independent estimate of the state. The result was a sort of pseudo-philosophy bent to the discovery of the best methods for the conduct of planning and administration. They were, thus, the managerial revolutionists, essentially nonideological, par excellence.

This can be put in even more general terms. The Fabians were not overly excited by the adventures of ideas, in the manner of a Russell or a Whitehead. Leonard Woolf attempted a philosophical treatment of the relationship between historical time and social values in his *Principia Politica*, but it failed to attract any response from the English intellectual audience. Shaw, too, essayed a general philosophical statement; but his play prefaces and books were more in the nature of brilliant monologues of teasing, paradoxical argumentation in the eighteenth-century Voltairian manner rather than systematic social and political theory. The main Fabian ideologues, including the Webbs, retained throughout a scepticism of such efforts and a distrust of metaphysical systems in general. Thereby, of course, they put aside philosophy as impatiently as they put aside faith. There resulted from that a failure to appreciate that all so-called practical attitudes are, however unconsciously, based upon some general theory of man, society, and nature. It is the great thinker, like Descartes or Rousseau or Hegel or Marx, who constructs such a theory and, in so doing, draws, as it were, an intellectual map of the human adventure. By thinking dialectically, he helps men to see beyond the world of immediate appearance to that of the underlying reality of first principle on which appearances are based. He confers design, meaning, purpose upon the mass of experience. He defines what is possible in the world of social endeavor. He may not be a household name like the soldier or the politician. But because he shapes, more than any other type, the climate of opinion, he helps fashion the unexamined assumptions on which men who may never have heard of him behave in their daily lives. Even in their own lifetime, then, it was the system of Marx rather than that of the Fabians that was already working the more profound and lasting impact. Likewise, in the second half of the twentieth century, the really important work in the construction of a philosophy that meets the new problems of the age has been done, and continues to be done, not by the English practitioners, who remain obdurately Fabian, but by the Continental Marxists—Sartre, Garaudy, Lukacs, Althusser, Gramsci—who, using the original rich deposit of Marxism, have presented modern man with a picture of the organic totality of relationships that holds together technology, science, philsophy, religion, and the arts.

"The experience of practical politics," a friendly Canadian critic has written, "shows that the Fabian process of permeation is one that can work both ways." Nothing illustrates the truth of that remark better than the ease with which the Fabians took over the characteristic viewpoint of the English ruling class in the sphere of international relations. They were incorrigibly English in their attitude to the outside world. They accepted the world-wide domination of the English industrial civilization as a fact of life, and the legend of England's superior excellence that went along with it. Throughout English history there has always been a play of subtle influences which have drawn about the minds subjected to them an invisible but impassable charmed circle beyond which no outlook or sentiment has been able to trespass. That has been the basis of the sense of being English, the hard core of English national patriotism. It has left its mark upon all political parties, the left as much as the right. The Fabians, and, after them, the Labour party had their full share of the sentiment.

That explains why the Fabians were rarely excited by the world outside. Wells wrote two perceptive books on America; but although the Webbs could suggest, as in their remarks on Wilson's *Congressional Government* book, that they could have written a fascinating volume on American government, the promise was never fulfilled, and it was left to Lord Bryce to perform the task. They paid little attention to Continental thought. It would be difficult to imagine them writing, say, on the French revolutionary tradition, and it was Belfort Bax who wrote in 1911 one of the very first serious English studies of the socialist element in that tradition, entitled *The Last Episode of the French Revolution*, an account of the conspiracy of Gracchus Babeuf. It is true that their historian recorded, with some pride, that the very first Fabian tract was written by the American worker, W. L. Phillips, who had worked in the slave "underground railway" movement of the American pre-Civil War period. But the implications of that fact were never followed through, and the Fabians never accepted the Marxist concept of the international civil war between capital and labor. They thus never in any real sense appreciated the truth that socialism was an international struggle, a truth summed up in the observation of Graham Wallas that socialism should become a "world-purpose in whose light the death and maiming of a whole generation of young men in war may be seen as resulting from the same failure of imagination and sympathy as that which produces Chicago slums and Mexican peonage. . . ."

That insular temper was of course typically expressed in

the Fabian attitudes to the emergent imperialism of their time. The society was in fact only reluctantly drawn into a discussion of imperialism by the outbreak of the Boer War, which precipitated a division of its membership between anti-imperialist and proimperialist groups. Significantly, it was the proimperialist group that won out, with its views expressed in Shaw's pamphlet, *Fabianism and the Empire*. After that event, the Fabians turned with relief to domestic problems, almost as if the war had simply been a minor aberration. Graham Wallas could charge in 1916 that he did not think the society had ever published a word on its own responsibility about India. It is true that, later on, with the establishment of the Fabian Colonial Research Bureau, the society preoccupied itself much more with colonial problems. But it still saw those problems as simply a matter of the improvement of the colonial service in its task of white trusteeship; and a Fabian colonial expert like Rita Hinden believed as much as a conservative colonial expert like Marjery Perham that the British imperial task was to transfer the methods of British parliamentary democracy to Africa and Asia, without much comprehension of the anthropological inappropriateness of such a policy. An extreme example can be found in the curious book written by one of the early members of the society, Cunninghame Graham, on one of his eighteenth-century ancestors, Robert Graham of Gartmore, who had been a Jamaican planter. The Jamaican plantocracy of that time, wrote Cunninghame Graham admiringly, were "empire builders" leading the life of the English squirearchy overseas, with the slaves constituting a mass of bogus Christians from "warlike races," who bellowed their hymns in the daytime and resorted to evil obeah practices at night.

There were, admittedly, individual and remarkable exceptions to this outlook. Olivier, a founder member, later became Governor of Jamaica, and in that position wrote a series of able books on Jamaica, and Leonard Woolf, as a colonial district administrator in Ceylon, was ultimately driven to resignation because he recognized the gross moral inconsistency between empire and democracy. Even so, they were both voices crying in the wilderness. Olivier has described how his books were only too often regarded by even educated members of his own class as merely tourist guides instead of as serious analysis of the colonial social problem; while Leonard Woolf has described in his engaging memoirs how difficult he found it, after his return to England, to interest his Fabian friends in the colonial issue. The reader who wants to know something, then, about the historic encounter of East and West, going back to the early travels of the Jesuit missionaries of the late medieval and early modern period, must go to the fascinating books of a writer like Maurice Collis; and how little this sort of thing had to do with ideological preferences in domestic politics is evident from the amusing fact that Collis was a homebred conservative and an intimate friend of Lord Astor and the neofascist "Cliveden set" of the England of the 1930s.

When it came to the issues of colonialism, imperialism, race, and color, then, the Fabians were the least revolutionary of people. They believed in efficient and large units of government, from which it followed that imperial control and utilization of non-European territories was justified since they could be conceived as embryonic forms of international organization. There was inherent in history, as they saw it, an evolutionary process toward world "civilization," and any country that stood in its way, by reason of a false and romantic appeal to "nationalism," could justifiably be forced to surrender to that higher force. They were for Home Rule for Ireland, therefore, but not for Irish independence. Their test of "civilization" was implicitly that of industrial and technological Europe, which came perilously near to the American doctrine of manifest destiny, with its conviction that American "civilization" had almost a divine right to absorb all those "less civilized" elements, from the Plains Indians to South American republics, that stood in the way of the rational exploitation of the natural resources of the world. Their belief in free trade reinforced that conviction, so that inferentially Europe became justified in forcing countries like India and China to open up their frontiers to the beneficent effects of international trade and commerce. No individual nation, as Shaw's pamphlet argued in a question-begging analogy, had the right to do what it pleased with its own territory without reference to world interests any more than a landlord had the right to do what he liked with his property without reference to the interests of his neighbors. The flaw of the argument was that it assumed the existence of a higher world-authority to enforce that obligation, so that in the end result the argument implicitly legitimized the temptation of the big imperialist power, within the framework of the international anarchy, to impose its will upon a weaker country. It is true that once a higher international authority did appear, later on, with the birth of the League of Nations, the Fabians ardently supported it. Shaw's later Fabian tract of 1929 argued cogently that the most vital aspect of the new body was not so much its diplomatic activities as the growth within it of a genuinely international public service, thus becoming a school, as it were, for a new international statesmanship as against the old and dying Foreign Office diplomacy and its obsolete practitioners after the manner of the type of Sir Eric Drummond. Yet even then the old Fabian passion for organized uniformity asserted itself once more in Shaw's complaint that things like Nordic and Latin "temperaments" hindered the new style, and that the league would not succeed until mankind became a much less miscellaneous lot than it was at present.

For the most part, then, the Fabians, even when they supported the idea of a world order, assumed an order along European lines. It was hardly surprising, then—to take a few examples only—that the society did not think it necessary to issue a definitive statement of its attitude to the war of 1914–1918; that Sidney Webb, as colonial secretary in the 1929 Labour cabinet, sided with his departmental officials in upholding the privileged status of the white settler group in the East African colonies; and that in the later period of the 1930s and 1940s the society supported the policy, with the single exception of independence for India, of merely granting internal self-government for the colonial possessions within the framework of continuing British control. As the

Trinidadian labor leader, Captain Cipriani, bitterly complained, the Labour party in opposition was one thing, in office quite a different thing. The outcome of this narrow-minded attitude was that the labor movement was completely unprepared for the great wave of anti-imperialist nationalism that swept through the colonial world like a prairie fire after 1945.

Yet this cultural Europocentrist bias went even further than that. The theoretical basis of Fabian social imperialism was that of a virulent eugenicism. The dining club known as the "coefficients" established early on by the Webbs openly sought to promote the causes of empire and national efficiency based on the idea of a planned population policy designed to weed out the "weak" and encourage the "strong." Much of the completely unscientific argumentation of the policy was drawn from the race-selection writings of Karl Pearson. Sidney Webb's pamphlet, *The Decline of the Birth Rate*, warned of the national "degeneration" of stock if the Jews and the Irish were allowed to become a preponderant element, thus frustrating the great purpose of raising "an imperial race." The note of class and race elitism was echoed in the writings of all the early directors of the London School of Economics, all of them handpicked by Webb himself as part of the Fabian strategy. W. A. S. Hewins wrote an autobiography, *Apologia of an Imperialist*, in which he boasted of the fact that the school was the first institution to undertake teaching and research on the policy and administration of the empire. Halford MacKinder fashioned a strange theory of geopolitics in which the British were destined to undertake, as trustees, the education of "the half-civilized millions" of the world through the medium of a strong, white Commonwealth. William Pember-Reeves, a confessed New Zealand racist, could manage to write that "the average colonist regards a Mongolian with repulsion, a Negro with contempt, and looks on an Australian black as very near to a wild beast; but he likes the Maori and treats them in many respects as his equals . . . the finest race of savages the world has ever seen." The contribution of William Beveridge, in his turn, was to argue, in a volume edited by the Webbs, for the sterilization of those workers deemed "unfit" for efficient employment; while Carr-Saunders added to this a pseudo-biological theory attempting to show not only that the white "races" were superior to all others, but also that there were biological differences between various strata of the domestic social structure of Britain, thus completing a general line of argument in which racist and genetic myths were employed to justify both internal and international inequities of social reward.

Since most of the histories of Fabianism have generally overlooked this preoccupation with the idea that genetics could play in biology the role that relativity was coming to play in physics, it deserves a little elaboration. Both Wells and Shaw, as already noted, had toyed with the idea, envisaging a "new eugenics" which would experiment with the human genetic endowment as a means of human species improvement. Wells's novel, *The Island of Dr. Moreau*, painted a picture of what this could mean in terms of a new "genetic surgery." Many of its Fabian protagonists no doubt saw it only as a mechanism for curing disease. But only too often others saw it, more ambitiously, as a mechanism for "improving" the human species, not sufficiently perceiving that it could lead to the danger of a genetically controlled society, replete with new and more subtle tools of social controls; social controls, moreover, which could be used against "inferior" classes and races. The Fabians who entertained this frightening dream thus failed to appreciate the lesson that the technologically possible is not always the ethically acceptable. Nor did they see that by thus violating the line that must be drawn between the uses and the abuses of science they were giving fresh ammunition to those capitalist mass media, especially the movies, that over the last fifty years or so have used the "mad scientist" syndrome to further their anti-intellectual message.

Looked at from this angle, the Fabians were characteristically little more than the liberal allies of the British imperialist ruling class. They were part and parcel of the general process whereby European socialist movements in the modern century have helped the Western industrial technology to destroy native economic and cultural systems throughout Asia and Africa with little effort to prevent, even to ameliorate, the economic misery and the cultural dislocation which overwhelmed them. They blindly accepted the classical European model of "development" without seeing that it really meant at once the elimination of native civilizations that predated the advent of the white man to Asia or Africa or the Americas by centuries and the destruction of viable agricultural economies on the altar of the Western adoration—shared by European left and right alike—of machine technology. Shaw could write a piece on *The Little Black Girl in Search of God*. But it was nothing more than a typical exercise of Shavian mocking of all world religions; it failed utterly to see that the black girl was the outcome of a detribalizing and deculturating movement set in motion by European capitalism with the "scramble for Africa" that developed during the last quarter of the nineteenth century. The Fabians, all in all, as far as their internationalism was concerned, saw the world from the perspective of the colonizer, not from the perspective of the colonized. They saw China, for example, as simply the "yellow peril," so that it was left to great journalists like Edgar Snow to reveal to the Western world the tremendous, earthshaking implications of the Chinese Communist revolt led by Mao Tse-tung and Chou En-lai. They were, in brief, typical of that process whereby, in the history of the European socialist movements, the ideology of a genuine socialist internationalism has been sacrificed, at every crucial moment, to the xenophobia of the nationalist spirit.

It could be argued that the Webbs' visit to the Soviet Union and the book that the visit produced, in the twilight of their lives, belies that generalization. Yet in a very real sense that book, to the contrary, is still further evidence of the Fabian insularist temper. Trotsky's judgment on "socialism for radical tourists" may be too unjust; yet it is not altogether inaccurate. For it is not too much to say that the book interpreted the Soviet Union from the viewpoint of the English liberal metaphysics of which Fabianism was only a particular expression. It led, then, to disastrous errors of judgment about the Soviet experiment. Its authors saw, rightly enough, the positive side of the experiment. What they termed the "vocation of leadership" in the Communist party—with its dynamic enthusiasm, its zealous sacrifice of private life to the public good, the opportunity offered to talent, the appreciation of science in the new education, the moral austerity of party members—appealed to their instinctive asceticism. They saw that planned production for community consumption was the principle for which they had themselves fought within the English experience. Yet at the same time they saw all of this through alien, English eyes. They saw the Russian communist as some sort of Soviet Fabian. They were thus only too easily blinded to the fact that their English assumption that reasonable men will always use power reasonably did not fit into the Russian pattern. They accepted a literary theory of the Soviet Constitution. To argue that Stalin was only the secretary-general of the party, comparable to the position of the American president, overlooked the fact that he was, in reality, a popular dictator, not to mention the fact that, if the Webbs were right, their interpretation failed to explain the Oriental-like veneration of his person already much in evidence at the time of their visit.

To argue, again, as they did, that the device of "democratic centralism" provided for free speech within the regime neglected to note that, historically, such freedom requires that dissenters be able to carry their case to an unfettered public opinion and that, further, they be permitted to organize their dissent within the framework of the party organization: both of them conditions that had effectively been eliminated with the ouster of Trotsky and his colleagues. It is true that the Webbs noted the "disease of orthodoxy" in the regime. They failed to appreciate, however, that this was no accident but an inevitable outcome of the sclerotic rigidity of

Stalinist communism, and that as long as dissent was viewed as a heretical challenge to the state authority rather than as an honest criticism of party policy, the gradual liberalization of the regime which they anticipated would be highly unlikely to develop; as, indeed, the later Stalinist purges grimly proved. It says much for the more prescient insight of H. G. Wells that in his 1934 conversations with Stalin he perceived the symptoms of paranoia in the Russian leader which the Webbs were incapable of recognizing.

The major error of the Webbs, as of the international socialist movement of the period, was to see the Russian experience through ideological eyes instead of evaluating it in terms of the Russian historical tradition. The year 1917 was not the open break with the past it was so easily assumed to be. No revolution, however extreme, creates a tabula rasa on which new cultural forms and habits can be imprinted. The Stalinist temper can thus only be understood as a continuation of the old czarist temper dressed up in revolutionary rhetoric. It was a temper deeply rooted in Byzantine origins. It escaped the influence of Greco-Roman rationalism. It missed the Reformation and the enthronement of individual conscience that was, if only indirectly, the final result of that event. The Greek Orthodox church shaped its concept of authority. It has thought of power, accordingly, in theological terms rather than in terms of the western European tradition of reason. In this light, the theory and practice of Russian communism have been more Russian than Marxist. They exhibit the pervasive sense of sin, the sick conscience, the yearning for expiation, the passion for martyrdom, that haunt the Russian literature of the nineteenth century. The antirationalism of Dostoevsky, the Slavophilism which even influenced Westernizers like Belinsky, the nihilism which persuaded men like Bakunin that all institutions were evil, all share the influence. The Stalinist concept of the party, in its turn, goes back to the czarist period under which revolutionary groups, as in Dostoevsky's *The Possessed,* were obscure and underground conspiracies disciplined by mutual fear; and Tchakev's well-known letter to Engels, in which he advocated a guiding cadre founded on a Jesuit discipline, was inspired by Bakunin's revolutionary insurrectionism. It is in the work of other scholars—the various books of Sir John Maynard, for example —rather than in the Webbs' volume, that this background is more fully appreciated. In much the same way, it might be added, the new post-1949 China, despite things like the anti-Confucian campaign of the Cultural Revolution, can only fully be understood if it is remembered that the Chinese attitude to the outside world still remains rooted in the powerful ethnocentrism of the Middle Kingdom tradition, and the new post-1959 Cuba can only fully be understood if it is remembered that, notwithstanding the official Marxist-Leninist language, the *fidelista* revolution has its intellectual roots in the proud *cubanidad* of nineteenth-century thinkers like Saco and Martí. It is difficult not to feel that the Fabians made the pilgrimage to Moscow, just as before them the Tractarians had taken the road to Rome, in order to find consolation and comfort in a foreign faith denied to them at home.

What, then, must be the final verdict on the Fabians? For fifty years or more they were the main catalyst of the British labor movement. When the balance sheet, on both the credit and debit sides, has been drawn up, it is clear that their most lasting achievement was to help bring into being the British form of welfare-state capitalism as it stands today. It was, of course, a limited achievement, for there was nothing really fully socialist in it, either in a domestic or an international sense. But for all that, nonetheless, it was something. It helped persuade the liberal sector of the ruling class that if it wanted to avoid revolution it would have to accept reform. The analogy with the slavery abolitionist movement of the earlier period is apposite. The abolitionists, for all of their defects, managed to persuade the ruling class of their period that if slavery was not terminated by constitutional means it would be terminated by violence, with the result that abolition, in the English case, was achieved by parliamentary enactment which the West Indian plantocracy was obliged to accept, whereas in the American case abolition was only finally achieved through civil war. Similarly, the Fabians persuaded the ruling class of the later period that a social-welfare program would have to be accepted, albeit reluctantly, or else an openly revolutionary movement would bring it about; by contrast, the French and the German ruling classes chose to ignore that lesson, with the result that they were overwhelmed, in the French case, by the war of 1940 and, in the German case, by the Nazi revolution of 1932. To have saved England from a similar catastrophe was no mean achievement. The Fabians, on the evidence, are entitled to the claim that the achievement, in large part, is a monument to their work.

[Chapter 7]

Churchill as Historian:
The Response of the Master Class

No discussion of radical thought can be complete without some consideration of the response that it evokes in the master class of the society. For there takes place a continuing dialectic between those groups seeking fundamental change and those that resist it. To employ the suggestive conceptual framework elaborated by Karl Mannheim, the ruling groups concerned with the continuing stability of a given social order develop an "ideology," a series of ideas and institutive principles designed to legitimize their concrete social and economic interests; while those groups seeking to transform the given social order construct a "utopia." The first phenomenon seeks to conceal the reality of the present by comprehending it in terms of the past; the second seeks to transcend the present by orienting its analysis to the future. Both "ideology" and "utopia" thought-systems, in their turn, must be seen as expressions only to be fully comprehended as they are seen as set within the sociohistorical conditions of their given time period. Both of them, in Mannheim's terms, contain the imperative that every idea must be tested by its congruence with reality. Both of them see reality from different perspectives. Two important conclusions flow from this analysis. First, as a subordinate group or social class becomes, by one means or another, the master class in a given society, its utopian mode of thought becomes transmuted into an ideological mode of thought. Secondly, it is impossible to establish absolute truth, because the "sociology of knowledge" is in effect the sociology of the struggle between different social groups.

How does this fit into the English historical experience? The primary historical fact shaping English ruling-class "ideology" is that, since 1689, there has existed no serious challenge to its domination of the national life. The blend of aristocratic conservatism and bourgeois liberalism cemented an alliance which made possible the rise of the capitalist order without any real resistance either from a displaced nobility or a class-conscious rebellious proletariat. It followed, resultantly, that there existed no real objective necessity to develop a coherent "ideology." It was only necessary to develop a sociopolitical theory of accommodational adjustment to each particular historical moment as it arose. For the aristocratic component of the ruling alliance that theory was constructed by Burke, with his skepticism of general ideas; for the component of the liberal-democratic bourgeoisie, it was constructed by John Stuart Mill, with his defense of liberal individualism. The two elements combined to produce the well-known English pragmatic temper, with its distrust of abstract categories and principles of social organization. It produced, in turn, the special myth that the English, by some mystique of "national character," were an empirically minded people. The truth, on the contrary, is that the absence of profound challenge to the ruling aristocratic-bourgeois alliance after 1689 negated the necessity to construct either an abstract philosophical system or an abstract theory of politics. The French and German cases were different, because the rising bourgeoisie faced throughout the serious threat of destruction from both left and right, as the history, respectively, of the French Third Republic and the German Weimar Republic demonstrated. That explains why the dominant thought-system in eighteenth-century England was Burke, not Hegel, and in nineteenth-century England John Stuart Mill and not Marx. It explains the difference between Hume and Diderot, between Stubbs and Ranke. It explains why English political philosophy has rarely examined the foundations of the social order, with the single exception of Hobbes, who was driven to such an examination by the trauma of the Civil War of 1640. It explains, all in all, the stubborn parochialism of English thought in all of its departments: philosophy, political theory, anthropology, sociology; and why, up to the present day, the leading institutions of the society—the church, the universities, the civil service, the political parties—exhibit the same temper of Podsnappian self-satisfaction.

The English intellectual scene has in its own turn reflected this. It is no accident that the effort, in sociology, to refute Marx has been the work of the Continental bourgeois scholars—Simmel, Max Weber, Durkheim—who in the very process of their refutation testify to the profound influence of Marx himself on their theoretical statements. It is no accident, either, that the effort of Marxist scholars to bring Marx up to date has been one, again, of Continental theoreticians from Rosa Luxemburg to Gramsci, Lukacs, and Adorno. The failure, in turn, despite the early effort of Herbert Spencer, to fashion a classical sociology pregnant with a coherent world-perspective can be traced to the inbred provincialism of the English university culture; and even when such a synthetic grand design grew up in the associated field of anthropology it is explained by the fact that anthropological studies were notoriously developed as an intellectual justification for British imperial rule. All this, in turn, was facilitated by the fact that the university intelligentsia, from the beginning, were coopted by the ruling class, with the Oxbridge system becoming at once a nursery for the training of the administrative cadre of the system, both domestic and colonial, and cultivating intellectual habits of thought openly skeptical of iconoclastic speculation. The typical university scholar thus became a busy antiquary cultivating his own private field of "research," to be finally rewarded, if he gained eminence in his speciality, with a knighthood or the Order of Merit. It has been a rare scholar, like Collingwood, for example, who has used his historical insight to move forward to a radical stance on the social issues of the day. For the rest, scholarship, as in the work of Namier, has been a nostalgic apologetic contrasting the unbearable anarchy of the modern world with the quiet

[267]

social stability of eighteenth-century England. The genuinely radical scholar, who uses his analytical tools to criticize the contemporary bourgeois society, as Deutscher in his Marxist and Soviet studies, has been ostracized with that genius for isolating the outsider which the English have developed to a fine art; the Marxist historian who does not so suffer, like Christopher Hill, is accepted because studies, however radical, of seventeenth-century Puritanism are hardly calculated to seriously embarrass the politico-academic ruling clique. So, it was left to Harvard University, in an inspired moment, to recruit the great socialist humanist, A. N. Whitehead, to its faculty after his retirement from Imperial College, London; and there is equal significance in the fact—so damning a comment is it on the elegant and tired conservatism of the English closed university world— that so many of the literati who satirized the cultural atrophy of English life—Henry James, Shaw, Wells—were denied access to that world.

It is against this background that the figure of Mr. Churchill as the historian of capitalism and imperialism must be set. Spurious collective cultures breed spurious personal reputations. The collective Churchill opus, from the early *World Crisis* to the *History of the Second World War*, and on to the four volumes of the *History of the English Speaking Peoples*, has been applauded by the academic mandarins while, by contrast, the academic world, a generation earlier, scoffed at Wells's pioneering *Outline of World History* because it attempted a global, syncretic analysis of world civilizations going beyond the English insular outlook. The Churchillian work is therefore rewarding of study because, with all of its naive aplomb, it accurately reports the response of the English ruling class to the cataclysmic changes that have overtaken that class over the last fifty years or so. Because, too, he is not the professional historian like Bryce or Acton but the popular historian like Froude or Trevelyan, he reflects

English pride and prejudice in all of their pure form. He seeks, not to analyze the English national experience, but to celebrate it.

In the twin histories of the two world wars the reader is listening, of course, to the great political actor whose experience in practical affairs no historican can hope to recapture. Like Lloyd George's *Memoirs*, they are the partisan defense of wartime politico-military strategies advanced by an active participant, in the case of World War II of the prime minister himself. As such, they are necessarily one-sided, for if the *Crisis* volume is a self-justificatory defense of the politicians against the soldiers, the *History of the Second World War* is an apologetic for the Churchillian national leadership, accompanied by fierce prejudices and personal animosities, as the publication of the Alanbrooke *Diaries* has shown. In much the same way, recent critical scholarship has shown how the young Churchill, as newspaper correspondent, irresponsibly exaggerated his adventures when he portrayed himself as a sort of James Bond character riding with the famous Spanish general Martinez Campos against Cuban rebels, fighting Pathan tribesmen with the Bengal Lancers, joining the cavalry charge at Omdurman in 1898 against the forces of the Dervish empire, and marching with Buller to the relief of Ladysmith. The *History of the English Speaking Peoples*, on the other hand, is an attempt to apply the perspective of the amateur historian to the history of a thousand years. The two efforts are naturally interrelated, for if a military historian like Captain Liddell-Hart gained much of his understanding of strategy and tactics from his personal experience in World War I, Mr. Churchill can describe the great soldier or the decisive battle as one who himself personally participated in military campaigns, however much he might have romanticized his remembrance of the experience. The interrelationship, of course, can at times produce dubious historical analogy; when, for example, the Tories who opposed the war policies of William III are compared to the Conservative party isolationists of the Baldwin-Chamberlain period of the 1930s it is evident that the historian has been replaced by the politician.

History in the Churchillian style, it goes without saying, is generously conceived. It defies the professionalist assumption that with the advance of research and specialization, history in the grand manner has to be relegated to the lumber room. Lucid narrative, architectonic style, vivid description are married to a wisely tolerant spirit ready to forgive most everything except the betrayal, in men or nations, of the ultimate verities within them. There is the perfect connection between form and thesis naturally to be expected from the great parliamentary orator. There is the power to describe in unforgettable phrase the deeper resolution of the national spirit. It is not in itself insignificant that the seminal moments of the various works are those five momentous periods within the last four centuries when England has been challenged to defend herself against a Continental rival—Philip II, Louis XIV, Napoleon, Imperial Germany, and, lastly, the Axis powers. There, Mr. Churchill rises to his most supreme heights because nothing stirs him so profoundly as the sense of the British "mission." half in Europe, half extending over the world, as it sets itself against mighty protagonists to reach forward to its opulence and dominion. Born into the aristocratic tradition, he has all of the gentleman's determination to crush the enemy who dares challenge him, yet at the same time the gentleman's respect for a brave opponent; so that the prime minister's act of stretching across the havoc of war in 1942 to acclaim the greatness of Marshal Rommel is matched by the historian's portraiture of men like Washington and Napoleon and Lee, all of them in their different ways enemies of British imperialism. Indeed, he can see in the defeat of his enemies, as Milton with Satan, the tragic majesty of their fall rather than an occasion for the victor's boast. Few statesmen of his age, in fact, grasped so fully as he the nature of the relationship between war and politics. He has learned that the statesman fights hard and forgives readily. His remark that "I have always been against the pacifists during the quarrel, and against the Jingoes at its close," is of the essence of wisdom; it saved him from the *revanchiste* feeling after 1918 and the spirit of vengeful Vansittartism after 1945. This dual training in war and politics has meant that the politicians have not been able to dismiss him as an "outsider," the soldiers in the field have not been able to dismiss him as an "office wallah." It is this combination of gifts and experience that make his history still so fascinating to read.

There is even more than this, speaking still of the credit side of the Churchillian balance. Mr. Churchill is, essentially, the historian of nationalism and the nationalist spirit. As a person, he is the *homo anglicanus* embodied: a being with all kinds of crotchety prejudices, frequently wrong in his opinions, rarely mean in his battles, suspicious of general ideas, with admiration for the courage that stands up for what it believes in, with no pity for the weakness that cringes before danger, possessed of a capacity to be curiously sentimental and passionately angry. As a historian, he writes in that vein. He understands the deep power of national pride. That does not mean, of course, that he hates all foreigners. His love for France has been a lifelong passion. But his deliberate mispronunciation of foreign names appeals to English insularity, that they are a people apart, and it is not for nothing that his finest hour, like theirs, was in 1940 when both of them felt an almost perverse exhilaration in the knowledge that they stood alone, that they had the war all to themselves. He would have applauded Tim Healy's admonition to Lord Hugh Cecil that "nationality is something that men die for. Even the noble lord would not die for the meridian of Greenwich." He may embrace projects like European federalism, but it means less an intellectual recognition of the obsolescence of national sovereignty than a mystic feeling about the grand interests of European society. His internationalism is more an eighteenth-century passion for the comradeship of great and ancient states in alliance and less a liking for schemes of supranational authority. It is true that this has been a reactionary nationalism, not in any way

[271]

phrased in socially progressive terms. Yet it implicitly recognizes the deep emotive power of nationalism in human affairs. The postwar experience, it might be added, supports the lesson that the satisfaction of that emotive power, even in the postindependence excolonial socialist states, has seemed far more urgent than obedience to socialist-internationalist principle. The collapse of the pan-African movement, the failure to develop a viable Caribbean community, the resurgence of Chinese and Indian nationalism, the upsurge of a new, vibrant regional nationalism in Wales and Scotland, Quebec, and the Basque country, all are witness to the power of nationalist sentiment to appeal to human nature. Marx undoubtedly underestimated that power. It is ironic that an imperialist apologist like Churchill should have recognized it, albeit more through sentiment than rational analysis.

It will obviously be the task of the new thought systems of the non-Western world—black Marxism, African socialism, Chinese radical populism—to work out a new mixture of "ideology" and "utopia" which will accommodate the various components of nationalism, socialism, and internationalism into a new praxis. For that task, clearly enough, the Churchillian history-making is fatally ill-equipped. Its debit side is too glaringly obvious.

That debit side starts, perhaps, from Mr. Churchill's own self-image. He has always seen himself as the man of action. In his political career he has seen himself, romantically, as the great hero who treads the boards of history, as the orator who hears the sweet music of parliamentary cheers, as the statesman who "shapes the whisper of the throne" and who can "walk with kings nor lose the common touch." To command men in the grand manner, to be the big actor in the big production, to have some formidable challenge to meet, some tremendous task to organize, this, for Churchill, is life enriched, life made whole and meaningful. In the theater of his mind, in one critic's phrase, it is always the hour of fate and the crack of doom. But in truth all that does not make him a man of action. For, regarded psychologically, he is much more the man of letters deeply anxious, in the Hemingwayesque fashion, to pose as the conquistador in a cult of masculine toughness he cannot really carry out because his inner nature ill-equips him for the role. That contradiction in his psychological make-up has in turn been sharpened by his knowledge that, in the value framework of his own class, to write a book is almost an index of mental weakness. That class was willing to forgive the father, Randolph Churchill, for marrying a rich American heiress, for that, after all, as the vulgar saying has it, was money in the bank; it was far less willing to forgive the son for writing books.

The outcome of these contradictions is that Mr. Churchill can never quite make up his mind whether he is the historian writing about politics or the politician writing about history. He is not, like the Webbs, the patient excavator of facts long forgotten in trade-union records or municipal files. Nor is he, like Tawney, the scholarly annotator of the complicated movement of seminal ideas like Puritanism and capitalism. In part, his writing is a brilliant and evocative higher journalism, with the genius of the great newspaperman for grasping the telling story, the compelling headline, carrying a personal zest that is far removed from the Olympian detachment of a Gibbon or a Toynbee. In part, again, it is something in the belles-lettres tradition of the Augustan gentleman-writer, Pope perhaps, or Horace Walpole, polishing a phrase until it is a glittering perfection of art, or shaping the sentence which can become a quotable gem for the historians of a later age. In part, yet again, it is an old-fashioned type of history as an exercise in biography, so that if his *Lord Randolph Churchill* is an effort of filial loyalty to defend the tarnished reputation of his father, the volume on *Marlborough: His Life and Times* is at once a rebuttal of Macaulay's well-known critical portrait of the great duke and an expression of the Churchillian theory of history as a splendid pageant through which great and famous men move to the applause of the crowd.

These are serious defects. Yet they are defects that relate to the Churchillian personality only. They are defects, in his literary work, that reflect the defects in his politics. As a politician, he has never been a party "regular." He broke with the Conservatives in 1903 and with the Liberals in 1924, parting with each group, it is worth adding, on the very eve of its decline from power. It is small wonder that the party managers have rewarded him with ostracism. For the British party system works, necessarily, on the basis of loyalty and discipline. It rightly distrusts overnight transmutations of political faith; and the spectacle of Mr. Churchill talking the wild language of Lloyd George in 1910 and espousing a melodramatic crusade against Bolshevik revolution in 1924 was hardly calculated to reassure anybody about the sincerity of his motives. He could quote in his own defense Lord Halifax's seventeenth-century celebrated aphorism that "I trim as the temperate zone trims between the climate in which men are roasted and the climate in which they are frozen." But to many observers it seemed less a gift for responding to the necessary flexibility of politics than an incapacity for working harmoniously with others and, even more serious, as Harcourt noted, a real lack of judgment about the proper proportion of things. It is misleading, then, to see him, as Esmé Wingfield-Stratford sees him in *Churchill: The Making of a Hero*, as a man of destiny denied too frequently by lesser men the eminence that is rightfully his, or, as René Kraus sees him in *Winston Churchill: A Biography*, as a great hero struggling in the cause of property and empire against second-rate rivals and a democratic mob. That is to accept Mr. Churchill at his own face value, as set out in his own autobiography. The real truth is that he has had too much a passion for going his own way and a dislike of party control and responsibility. "He has truly brilliant gifts," Harold Begbie wrote, early on, "but you cannot quite depend on them. His love for danger runs away with his discretion. His passion for adventure makes him forget the importance of the goal. Mr. Churchill carries great guns, but his navigation is uncertain. His effect on men is one of interest and curiosity, not of admiration and loyalty. His power is the power of gifts, not of character. Men watch him, but do not follow him. He beguiles their reason, but never warms their emotions." That combination of irresponsible judgment and reckless adventure explains why, in his long political history, he was so monumentally wrong in so many of the crucial issues that he confronted: the military strategy of World War I, the Russian Revolution, the growth of socialism, the royal abdication crisis of 1936, India, and, after 1945, Soviet-Western relationships.

The more serious defects of the Churchillian historiography, however, go deeper than this. His general framework of reference is that of the great English Whig tradition. It is true that he is thereby saved from writing about the Stuart despotism, for example, in the ultraroyalist manner of Sir Charles Petrie; and that, too, he escapes some of the more obvious errors of Whiggism—he can thus dismiss the Victorian myth of the Anglo-Saxon genesis of English liberties, and goes beyond May in writing what Maitland termed a "history of results" as distinct from a "history of efforts and projects." Yet it remains the fact that, substantially, the Churchillian world is still that of Hallam and Stubbs and Freeman. English history from the Conquest to the Glorious Revolution is once again presented as a struggle of popular liberty against the aggressions of arbitrary royal power. The myth of a "constitutional opposition" is again traced back to the Plantaganet period. The Victorian civil service is once again portrayed as beginning under Henry I. Runnymede once more becomes the fount of national freedom rather than the effort of a feudal baronage to resist the growth of a strong, centralized monarchy. Men like Cromwell are presented, after the manner of Gardiner's Victorian portrait, as seventeenth-century anticipations of Gladstonian liberalism; 1689 is rewritten as Locke saw it and not as Hume's political skepticism saw it. The reader sees the eighteenth-century struggle between George III and Parliament over again through the eyes of Burke, notwithstanding the fact that the revisionist work of the Namier school has revolutionized the assumptions of scholarship on that period. Mr. Churchill, indeed, seems to be unaware of the meaning of Sir Richard Pares's remark that only the consecration of political party by the success of the two-party system in Victoria's day has deceived posterity into thinking that Burke had the better of the argument in his own generation with respect to that issue. No historian, concededly, writes without bias. Yet it is astonishing that the Churchillian account, so late in the day, can still uncritically embrace the Whiggite assumptions. It manages still to conceive the story it relates as, teleologically, the gradual unfolding of a principle of political liberty which is, in Hallam's phrase, "the slow fruit of ages, still waiting a happier season for its perfect ripeness." Like some other Marcus Aurelius, he puts together the matured statement of a philosophy at the very moment when the crumbling world around him testifies to its pathetic obsolescence.

The basic argument, this is to say, is that of a constitutionalist gradualism. Yet it is illogically fused with the Churchillian preoccupation with conflict as the creative, energizing element of the historical process. This is not to say, with some of his critics, that Mr. Churchill is a warmonger but rather that for him war leads to the upsurge of patriotism, the best passion of men. The illogicality arises because if the germs of constitutionalism were already present in the medieval past it is difficult to understand why their final consummation should have required the motivating forces of war and battle. However that may be, there is little doubt that Mr. Churchill obviously enjoys himself most when he is cataloguing the movement of war. The great events are England's foreign wars. The primary hero-figure is the great soldier, even more than the great statesman. The political leader who makes peace his final goal is almost contemptuously dismissed as pusillanimous or self-interested. In domestic politics, Mr. Churchill prefers the controversial figure to the figure who seeks peace at any price; that is why he prefers Disraeli to Gladstone. Action almost for action's sake is the breath of history to him, and when the campaigns are over he writes with a sense of regret for which his consolation is the happy remembrance of the exhilarating moments they have brought to the protagonists. Thus the glory of war half-blinds him to its terrible price in human suffering. We are invited to admire the bloody campaigns of Marlborough which in their own day even shocked the conscience of an age that took life lightly. The author, it is true, does not go so far as to echo the Carlylean praise of the awful butchery of Cromwell's campaigns in Ireland and Scotland. But he almost comes near to repeating the curious idea that the greatest battle is the one that produces the most frightful carnage. He is only deterred in this by the aristocrat's feeling that modern democracy has brutalized the gentleman's trade of war. "The wars of peoples," he writes, "will be more terrible than the wars of kings." It does not seem to have occurred to him that the common soldier of the eighteenth century, as described, for example, in Thackeray's *Henry Esmond*, might have felt differently about the matter; or that the difference might be traceable not to the advance of democracy but to the advance of weapon technology.

Mr. Churchill, in brief, is obsessed with the glamor of the British imperial epic. The drive of imperial expansion, Pitt's aim to "make the Union Jack supreme in every ocean," is taken for granted. He can smile ironically at the needlessness of the Mexican War of 1846 as an expression of American manifest destiny; he cannot see that by the same token the British military adventures in Canada and Africa and India ought to be equally condemned. The French Revolution seems to have little meaning for him save as it sets the Continental stage for the Napoleonic glory. Its leaders, for him as they were for Burke, are contemptuous adventurers whose crime is only mitigated by the genius of the military leadership discovered in the army of the republic. He may, in turn, deplore the Revolutionary War of the thirteen colonies as an unhappy rupture of the Anglo-Saxon fraternity; but what moves him is not so much the opposition of Burke and Fox to the war (an opposition which he dismisses in one curious phrase) as the ineptitudes of the British military strategy. In similar fashion, it is Napier's famous description of the death of Sir John Moore that constitutes for him the finest story of the Peninsular War. This is not to say that for Mr. Churchill there are not good wars and bad wars. Because, in his outlook, war ought to serve some great purpose to give it nobility. He can be bitterly critical of misguided adventurism, as in his recognition of the truth that when Henry V revived the English claims to France he opened the "greatest tragedy in our mediaeval history." But even that does not deter him from a vivid and prolonged description of the famous battles of the Hundred Years War. He can at times half-perceive the sheer imbecility of war—the mass slaughter of the Marne trenches, after all, left an indelible impression upon his mind—but in the final analysis he will conclude that it is the turn of fate, the twist of chance, which determines these things, and that men have little control over the wheel of destiny.

For Mr. Churchill is the eighteenth-century English gentleman, at once something of a moralist and something of a gambler. He is as much the partisan of the superb failure, the unlucky turn of the wheel, as he is of the famous victory. Where the Victorian imperialist historians, such as Froude, saw the enemy self-righteously as the villain, Mr. Churchill sees him, with rare exceptions, as a worthy opponent in the world drama. The figure of Lee thus becomes the Achilles of the American Civil War, and Lincoln only a brooding omnipresence over the battlefields. Once again, the theoretical contradictions of the argument become clear. For this sense of the throw of the dice in human affairs is not logically reconcilable with the belief in the irresistible march of liberty and empire, and if there is anything such as a philosophy of history in the argument, it oscillates, unsatisfactorily, between the twin concepts of accident and purpose. What holds those two conflicting concepts together, at best, is the Churchillian conviction that purpose produces the general sociohistorical environment and accident the great leader-figures who give it direction. He thinks of history in the graphic fashion of the leader who may or may not comprehend the general forces that have pushed him forward but who has, inexorably, to act and is caught between principle and fortune.

The life of the great statesman, like Gladstone or Lincoln, is held together by a sustained adherence to a great principle never lost sight of. Yet here again a further contradiction intrudes, since Mr. Churchill in his own political career has been too much of an opportunist to adhere loyally to any one such principle. There was, it is true, his brief flirtation with Tory Democracy. But that, as Lord Rosebery observed, has been nothing more than a convenient resource for any politician who discovered himself entertaining radical opinions within the Tory party, and who did not wish to leave it. It follows from all this that the "people" are seen only as the faceless audience in the theater of history, never as actors in their own right. Mr. Churchill, as historian, may regret at times their sufferings. But he is firmly convinced that they are necessary sufferings. He does not see the hidden social and economic roots of national action, only their military and diplomatic consequences. That explains why—to take an example only—he can complain that the House of Commons has lost its pristine greatness because it saw fit to devote two days of debate to television policy and only one day to foreign affairs. War and diplomacy are for him the most splendid expressions of the national "spirit." He thus cannot appreciate the aversion to war that soldiers as different as Wellington and Sherman felt, let alone appreciate the opposition to war that statesmen like John Bright felt. He can applaud the religious mind, in turn, so long as it leads to great action, as with the princes of the church, but as an inner mystic experience it is beyond his ken. As Mrs. Webb aptly noted, the foundation of these weaknesses is that he has all of the American's capacity for the quick appreciation and rapid execution of ideas, while barely comprehending the philosophy beneath them.

Mr. Churchill, in short, is the chronicler of the English ruling class. He accepts the values of that class without question. Imperial expansion, the aristocrat's secret diplomacy, the British "mission," all are taken for granted. Those who have challenged them are given short shrift. There is the hostility of the gentleman's club to the outsider, aptly epitomized in Mr. Churchill's account in his war memoirs of the formation of his war cabinet of 1940, in which he fails to accept the fact that that cabinet would have been impossible without the readiness of the Labour party to participate in it. He can catalogue the liberalism of the English polity and the tolerance of the English constitutional tradition, but he misinterprets them as a conscious search on the part of the national ruling class, whereas in fact they have been simply a by-product of its possession of power. He dislikes really radical breaks with historical continuity so that, for all of his American qualities, he cannot see that the American tradition, at its best, has been the ability to make traditions anew. His conservative historicism, similarly, sees the personality, not the social class or the economic group, as the basic component of the historical process. He understands Andrew Carnegie, but not capitalism; John Burns, but not trade unionism; Cromwell, but not revolutionary republicanism; Aneurin Bevan, but not socialism; Lenin, but not communism. He notes, again, the growth of rationalistic liberalism. But the fact that nearly one-third of his volume on the nineteenth century is devoted to the theme of the American Civil War indicates his difficulty in identifying himself with the nature of ideas in any sympathetic fashion. The liberal attitude toward conflict in social issues, indeed, irritates him; and he would deeply resent John Bright's well-known assertion that "this foreign policy, this regard for the 'liberties of Europe,' this care at one time for the 'Protestant interests,' this excessive love for the 'balance of power,' is neither more nor less than a gigantic system of outdoor relief for the aristocracy of Great Britain." The outcome of all this is that Mr. Churchill has written the history of the English-speaking peoples as a civilization only as he knows it. He has not written about the enlargement of its boundaries because its ruling class, to which he belongs, believes that the final stage of the march forward has already been reached.

What the historian omits is oftentimes as revealing as what he includes. The startling fact about the Churchill volumes is that they almost wholly omit entire regions of the national experience that cannot be regarded as either trivial or unimportant. They have little to say about either socioeconomic or intellectual history. Science and technology are almost entirely neglected. There is no awareness that the invention of radio or the formation of the first trade union are in themselves as decisive events as Blenheim or Waterloo. We hear little of the novelist; one has to go, say, to a book like Lord David Cecil's *Early Victorian Novelists* to understand that aspect of English thought. The contribution of dissent to the English character is largely slurred over by an author who belongs, if he ever thought about religion at all, to the official church-state establishment. Nor is it sufficient, to excuse these omissions, to say that he is writing not as a specialist but as a generalist, for an English history that omits such seminal topics is patently Hamlet without the Prince of Denmark. By comparison, a volume such as Professor Hamilton's wartime *History of the Homeland* amply illustrates how a genuinely popularizing history can deal fully not only with politics and statecraft but also with all of the social, cultural, and technological changes that have shaped both the national experience and the national character.

The manner in which social and economic history is treated is particularly revealing. The work of the great economic historians is recognizable enough in the chapter on the Black Death, but the Peasants' Revolt of 1381 is seen as a struggle between "vulgar lawlessness" and "reconstructed authority," and the observations on its leaders almost summon up the spectacle of an excited Mr. Churchill facing the miners and the railwaymen in the general strike of 1926. Little attention is paid to Sir John Neale's definitive work on the Elizabethan parliaments; similarly, there is no recognition of Professor Nef's discoveries about the Tudor commercial-industrial revolution. There is a curt reference to the "deep-cutting convictions" of the left-wing elements of the

1640 revolution, but nothing more, so that the neglect of those elements on the part of the Victorian historians is inexcusably repeated, almost as if the Putney debates of the New Model army in 1647 had never taken place. The economic causes of the French Revolution are duly noted, but its long-term economic effects are passed over. The portrait offered of 1789, indeed, here differs very little from the grotesquely misleading account of the event imposed by Carlyle and Dickens upon a Victorian bourgeoisie frightened by Chartism, and which the English public has never really quite given up. It is almost as if Mr. Churchill were not so much writing about the real event as reenacting the melodrama of the Scarlet Pimpernel. Coming back to the English theme, there is little appreciation of the conditions of inhuman brutality that characterized the life of the ordinary British soldier and sailor in the eighteenth-century period, and that culminated in the Nore and Spithead naval mutinies of 1797. For Mr. Churchill has the mentality of a first lord of the admiralty, and it would be psychologically unbearable for him even to entertain the thought that an English sailor would wish to mutiny against the Captain Blighs of the fleet. It would be equally impossible to imagine him reading, say, the classic account of the 1797 episode contained in *The Floating Republic* by Dobrée and Manwaring. There is still less appreciation of the terrible price, as recorded in the books of the Hammonds, that the English peasant and craftsman had to pay for the victory of the industrial revolution; that aspect, indeed, is passed over almost as if it had never happened.

"A constitutional statesman," wrote Bagehot in his essay on *The Character of Sir Robert Peel*, "must sympathise in the ideas of the many." Mr. Churchill lacks that sympathy. Or, more properly speaking, if he possesses any of it, it is the aristocrat's compassion for the poor rather than an identification with the aspirations of the poor. The "agitator" is applauded if he contributes, like Wycliffe or John Wilkes, to the rising tide of national feeling, but denounced if his sentiments challenge in any fundamental fashion the basic elements of the social order. The prejudice can understand a political revolution, but recoils in horror from a social revolution. It hates radical ideas; so, it can write about the French Revolution with only a brief half-paragraph on the philosophies of the Enlightenment, just as Shakespeare could write a whole play on King John without mentioning the Magna Carta. It writes at its most plangent and persuasive when it deals with a period, such as Victorian England, of political battles conducted by parliamentary leaders within a context of tolerant and enlightened middle-class civilization. It is a viewpoint unsympathetic to social and economic problems, which explains why Mr. Churchill could tell a select committee in 1931 that English politics had ceased to be "dramatic" and "controversial" because political questions had become subordinated to economic questions, reflecting a changed electorate that had replaced the old noble passion for politics with a vulgar passion for football matches. All this helps the reader, then, to understand why the closing chapter of the Churchillian *History* is full of sad comment upon the folly of a postwar people, after 1945, who do not know how to garner the fruits of victory, complemented by the suspicion that the emergence of the Labour party has put an end once and for all to the politics of the golden afternoon and the summer twilight of the Victorian period.

All ruling-class history, it is another way of saying all this, is traditionalist history. It is the flow of history, not its depth or its structure, that appeals to the ruling-class mind. Mr. Churchill is thus driven, perhaps only half-consciously, to twist the evidence into a mold of spurious historical continuity. So, he presents the modern world, once again, in the old-fashioned manner, as beginning with the Reformation. The notion, developed in the work of Tillyard, that the Elizabethan world-picture was still half-medieval in its assumptions, the further notion, made orthodox by Whitehead, that the real watershed separating the medieval from the modern world was the scientific revolution of the seventeenth century, are cavalierly ignored. The Churchillian treatment of the great modern bourgeois revolutions reveals a similar blindness of perspective. The Revolution of 1689 is canonized into a conservative movement in the manner of Burke's famous defense of it in his *Appeal from the New to the Old Whigs*, so that the disciple of Burke no more than Burke himself appreciates the fact that the deposition of the king by force was correctly seen by contemporary groups like the Non-Jurors as an outright violation of the doctrine of legitimacy. Similarly, the American Revolution is presented as an equally conservative movement based upon "an old English doctrine freshly formulated to meet an urgent American need," whereas of course its break with legitimacy and its republicanism were regarded correctly by both British Tory and American Loyalist alike at the time as revolutionary ideology. Indeed, the publication of Paine's *Common Sense* marked the point where the colonial movement consciously became a radical nationalism, rejecting the whole structure of British royal-parliamentary authority, as contemporary thinkers like Leonard and Boucher properly recognized. But with Mr. Churchill we are back once more in the patriotic mythology of Story and Bancroft before it was decisively shattered by the critical scholarship of Smith and Beard. It is the mental framework of the English conservative outlook, sedulously cultivating the legend that political doctrine is a Continental disease that the "English-speaking peoples" never catch. The legend is believable only so long as the historian reconstructs Anglo-American revolutionary history in such a way as to play down all the theories and theoretical debates that have accompanied it—radical Puritanism, the Putney *Debates*, Filmer and Locke, the American natural-law concepts, and the rest. It is only believable, too, if the secondary myth is cultivated that the English are a "practical" people as compared to "intellectual" peoples like the French or the Germans: a myth illustrated by Mr. Churchill's inaccurate assertion, in a brief reference to the Fabians, that Marx had no influence at all upon them. Mr. Churchill, in brief, writes the sort of history comparable to a history of English literature which would overlook, say, the influence of Rousseau on Richardson or the influence of Ibsen on Shaw.

"When the historian of aristocratic ages," wrote de Tocqueville, "surveys the theatre of the world, he at once perceives a very small number of prominent actors, who manage the whole piece. These great personages, who occupy the front of the stage, arrest the observation, and fix it on themselves; and whilst the historian is bent on penetrating the secret motives which make them speak and act, the rest escape his memory." The passage illustrates yet another weakness of the Churchillian history: its narrow, elitist bias. Mr. Churchill is the type of court memorialist—Froissart, St. Simon, Croker—who catalogues the achievements of the great and famous and who annotates the history of court and parliamentary intrigues. The virtues he applauds—integrity, energy, courage, tenacity, truthfulness—are those of the outstanding individual. It is the model of Plutarch's *Lives*—to set before the reader examples of noble action, to disinter a moral tale for the benefit of future generations who might have strayed from the old and trusted paths.

There are grievous pitfalls in this mode of historical writing. There is, to start with, no really satisfactory definition of "greatness" contained in the argument. At times, the Churchillian answer appears to be the ability of a leader to refuse to bow to circumstances, even at the cost of enormous sacrifice. Thus Lee is praised for continuing the fight after 1863, when it was already clear that the South could not win and when his resolution could only mean the continuation of useless slaughter. Similarly, Mr. Churchill can approve, later, of President Roosevelt's decision, based upon a half-remembered echo from the same Civil War, to insist upon an "unconditional surrender" attitude in 1943, despite the fact that such a policy decision can only have determined the Axis enemy to fight on to the bitter end. At other times, "greatness," in the Churchillian outlook, seems to be nothing less than a romantic admiration for the mythical culture-hero, such as King Arthur and his knights; and its author seems to be unaware of the truth, advanced in Lord Raglan's book on *The Hero*, that dramatic truth rather than historical fact has always been the basis for that mythology. Then there are times, even more—as in the description of the Duke of Marlborough—when "greatness" takes on the guise of an unscientific thesis of family eugenics, in the manner of A. L. Rowse's book on *The Early Churchills*, as if its secret resided in the mating habits of lusty ancestors. The entire question, indeed, of what constitutes "greatness" is begged by the assumption that moral elevation is a function of historical eminence. Nor is any light thrown on the problem by the effective use of psychohistorical analysis, for if Mr. Churchill knows little about the economic foundations of social behavior he knows even less about its psychological foundations. The pen portraits he paints, consequently, are of one-dimensional men, motivated, according to their historian, by things such as "race," or "destiny," or "character," conceptual determinants never carefully defined or rigorously analyzed. If, then, as Collingwood has urged, the task of the historian is at once to investigate both the "outside" and the "inside" of an event, Mr. Churchill fails dismally to meet the test because the flat surface of events is only imperfectly illuminated by insight into their inner sociopsychological dynamics. He composes history, in brief, in the manner of a playwright constructing a play, wherein each scene is depicted with the *grand denouement* already consciously present in the mind of the actors, and the function of the author, as it were, is that of a Grecian chorus declaiming the tragic lessons of the drama. Certain vague, cosmic forces are continuously invoked. But how individual or collective experience, as men know it, is related to those forces is never really explained or critically examined.

The Churchillian view of "greatness" seems to be, quite simply, one of historical accident. The great crisis produces the great man; and the great man is the means whereby providence raises a nation to greatness. It is an argument at once profoundly inadequate and incomplete. The impact of personality on historical development is, of course, undeniable; that both Henry and Elizabeth Tudor were strong-willed monarchs no doubt contributed much to the final victory of sixteenth-century England against the Catholic reaction. But no less undeniable is the fact that such impact can only occur in certain given historical situations. It is the total parallelogram of socio-economic-cultural forces which at any given moment explains and conditions the influence any individual person exercises on the historical process. The character of an individual, however outstanding, is a factor in that process only to the degree that those forces permit it to be so. It is true that, within that framework, that factor will have enormous influence; so that when Mr. Churchill, for example, emphasizes the tireless search for power, the demonic energy, the ruthless ambition of men like Henry VIII or Wolsey or Cromwell, he is utterly right in the emphasis. Yet before such personal drives can in any measure influence the course of events they must, first, be conformable to the primary needs of the time and, secondly, fully deployable under the prevailing conditions of the times. Had the *ancien régime* survived another generation in France Napoleon would most certainly have died as an obscure though talented sergeant of the royal armies; likewise, Nelson would have lived out an obscure career in the West Indian and Mediterranean naval stations had not the social contradictions of the *ancien régime* given rise to a French revolutionary nationalism that came to threaten the commercial supremacy of Britain. It is misleading, then, to see the outstanding individual as the prime shaper of events. He is, rather, the product and agent of impersonal forces. He may take the initiative in certain directions of action and policy; he may see further than others; he may dramatize in his person the requirements of a new class or a new nation. But, all along, he is the instrument, albeit unconsciously, of the inherent logic of social forces and economic structures. Because Mr. Churchill neglects this dialectical relationship between individual and society he is able to write still as an eighteenth-century historian for whom casual phenomena and the personal traits of celebrated people are more important than general causes.

The problem, however, is not only one of historical science.

It is even more, one of historical morality. The Acton-Creighton controversy comes to mind as one reads the Churchillian defense of the great and famous. It is not so much that the Churchillian method objects to Acton's dictum that the historian must be judge as well as witness, for there is sufficient Victorian moral earnestness in its author to ensure his agreement with the dictum. Yet he fulfills the dictum only imperfectly. Throughout the four lengthy volumes of his history there is a distinct temptation and readiness to excuse the moral shortcomings of their hero-figures. If Creighton failed to pass proper moral judgment upon the inquisitorial policies of the medieval popes, Mr. Churchill cannot bring himself to echo even the criticisms of contemporaries such as Erasmus and More on the Machiavellian statecraft of Henry VIII. He does not note the moral evil of war, as even Frederick the Great could see the fallacies involved in the pursuit of power and authority. The art of civilization, only too frequently, is identified with the success of forceful leaders who shape and create a viable state polity.

Against such a view of history at least three criticisms may be directed. The first is historical: it does not provide us with a veracious portrait of the past. The second is ethical: it is not morally elevating. The art of conflict is not the greatest task facing men, for, as Whitehead insisted, civilization means the replacement of force with persuasion. The third is utilitarian: it is by no means a self-evident truth that the sovereign nation-state eulogized in the Churchillian viewpoint can serve any further useful purpose in a world in which the whole globe itself is the only viable economic unit. Mr. Churchill properly appreciates the emotive power of national self-identity; he fails to see that in a world that increasingly is functionally international that power will have to seek its fulfillment more and more on the cultural plane, and less and less on the economic and political plane. The epoch of bourgeois supremacy is rapidly drawing to a close, which means that its more narcissistic expression in the phenomenon of a narrow, inward-turned political nationalism becomes increasingly anachronistic and therefore increasingly dangerous.

Confronted with this line of criticism, the conservative historian retreats into the argument of "mystery." He urges that there are irrational realms beyond the comprehension of critical examination, that the impulsive and accidental factors in history are so large that men must be content, in Burke's phrase, to venerate what they do not presently comprehend. So, the Churchillian outlook sees man not so much as the master of nature as the rebel against nature. It cannot understand or appreciate the effort of thinkers, such as the philosopher-scientists of the seventeenth century, to conceive of science and philosophy as instruments whereby man may become the controller rather than the servant of the relationships in which he is involved. It envisages man, not as a force mastering nature, but, Machiavellian-like, as a spirit juggling with fate. It is impatient with the utopian element in history. Thus when Mr. Churchill comes to write about his *Great Contemporaries*, it is to admire the liberal, pragmatic statesmen of the pre-1914 period—Rosebery, Morley, Asquith, Balfour—and to chastise those, such as Shaw and Trotsky, who criticize the foundations of the social order. Ideas, for him, are at best useful instruments of political warfare, at worst subversive doctrines. He can shrewdly estimate a revolutionary leader, like Robespierre or Lenin, yet fail utterly to explain their devotion to a dialectical view of the universe for which they are prepared to sacrifice all. His theory of motive is thus disastrously parochial. His history, accordingly, is not held together, as are those of Gibbon or Mommsen or Toynbee, by a seminal intellectual principle that confers upon the historical experience unity and purpose; rather, it is a chronological narrative that rises to its climactic moments when it arrives at the momentous battle, the grandiloquent gesture, the supreme challenge. Its author does not stand, as do the really great historians, in an attitude of almost timeless detachment to his subject matter. Instead, he enters with cavalier gusto into its disputes and identifies himself unashamedly with its partisans. His work, like that of Belloc or Froude, is utterly *parti pris*. He is ready with genuine feeling to weep, like Xerxes on the eve of Thermopylae, over the fate of the massive forces he has helped to put together. But he is unable to believe that men can do much to avoid that fate or shape its predestined course.

This concept of fate is allied to the other concepts of race and national character, the twin lodestars of the Anglo-Saxon racial entity that plays so large a part in the Churchillian story. Both of them illustrate at once the latent racism and the blatant Europocentrism of the Churchillian outlook and, together, they constitute an absurd and dangerous farrago of stereotypes, rationalizations, and casuistical argumentation. It is true that there is a very real generosity in the Churchillian presentation of all this. He can see the valor of an enemy. He understands that all power without responsibility is dangerous, and his constitutionalist instinct is fully alive to the awful cruelties that power can generate in the hands of irresponsible men. Even so, in his viewpoint, that responsibility can arise not out of democratic government but out of a sense of moral trusteeship on the part of a governing class. He does not pause to enquire whether such a sense of responsibility may be a guarantee against faults of personal conduct and yet fail to be a guarantee against major errors of policy. Race and character, he assumes, will be enough to keep the English ruling class within the limits of decent behavior.

How utterly implausible all this is can be seen when it expresses itself with reference (1) to the concept of the Anglo-American union, and (2) to the concept of the world outside of that union. With reference to the first, it is based, palpably, upon extremely dubious ethno-racial assumptions. The ethnic composition of the American society of the twentieth century has become far too polyglot to justify its Churchillian description as a transatlantic expression of Anglo-Saxon civilization. It can only be seen as such if attention is studiously restricted to the philo-British circles of the upper class of the eastern, Atlantic-seaboard region. Churchillian America is in fact that of the world of the Boston Brahmin and the Washington political elites, of an Anglicized coterie of the rich and wellborn, of, in brief, an internationally minded eastern republicanism. The portrait never comes to terms with all of the America that is alien, even hostile, to those elements. Culturally and ethnically, America has grown less British since 1900, when Mr. Churchill first made its acquaintance; indeed, that was seen at the time by more perceptive observers like Henry James and H. G. Wells, albeit from different viewpoints. Mr. Churchill, in truth, ignores the seminal differences between the two societies, and especially the most seminal of all, that the American tradition, historically, has been democratic while the British has been aristocratic. America has been shaped, ineluctably—whatever the imperfections of reality might be—by the twin principles of the land of promise for those who are there and the land of refuge for those who come as immigrants; and they have generated, from the beginning, a sense of the American as a "new man" divorced, culturally and psychologically, from the European heritage.

There are, all in all, in American society, far too many features that cannot in any way recommend themselves to the Churchillian neoaristocratic, romantic prejudice: the earnest self-righteousness and the loud deference to public opinion; the gospel of group conformity that inhibits genuine eccentricity; the presence of many small ambitions and the absence of many great ambitions; the worship of money; the social aggressiveness of the American woman (Mr. Churchill did not fight the Pankhurst suffragist sisters for nothing); the appalling cultural philistinism; and the absence of manners in any European sense. Nor is the field of American politics any more appealing. For despite the fact that one of Mr. Churchill's earliest American acquaintances was Bourke Cockran, whose oratorical phillipics against Boss Croker of Tammany Hall were likened in his own day to Burke's speeches against Warren Hastings, he has never really understood the peculiar jungle of American politics.

Political America, in truth, must be distasteful to any temperament like the Churchillian. It was, after all, the younger Churchill who warned his Conservative party early on that if it accepted a policy of imperial protectionism it would mean that "the old Conservative Party with its religious convictions and constitutional principles will disappear and a new party will arise—like perhaps the Republican Party in the U.S.A. —rigid, materialist, and secular, whose opinions will turn on tariffs and will cause the lobbies to be crowded with the touts of protected industries"; and if anything has changed since that time it is certainly not the Republican party of the United States.

Nothing illustrates so well, perhaps, the fallacy of the Churchillian "Atlantic community" thesis than the sorry history of the so-called special relationship between London and Washington in the post-1945 period. Britain needed America in 1939; America did not need Britain after 1945. From being an ally Britain in effect became a satellite of the emergent American imperialism. Every prime minister who has counted on the "special relationship" has been rudely awakened to the facts of life. Mr. Churchill himself has told the story of how he learned the details of the hydrogen-bomb explosion at Eniwetok Atoll through reading a British newspaper report of a speech made by the chairman of the Joint Congressional Committee on Atomic Energy; the Anglo-French adventure against the Suez Canal in 1956 was brought to a humiliating halt through the intervention of the U.S. secretary of state; and the later Nixon rapprochement with Russia and China was undertaken without consultation with London. The Churchill-Roosevelt relationship early on revealed the deepening rift, for they rarely saw eye to eye on the basic issues in which they were involved. Nor was this due to the fact that, according to the American liberal legend, the prime minister was a reactionary imperialist and the president a Wilsonian liberal; a distorting picture painted in books like Elliott Roosevelt's *As He Saw It* and Louis Adamic's *Dinner at the White House*. It is more like the truth to say that both of them were fighting for the maintenance of the Western capitalist order. But whereas Britain, by 1945, was a declining imperialism, America was an expanding imperialism, developing its own global power politics, in search of new allies, and impatient with an outmoded Churchillian ambition no longer possessed of the politico-military power to back it up. The postwar anti-American temper that has infected British attitudes since that time can only be understood in terms of British resentment at that radical change in the balance of transatlantic power. A British prime minister dealing with an American president within the framework of that change must feel at times like nothing so much as a Greek Stoic philosopher facing the arrogant authority of the new Roman regimental centurion. Yet he would only have his addiction to the Churchillian romantic dream of an Anglo-American common destiny to blame for his predicament.

The second example that underscores the latent racism of the Churchillian mind is its attitude to the non-European world and the non-European peoples. For the "Atlantic community" is nothing much more than a euphemism for the hegemony of the white Euro-North American world. That world, for Churchill, is the climax of human experience. World "leadership," for him, means Western leadership. Unlike Burke, he is incapable of feeling the appeal of historic cultures older than his own, for in a way he has been too American to be conservative wholly in the Burkean manner. Both the Catholic and the Oriental world views are alien to his temper. He is thoroughly eighteenth-century in thus mistaking the transient conditions of one given historical age for the permanent conditions of human life. He entertains the crude fallacy that historical syndromes of culture and tradition can be identified as functions of pseudo-biological facts such as race and pedigree. Ecumenical history in the Hegelian manner is foreign to his spirit because it would not occur to him to believe that the golden age of English history he describes might simply be part of a single civilization destined, like twenty others before it, to final decline and disappearance. It has not been vouchsafed to him to experience the sort of Damascus Road illumination which in 1914 persuaded Arnold Toynbee of the grim contemporaneity of the history of Thucydides, or which in 1943 proved to Geoffrey Barraclough that the Battle of Stalingrad emphasized the importance of the Russian and Byzantine strands in the net of history. Russia, czarist or Soviet, he has always regarded as a barbarian intruder. His view of religion is English, and he would be incapable of constructing a theory of history, as Toynbee has done, around the theme of an architectonic religious syncretism. It is true that his lively mind drove him, as a young Fourth Hussars subaltern in the pre-1914 Kiplingesque colonial society of Bangalore, to a reading of Gibbon; but it was the style and not the skepticism of Gibbon that finally remained with him. Civilization, then, in his view, is Christian, as if there did not exist other world religions, such as Islam and Buddhism, that surpass in their vast followings the historic churches of the West.

All this infects his writing as he comes to treat the non-European world. He eulogizes the "white" Commonwealth; he barely disguises his contempt for the "black" Commonwealth. He sees the East through the eyes of Macaulay and Kipling. For him, Gandhi is "a seditious little Middle Temple lawyer, posing as a fakir of a type well known in the East." Nehru and his colleagues are "men of straw" incapable of responsible habits. He can understand "tough" personalities like Nasser or Kemal Ataturk or Ibn Saud. But he reserves his most fulsome praise for the "old" Commonwealth leaders like General Smuts, whose failure ever to face up boldly to the race problem in South Africa was in no small way responsible for the later growth of institutionalized apartheid in the republic. Likewise, he reserves his most excited passages for the European conqueror, Clive conquering the Mahratta Empire, Cortes defying the Aztec world with his handful of four hundred conquistadores, Livingstone opening up "darkest Africa," without appreciating that they all brought with them fiercely destructive forces fatal to that stability and continuity of ancient cultures that has always supposedly been the aim of conservatism to protect. The last word on the Warren Hastings trial is in favor of that "nabob" archcriminal; and it was that same bias, no doubt, that persuaded Churchill the politician to approve of Lord Morley's refusal, before 1914, to apply to India the principles of home rule and internal self-government which that latter-day Victorian liberal had been willing to grant to Ireland and South Africa. Despite the fact, indeed, that fifty years of domestic politics made Mr. Churchill into a *Realpolitiker*, his attitude to the non-English-speaking world has been one of hopeless and unrealistic romanticism, based on the unspoken assumption that the non-English-speaking peoples still need the enlightened despotism of European rule. Just, then, as the French historians of the right dream about the age of the great king, he dreams of the period between 1689 and 1914 when his own class of Englishmen persuaded themselves that they were the natural rulers of the world.

The Churchillian history of the "English-speaking peoples" thus becomes, astonishingly, the history of England from that class viewpoint. Scotland, Wales, and Ireland, as the smaller nationalities of the United Kingdom, are treated only insofar as they provide a stage for English arms. America is seen only as an outpost of Anglo-Saxon colonization. The Dominion peoples are described as the spokes that radiate out from the English axle. There is a complete inability to see the story from the viewpoint of the oppressed. There is hardly a word on slavery or the slave trade; the Caribbean is seen simply as a stage drop to the exploits of Nelson and Rodney. Mr. Churchill would thus no more be able to understand the observation of the Indian delegate to the United Nations General Assembly in 1954 that it is in Europe that the great wars of the modern period have all begun and that it is from Europe that they have been carried to other parts of the world than he would be able to understand why post-1945 Jewry can only see Europe as an accursed Egypt cancerous with the disease of anti-Semitism. It is true that his English sense of decency is outraged at the Nazi holocaust. But he cannot see that the English rape of Africa by means of the slave trade or the American destruction of the Indian tribal cultures in the generation following the Civil War were equally exercises in white genocide. He can see how, in the German case, the master-class becomes the master-nation and the master-nation becomes the master-race. He cannot see that from the African or Caribbean or Asian viewpoint that is equally the lesson of the English case. Fifty years of Europe are no longer more important, as they seemed in Tennyson's age, to a cycle of Cathay. The European age, in brief, is patently over and with it the world dominion of the European spirit: its racist arrogance, its technological leadership, its lust for adventure, its drive for expansion, its bland assumption that outside the European orbit there is no history worth speaking about. That history after the Churchillian fashion cannot see that is at once its tragedy and its crime.

Every ruling class maintains its dominion by some particular variant of the Platonic "noble lie": the American "manifest destiny," the French "civilizing mission," the British "imperial destiny." It is because Mr. Churchill is no great historian that he reveals so innocently the real character of the English ruling-class mentality. He does not disguise that character beneath the patina of any leading intellectual or philosophical principle, because a ruling class in the full plenitude of its power does not need such a principle; Lord Morley has observed even of Burke that there is no passage in all of the Burkean writings which reveals a philosophic estimation of the value of absolutely unfettered enquiry. The Churchillian history, in brief, is a frank apologetic for the neoaristocratic capitalist class. For if, as it argues, the secret of politics is its mystique, and if it can be acquired only through long experience over generations by its practitioners, it follows that this becomes a rationale for a governing class that has been in the saddle over such a lengthy period. It may well be that in its rodomontade, its rhetoric, and its braggadocio the Churchillian account transgresses much of the social code of behavior of that class. It remains true, nonetheless, that in the last resort it is the justification of its social and political power which constitutes the raison d'être of that account.

There is one final point. It might seem that, with the postwar decline of Churchillian imperialism, any comment on it must take on the form of an obituary. Yet that would be to gravely misunderstand the nature of postwar English society. For although the empire is dead there is much evidence to suggest that the Churchillian attitudes still remain deeply imbedded in the national psyche. The postimperial trauma, indeed, has if anything exacerbated them; for in a new world that has less time and patience for English claims the English have reacted by retreating into a reinvigorated "little England" nationalism that has a quality of mean small-mindedness about it unknown in the earlier Churchillian variant. That can be seen in a number of ways. It is there in a new popular literature of romantic imperialist nostalgia. It is there in the continuing and extensive vocabulary of denigration concerning European peoples. It is there in the new pro-European politics embraced by both major political parties, going hand in hand with the precipitous decline of the old pro-Commonwealth politics; the entry into Europe, indeed, can be seen as a search for new white friends as the new Commonwealth has become increasingly black. It is there, finally, in the wave of racist xenophobia that, since the 1960s, has engulfed the national public opinion as a frightened reaction to the influx of Asian-Caribbean immigrants and the establishment of a permanent colored ethnic minority in the society. Race and color have become preempted, in an American fashion, as new elements at once in the national communal psychology and in the national politics. The phenomenon constitutes, in effect, the return of the colonial native to the metropolitan economy, and thus commences a new chapter in the long history of the metropole-colony relationship. The future of British democracy may well rest on the ability of the English people, of all social classes and political persuasions, to rise above the heritage of a gigantic mythology of race, hitherto only latent and now become explicit, created by the imperial past and its Churchillian celebration.

[Chapter 8]

Race and Color in
Contemporary Britain:
The Return of the Native

It was easy to see, even at the time, that the war of 1939–1945 constituted one of the major watersheds of English social history. It has not been so easy to see that it was also the beginning of the intrusion of the new components of race and color into the national life. For those components, now so much a settled feature of the social landscape, go back to the wartime recruitment of the empire's colored peoples into industry and the armed services, followed after 1948 or so by a steadily mounting influx of peacetime Asian-Caribbean immigrants, reaching its peak in the late 1950s and early 1960s, and then later reinforced by the entry of Kenyan and Ugandan Indians following the Africanization policies of the newly independent East African states. As Britain thus enters the last quarter of the century its settled population includes permanent communities of Third World immigrant peoples—African, Indian, Pakistani, West Indian—who both by virtue of skin-color and cultural habit, although in varying degree, stand out in bold contrast to the massive ethnic homogeneity of the traditional white native majority. Their presence, of course, is the end result of a general postwar wave of international migration by the workers and peasants of the slums of empire responding to the magnetic pull of the British full-employment welfare state. For the Asiatic groups it has meant an intensely traumatic break from static and traditional societies, repeating on the metropolitan stage the earlier movement, the "new slavery," of indentured East Indian laborers to Trinidad and British Guiana that only ended in 1917. For the Caribbean groups it has meant just the latest chapter in the history of the vast circulatory movements that took them earlier to Cuba, Santo Domingo, the Aruba oil refineries, the Panama Canal Zone, and, of course, the United States. But for both of them the major propulsive motive has been economic, what Ravenstein in his celebrated paper on the laws of migration, read to the Royal Statistical Society in London in 1885, termed the desire inherent in men to better themselves in material respects.

The consequences of this general phenomenon have been profound and far-reaching. To begin with, it has resurrected the black physical presence, of a high profile, in English society, culture, and politics, which was ubiquitous in the eighteenth century and which disappeared in the nineteenth century. In part, this is due to the new geographical dispersal of the black immigrant-person, for whereas in the earlier interwar period of 1919-1939 he was more or less segregated in the older "colored quarters" of the dock areas of East London, Liverpool, and Cardiff (there was a time when Cardiff's Tiger Bay area almost constituted a sort of tourist section for the Welsh miners coming down from the valleys for their Saturday night sprees), today he is more evenly distributed and more variously employed throughout the three main employment regions of the national economy: the Greater London area, the sprawling West Midlands area, and the northern industrial townships. In that earlier period he was known, generally, as the transient seaman, the visiting student, the well-known cricketer, and so, in many ways, collectively inconspicuous. Today, by contrast, he constitutes a wider and more representative segment of the national working class: the construction worker, the factory laborer, the bus conductor, the nurse, the transport worker, the shop clerk, the market porter, the housing janitor, and the rest.

At a higher class level, the world of the esoteric dining-out restaurant, hitherto the preserve of earlier minority groups like the Greek and the Chinese, has been successfully invaded by the Indian and the Pakistani. The open-air public market of West Indian petty trade, catering to the West Indian housewife, has become a standard feature in districts like Brixton and Handsworth, thus giving the lie to the legend that the West Indian black Creole is by nature incapable of commercial enterprise. The black model, both male and female, has become fashionably ubiquitous. Over the years the mass media have celebrated the "firsts" of the examination results of the grueling competitive process through which the immigrant has been forced to pass: the first policeman, the first magistrate, the first university union president, the first county cricket captain (Garfield Sobers), the first fashion designer, the first table-tennis player to make the English ratings, the first recipient of a Trinity House pilot's certificate, the first TV interviewer, the first bride of an English aristocrat, the first feature film director, the first actor to appear in a major role with the Royal Shakespeare Theatre Company (in that case, the late Trinidadian actor Edric Connor), and so on. Or, again, there is the figure of the black teacher; and it is no accident that the most poignant accounts illustrating the agony of that teacher facing a white classroom—*To Sir, With Love*, from one viewpoint, and *Violence in the Toilets* from another viewpoint—have come from West Indian teachers in the state school system. State public service has also attracted the immigrant; as of 1968, for example, there were some 16,400 colored officers in the civil service, over 50 of them being members of the prestigious top administrative level. There is also the entry into the new official race-relations civil-service structure: as of 1970, there were at least 10 colored chairmen of community-relations councils and 24 colored community-relations officers serving those councils. The growth of race prejudice thus, ironically, creates new employment opportunities for the more educated of its victims.

These twin factors of wide geographical dispersal and growing occupational diversity—notwithstanding the fact that the first is threatened by efforts to control the distribution of immigrant labor and the second by prejudice in the promotional ladder—mean that the black presence makes itself increasingly felt. People who had never seen a black person before in their lives now rub shoulders with him, or her, in the street, in the "pub," in the cinema, on the factory floor, even as the neighbor next door. The black face becomes a familiar feature in the newspapers and on the TV screen. The world of pop culture in the new "permissive" society draws new inspiration from the rich Afro-American song and dance forms, so that the "Liverpool sound" is matched by the Jamaican *reggae* beat. A West Indian beauty wins the Miss World beauty contest in London, although not without setting off a bitter controversy with racial undertones. Agatha Christie, whose books have fed the English obsession with murder for two generations, writes a new mystery thriller with a Caribbean theme and location. A Trinidadian steel band plays in the annual Lord Mayor's show in London. A black troupe stages an electrifying black Macbeth at the London Roundhouse. Movies like *Sapphire*, again with a London setting, introduce the English moviegoer to the issue of racial prejudice, dealing in that particular case with the subsidiary phenomenon of racial "passing," while another movie like *Two Gentlemen Sharing* portrays the battleground between the disciplined English middle class and the more rambunctious scuttle-crab lives of a certain segment of the West Indian immigrant group. The West Indian Pentecostal church and the Muslim mosque make their appearance, so that it becomes more and more difficult to sustain the myth that England is a Christian society; the result is that one controversy after another, notably the prolonged fight over the claim of Sikh transport employees to wear turbans on duty, erupts to disturb the traditional religious complacency of the English. Nor is that disturbance assuaged in any way when the average Englishman is told by radical Christians like Canon Collins that Christ himself was of colored Mediterranean stock, or when he learns to his shock that many of the newcomers, with their fundamentalist religious quality, entertain a profound contempt for what they regard as the scandalous irreligiosity of the English people as a whole.

The English populace, in sum, have been made to realize over the last twenty years that a new social animal has appeared in their midst, the "black Englishman." That his arrival has generated for them a new source of traumatic anxiety is evident in a number of ways. It is there in the fact that it has produced a regular correspondence in the columns of the *Times*—the final accolade granted to the importance of any topic from the Establishment viewpoint. It is there in the way in which color has become a new frame of reference, even in the most commonplace of personal interrelationships; thus, a well-known left-handed politician can observe that being left-handed in a right-handed world is like being colored in a white society, while an equally well-known politician's wife can respond to an enquiry about her possible political candidacy with the remark that it is like being asked whether you would marry a black man; "you don't know until you are asked." It is there, again, in the growth of a new race-based politics, concerned with the preservation of English racial "purity"; and this, like the issues of imperialism and women's suffrage before it, is the sort of issue which, appearing every so often in British public life, cuts across existing lines of party faith and affiliation. There is, finally, the development of a new semiofficial "race relations" academic subindustry, a new species of academic empire-building, treating the immigrant-person, only too often, as an exotic exhibit in much the same way that American anthropology has looked at the reservation Indian; and it is no small irony that the leading center for the study of multiracial societies should be located at the new Sussex University, only a few miles distant from that astonishing Regency Brighton Pavilion among the rococo-Oriental buildings of which it is possible to stand and imagine briefly that one is in Gujarat or South Trinidad.

Clearly enough, Britain today is a multifaith, multiracial society. For three centuries or more English colonialism uprooted both African and Asiatic to become the labor army of slave and indentured servant in the Caribbean plantation economy. The wheel has now come full circle; the descendants of slave and indentured servant have now returned to the imperial center itself. It is an ironic twist of history, reproducing the Shakespearean Prospero-Caliban encounter in a new age in which the Shakespearean neomedieval world outlook that assumed a permanent inequality between the children of light and the children of darkness can no longer be accepted as a self-evident truth of nature. The colonial person is no longer out of sight, out of mind. He has become an integral part of the national community. Religion, politics, recreation, the arts, education—all feel the disturbing impact of his presence. Both on the political right and the political left, the most popular speakers—whether it is the audience of elderly townswomen's guilds in Hove and Eastbourne or of progressive liberals in Hampstead and Highgate—are those who choose the topics of race and immigration. Hardly a day passes in which the reading public is not reminded of what was said, or allegedly said, on those topics by Shakespeare, Blake, Sir Walter Scott, Dickens, and Trollope. Kingsley anticipated all of this in a prophetic passage of his book of 1869 on the West Indies. "Great exertions," he wrote at that time, "are made every London Season for the conversion of the Heathen and Negro and the abolition of their barbarous customs and dances. It is to be hoped that the West Indian Heathen and Negro will some day show their gratitude to us, by sending missionaries hither to convert the London Season, dances and all, and assist it to take the beam out of its own eye, in return for having the mote taken out of theirs." That process of "colonialism in reverse" is now finally taking place.

It is not too much to say, as a generalization, that the English response to all this has been, increasingly and step by step, one of suspicion, hostility, fear, even open hatred. Even a cursory reading of the huge documentary evidence that has accumulated throughout the last two decades—newspaper articles, academic theses, novels, official parliamentary committee reports, and immigrant testimonials—is enough to make the reader aware of the barriers of prejudice and discrimination that have faced the black immigrant at every turn. For if by prejudice—to give it an academic definition —is meant the presence of a collective subconscious disposition toward an ethnic group that can be proven fallacious, and if by discrimination—again to give it an academic definition—is meant the denial or frustration of the equal opportunities of a minority group in general categories such as work, law, politics, and social relations, solely on the basis of race, color, religion, or national origin, it is palpably clear that the Caribbean-Asiatic minority suffers from both of those stigmata to a degree that has almost become American at once in their quantitative measurement and in their qualitative character. The American dilemma has, in truth, become the British dilemma; so much so that even the most optimistic liberal will no longer deny it but unhappily deplore it.

The three strategic areas of employment, housing, and education are the battlegrounds on which prejudice and discrimination have most characteristically deployed themselves. For the immigrant shares with the average Englishman the values pertinent to those areas: to have a satisfying job, to possess a decent house, to be able to educate his children in the best manner possible. For he has been shaped, historically, by the Protestant ethic of the English colonizer— especially the West Indian who forms, numerically, the largest proportion of the total one-and-a-quarter million, both first and second generation, of the new minorities. Yet, in all of those cases skin-color has become a disabling mechanism as real as a physical deformity, relegating the black person, in the public mind, to a second-class citizenship and identified, in that mind, with the forgotten casualties, as it were, of the welfare state: gypsies, the aged, the homeless, the young outsiders, the unmarried mothers, the homosexuals, the drug addicts. In the phrase used by the National Council for Civil Liberties, either we are all equals, or we are a two-tier society of those who are here by right and those who are here on sufferance. There can be little doubt, reading the major reports—the Political and Economic Planning

Report of 1967, *Racial Discrimination in Britain*, the 1969 volume, *Colour and Citizenship*, put out by the Institute of Race Relations, the various publications of the Runnymede Trust, and many others—that the choice has already irrevocably been made, by governments and public opinion alike, in favor of the two-tier society. The evidence is all the more damning since all of those organizations have been manned by the type of the English white liberal, genuinely concerned with racial justice, in no way revolutionary, and convinced that people will respond affirmatively if only an appeal is made to "decency" and "tolerance" and a sense of "fair play"—all of them, incidentally, terms that have taken on the status of sacred incantations repeated, ad nauseam, by press, politicians, and "race-relations" workers with an increasingly anxious intensity.

Even a brief summary makes all this painfully evident. In the field of employment, the original findings of the PEP report are still valid for the 1970s: that some 40 percent of colored applicants for jobs are refused outright with a "no colored" declaration; that an equal proportion are refused, this time with typical English mendacity, with a "no vacancies" claim, when in fact there are; that an excessive power of discrimination is wielded by whites in minor positions—gatemen, commissionaires, receptionists, and secretaries—who thus become petty agents of discrimination; that many immigrants are forced to accept jobs beneath their qualifications; and that the majority of immigrants are thus shunted into the dirty and menial job the British worker does not want and will not take on. Once on the job, moreover, the immigrant faces the second barrier of refusal to promote, so that, to take an example only, the high proportion of colored personnel in the national health services rarely means that even the most competent will rise above the level of junior doctor into the more prestigious grades.

Four general results flow from all this: (1) the immigrants come to constitute, in large part, a sort of new proletarian helot class concentrated in the less pleasing, manual, and unskilled or semiskilled jobs of the more unattractive industries: the metal foundry worker, the cotton spinner, the canteen worker, the hotel kitchen help, the bus conductor (an arduous job in the English winter), the night-shift woolen worker (the "night shift from Pakistan" has become a local joke in the northern Lancashire and Yorkshire towns), and the workers, many of them Pakistani women, who daily go through the hell of the evil-smelling rubber factories of the Southall employment district; (2) a stereotype of the immigrant grows up in the employer mentality which acts as a face-saving rationale for discrimination; the stereotype, namely, of the immigrant as a homogeneous mass of unskilled persons. "The success and undoubted capacity of coloured workers in a whole variety of occupations," concluded the 1960 *Colour and Citizenship* report, "ranging from doctors to textile workers, from administrative class civil servants to London Transport staff, shows that within the coloured population all grades of skill and industry are present. Whether the distribution of these skills is present in the same proportions as for the local population is doubtful, but it does mean that individual coloured workers stand to suffer from the generally held stereotype of the unskilled. . . . Employers willing to accept coloured workers for reasons other than labour shortages, workers willing to accept coloured workers as fully equal, especially in regard to promotion, have been exceptions and not the rule"; (3) a process, consequently, of forced proletarianization takes place whereby the skilled immigrant, told that he is "overqualified," is compelled to accept a job beneath his merits, so that the figure of the well-educated professional person doing low-grade work appears, a phenomenon last seen on any large scale in the modern industrial societies during the Depression period of the 1930s; and (4) the principle of "last to be hired, first to be fired" creates, at the same time, a highly visible group of black unemployed youth whose unemployment rate, according to the 1970 Stevenson-Wallis report, is four times as high as the national average: a situa-

[307]

tion which creates in them, in a phrase used in that survey, an appearance of passivity that goes hand in hand with strong internal resentment.

The housing field reveals a similar dismal pattern. Even, perhaps, more dismal. For the newcomer could always find a job of sorts. But to find a house he has had to contend with possibly the most massive failure of the postwar welfare state: its inability, as a huge literature of exposure has shown, either to renovate a delapidated national housing stock or to deal with a housing system held in the vicious grip of rent, interest, and profit, and callously operated by the ground landlord, the speculative "development" company, the huge private insurance companies, and a rapacious real-estate lobby. The immigrant, in the first wave of the 1950s, naturally gravitated to the existing immigrant settlement areas, staying with friends already arrived, and using them as an "ethnic colony," a base from which to explore more pleasing accommodation. In that exploration, there existed, in the phrase of the monumental Milner Holland report on greater London housing, two "escape routes": the sector of owner-occupier housing, usually penetrated by means of the estate agency and the building society, and the sector of local authority housing, controlling access to the council housing estates, the citadels of English working-class solidarity.

Save for a favored few, both of those routes have been blocked by discriminatory practices, both overt and covert. An alliance of estate agent, building-society manager, solicitor, and construction firm, all of whom share the English obsession with maintaining the "tone" or "class" of residential neighborhoods, and see the prospective immigrant buyer as a threat to "standards," blocks the first escape route; and the hypocrisy of their argument about standards being "lowered" was made graphically evident in the fact that the very first case to be tried under the 1968 anti-discrimination legislation concerned the refusal of a Huddersfield building company to sell to a colored applicant whose social-occupational profile—a well-educated professional person, associate member of the Institute of Electrical Engineers, and a highly paid shift engineer with the Independent Television Authority—made him, apart of course from color, an eminently presentable candidate for entry into suburban villa society.

In similar fashion, the route to council housing has been blocked not only by the enormous bureaucratic complexity of the application-approval system, so little understood by the newcomer but, much worse, by the petty local council-man mentality, Labour and Conservative alike, which sees its first duty to its locally born, white, working-class elec-torate. That territorial imperative, hostile to the black ap-plicant, is reinforced by the still-continuing Victorian philosophy of British public housing that places a premium on the "deserving poor," that is to say, those who possess all the habits of social "respectability" it is assumed, utterly erroneously, that the black immigrants lack. It is enough to read Audrey Harvey's *Tenants in Danger* or Stanley Alder-son's bitter *Britain in the Sixties, Housing,* to appreciate how all of the agents of the welfare state—health inspector, public housing manager, rent tribunal official—reflect its elitist, patronizing tone, seeing the homeless, whether black or white, as delinquents to be morally rehabilitated rather than as in-nocent victims of a general system which still sees a house as a marketable commodity and not as a basic social right. The end result of these twin processes, of course, is that the black minorities get pushed back into the decaying inner cores of the industrial cities, not yet constituting, in the American fashion, a pure ghetto situation but rapidly approaching it.

Thirdly, the immigrant, and especially the immigrant child, becomes the unwitting victim of the English educa-tional system. The controversy set off in 1971 by Bernard Coard's booklet, *How the West Indian Child Is Made Educa-tionally Sub-normal in the British School System,* vividly illustrated how that victimization takes place by means of a triple bias: the English middle-class cultural bias, the emotional dis-turbance bias, and the intelligence-testing bias. The cultural bias works by means of imposing upon the immigrant school entrant (especially the Asian, for West Indians, by contrast, have always been the most culturally Anglicized of the colonial subject-peoples) a Protestant, middle-class behavioral code that is foreign to him or her. The emotional-disturbance bias works by means of exposing the newcomer, this time both West Indian and Asian, to the unsettling permissive character of the English school, so frighteningly different from the Victorian character of the old colonial school system: and knowledgeable West Indian specialists like Pansy Jeffrey and Elsa Walters have shown how the confrontation induces emotional bewilderment and dislocation that are then wrongly seen by the English teacher as evidence of mental deficiency. The intelligence-testing bias, finally, compounds all this by putting the immigrant child through the unfair ordeal of tests that use Western-type diagnostics to assess immigrant-child potential. The end result of all of these biases is to place—a fact statistically proven—a highly disproportionate percentage of immigrant children into the educationally subnormal school, which assures their permanent stigmatization as a product of the "nut" school.

Two other general factors, in turn, make things much worse. First, the quite appalling ignorance of most English staffroom members about the Asian-Caribbean cultural background leads them into disastrous misconceptions; thus, even a sympathetic writer—Roger Bell in his article in the Fabian pamphlet, *Policies for Racial Equality*—can propound the astonishing thesis that the contrast between modern Britain and the immigrant home background is greater than that between modern times and Shakespeare's time, so that most immigrants will be strangers to the radio, telephone, television, and medical services: an argument that reveals a profound ignorance of at least modern West Indian social realities. Secondly, the curious English obsession with polite diction as the hallmark of social respectability—the assumption, as the joke goes, that everybody ought to talk like middle-class Englishmen who speak as if they had the Elgin marbles in their mouth—denigrates the West Indian child's Creole patois as "bad English," forcing him to deny his own linguistic identity. A vital, rich, energizing language form, then, with an almost Elizabethan quality of formalized rhetoric, thus becomes converted into a condemned speech form.

It is sometimes argued that all this, put together, is only cultural prejudice, since the English working-class child also suffers from it. But cultural prejudice is twin cousin to racial prejudice. That can be seen from a book like Mrs. Whiteley's *The Uneducated English*, in which a chapter on immigrants manages to reproduce some of the worst slanders of the old proslavery literature. West Indians come from a "sunny climate" and a "free relaxed life"; their sexual habits are "unreliable"; their children speak a Creole dialect "with such slovenly diction and mangled syntax that English people cannot understand what they say"; even worse, the children are intellectually "dense," combining "slow wittedness with their bounce of high spirits," and are guilty of petty thievery, wanton lying, and various sexual irregularities; while as for Asian children, they bring with them the un-English traits of graft and bribery, traceable to "Oriental deviousness." The whole exercise demonstrates how the English liberal spirit—for the author is a reformist who vigorously attacks, for example, the evils of the authoritarian headmastership system in English schools—can slip into a hysterical racialist vein once it is confronted with the unsettling issue of color.

It is eminently clear from all this that racism has gradually moved from the casual to the institutionalized stage in Britain. No better evidence could be advanced than the growth in both of the Establishment parties of a race-based politics. It took the form, most notoriously, of the series of so-called race relations acts—1962, 1968, 1971—which, step by step, set up an immigration-control machinery having as its end result (1) the almost complete abrogation of the Commonwealth citizenship concept, with its corollary of free entry into Britain, and (2) the subjection of the immigrant, hitherto regarded as an equal member of the Commonwealth

[311]

familia, to the Draconian regime of statutory law and administrative discretion governing the alien person. Politically, that meant the surrender of the party leaderships to the crypto-racialist grass-roots pressures emerging from the local constituencies, constituting as did those pressures a "white backlash" whose racist paranoia saw the immigrant-person, against all the evidence, as the primal cause of all the defects of the welfare state, making him, in brief, the malefactor-scapegoat of the society. How that surrender took place, yielding inexorably to the chauvinist and xenophobic elements of the national psyche, has been fully documented in books like Paul Foot's spirited polemic, *Immigration and Race in British Politics*. There took place a squalid Dutch auction in which each party sought to defend itself against the charge—so dangerous from the electoral viewpoint—that it was "soft" on immigration by preempting the anti-immigrant prescriptions of its hard-line extremist minority groups. By the middle 1960s both had adopted a "little England" position, by the early 1970s a "keep Britain white" position, while protesting their liberalism on the issue at the same time.

For the Conservatives, it was a not too difficult transition, for British Toryism has never really accepted the ethic of imperial trusteeship enunciated by Burke in 1783. For Labour, it was a more agonizing reappraisal, for it meant the ultimate betrayal of the doctrine of interracial socialist fraternity so movingly defended by Hugh Gaitskell in the early debates of 1961-1962. Harold Wilson, as Labour prime minister, in a famous parliamentary moment could castigate the Conservative victor of the race-motivated Smethwick by-election of 1964 as a "parliamentary leper," yet proceed himself in 1968 to break the word of a British government in the Kenyan-Asian crisis of that year, eliciting from Lord Foot the bitter comment that it was fortunate that the Children of Israel did not have to rely upon a covenant from the British government, or they would not have got beyond the Red Sea. It became generally accepted strategy for each party to cover up its own appeasement of its right-wing Neanderthal elements by hypocritically attacking the record of its rival, so that Harold Wilson, again, could comment, in his prolix memoirs of 1971, that on the issue of race the right-wing Monday Club had taken over the conscience of the Tory party, without bothering to ask himself if the conscience of the Labour party was in any better hands. It was, all in all, a sad politics of appeasement. The real victim, of course, was the immigrant. The literature of his disillusionment with the "mother country" will by now fill a large shelf; summed up in the disgusted remark of a Jamaican from Nottingham: "In 1944 I was a serviceman in the British Air Force fighting for freedom and democracy. In 1947 I became a settler in Nottingham. In the 1958 race riots I became a coloured man. In the 1962 Commonwealth Immigrants Act I became a coloured immigrant. And in 1968 I'm an unwanted coloured immigrant. You tell me what's going to happen to me in 1970."

The colored minorities are thus, in the 1970s, caught in the middle of a racial hurricane of truly Caribbean proportions. The eye of the hurricane is, of course, the enigmatic figure of Enoch Powell. It has been fashionable among his liberal critics to compare him either with Oswald Mosley, in the English case, or with Governor George Wallace, in the American case. Yet the phenomenology of Powellism can lend itself to mistaken theoretical interpretation if those analogies are accepted. In the first place, the American analogy is inappropriate because Governor Wallace remains still a regional figure of the old Southern white "bible belt," speaking the rough language of the county courthouse, the last, as it were, of the white populist demagogues of the Huey Long variety. Powell, by contrast, is psychologically a much more complex person, a bourgeois pseudo-intellectual possessed of wit, classical education, and a mastery of languages, and, despite his West Midlands stronghold, a politician who commands a genuine national following; in addition to which he is not, like Governor Wallace, a potential third-party maverick working outside of the established national parties, but an integral element of his own Tory party (notwithstanding his later transference of allegiance to the Ulster Unionists, the most ultra-Tory group in the House of Commons, for the presence of Powell himself is not necessary to the continuing influence of Powellism in the major Conservative elements).

The comparison with Mosley is inappropriate for another reason. Beyond doubt, there are obvious similarities. Both Mosleyite anti-Semitism and Powellite Negrophobia have similar roots: the one, in part, in the working-class anti-Semite; the other, in part, in the working-class racist. The long-term explanation for those roots is to be found in the success of Victorian conservatism, after 1867, in establishing a secure grip on the newly emancipated working-class voter by means of an extensive imperialist and racist propaganda, a process described in the study of McKenzie and Silver, *Angels in Marble: Working Class Conservatives in Urban England.* There is even a certain linear connection between the two movements, for something like Colin Jordan's Greater Britain movement can be seen as a link between the two. Yet, even so, the differences are perhaps more important. Mosley never became anything much more than a lost leader on the margins of the party system, disavowed by all progressive opinion—the parties themselves, the trade-union movement, the national press. His influence was restricted more or less to the east London region, where his Jewish target was most recognizable. Powellism, by contrast, enjoys a vast national support in all social classes. His target, the black man, is phenotypically a more visible target. He appeals to dark, psychic fears in the white population as a whole which explains why his party leadership dare not disavow him.

And of the fact that those fears are real there can be little doubt. The Shylock fixation, after all, is based on economic and religious factors susceptible to fairly rapid evaporation. British Jewry, unlike American Jewry, is not well-known for its Zionist sympathies, and much of it has been assimilated into the social and financial structure of English life, notwithstanding the fact that in friendship and marriage patterns it retains a certain segregationist pattern. The Othello fixation, by contrast, feeding on the black man-white woman miscegenative vision, is far more terribly intractable. In part, it is the demonstrable fact of Euro-Caucasian reactions to dark skin color. In part, it is the inherited legacy of attitudes created out of the imperialist experience. In part, again, it is the fact that since 1945 the main feature of European racism has been a movement away from the anti-Semitism of the fascist era toward a greater concern with color as colored Mediterranean-Caribbean-African stocks have become the lumpenproletariat mainstay of the revived western European capitalist economy. The outcome of all these factors is that the Shylock fixation has given way to the Othello fixation. The Jew can only take away your money; the black can take away your woman. You can recover your money, clean; your woman will come back, contaminated. And that this is the main drift of the Powellite appeal is evident enough from a substantive and linguistic analysis of the Powellite speeches since 1968. Their metaphors are militaristic and violent. A general paraphrase would read that there are entire detachments of Asians and West Indians encamped as outposts of alien territory in English cities, an alien wedge which will irrevocably pollute the native stock. The stranger at the door has become the barbarian at the gates. This will end in racial warfare, in "rivers of blood," if the English people are so mad and insane as to continue to accept it. It is a call to a holy war against evil, with each prescription of cure escalating in severity, culminating in the Powellite recommendation for an Orwellian Ministry of Repatriation.

There are three general points to make about the Powellite phenomenon. First, both public-opinion polls and newspaper correspondence over the years make it clear that Powellism has operated as an escape valve for the open public expression of attitudes hitherto deemed to be too outrageous to declare publicly. It made it possible for ambiguous attitudes to harden into well-defined and raucous prejudice. It helped break down that English attitude of kindly tolerance supposed to be the "decent thing" and replace it with an incredible mixture of ethnocentric nativism, authoritarianism, and open racism. It laid the imprimatur of legitimacy upon at once the strident obscenities of the working class and the more polite euphemisms of the bourgeois class. It made possible, further, and more easy, the emergence, in groups like the National Front, of neo-Nazi, postfascist elements propounding a new hate-literature and fomenting a politics of street violence last seen in England in the 1930s. In all of these ways, then, Powell can lay claim, as the Anand Ridley pamphlet, *The Enigma of Enoch Powell*, puts it, to an authentic status as the prophet of a new epoch in British political evolution.

Secondly, Powellism is to be seen not, simplistically, as the handiwork of an "evil" man but as the explosion of certain prepotent forces in the national life. The cowardly surrender of the party machines to Powellism has to be seen within the framework of the changing socioeconomic structure of the party memberships, reflecting postwar social changes. In both parties, the older groups have been increasingly replaced by the new, rising meritocracy of the welfare state, generating a noticeable *embourgeoisement* in both cases. With the Tories, that has meant the replacement of the old Toryism of birth and status with a new and younger type concerned more with technocratic efficiency; in one critic's acid phrase, they are the directors, as they see themselves, of Great Britain Limited, and they have five-year service contracts. They espouse the Manchester school of laissez-faire economics, with its antistatist bias; and in that sense, despite the fact that they are not the rabid rabble-rousers of the Powellite new right, they join hands with the Powellite attack upon the welfare state. They would not agree with the tone, but would agree with the argument, of a booklet like Andrew Elliot's *The Guilty Men of Whitehall* (with an introduction by Powell himself), which is nothing less than an angry portrayal of the welfare state as an evil conspiracy of power-made politicians and scheming civil servants working against an honest, white citizenry. In a similar fashion, the grand strategy of Labour in the 1960s was to court the same meritocratic group, so that the old working-class Member of Parliament has been gradually replaced to a large degree by the new middle-class professional member, operating a new program of managerial Fabian efficiency, ideological revisionism, and an American-style image-making politics.

So, just as with the Conservatives the older type of MacMillan-like gentleman, who could entertain a certain kind of patrician concern for the lowly, including the immigrant, has been supplanted by the new type of the city stockbroker, the estate agent, the company executive, and the garage proprietor, in the Labour group the older socialist zeal has been replaced with the type of ambitious university careerists who feature so much in the novels of C. P. Snow. On both sides, it has generated a temper of mind which has to see immigration not as a moral issue but as an issue to be reduced to electoral gimmickry. So, Tory Powellism was matched by Labour Powellism. And that was no accident, for both sides were appealing, in the British consensus-politics scheme, to the same constituency; it is no accident that both Ted Heath and Harold Wilson come from the same lower middle-class, grammar-school stratum whose newly found status and affluence can hardly be the most fertile ground for the development of a compassionate regard for other groups less lucky, like immigrants, in the ratrace of the "opportunity society." The new party managerialists thus come to see the race-color issue as an irritating nuisance, to be swept under the rug as discreetly as possible. The temper infected even the most liberally minded, evidenced in the suggestive fact that when Roy Jenkins (whose brief "liberal hour" at the Home Office deservedly gave him the reputation of being the most concerned home secretary about the immigrant tragedy throughout the last twenty years) finally came to resign his position in the Parliamentary Labour Party it was not on the issue of immigration control but on the quite different issue of the European Common Market.

The third point—which flows with relentless logic from these two previous points—is that all strata of modern English society are infected, one way or another, with the racialist poison. Being still a highly differentiated class society, the poison expresses itself in different ways. At the worker level, it takes the form of a rough outspokenness which may be seen as total insensitivity about the feelings of the black worker rather than deliberate malice. But it is nonetheless a racist exercise since it ascribes to the black worker on the factory floor a prescribed role he is supposed to play in terms of assumed collective characteristics. He is accepted. But it is an acceptance set within that role-ascription imposed upon him. "One West African has remarked to me," a Manchester personnel officer has reported, "that this acceptance is a sort of patronage of a weaker being until the coloured man has proved by his wit and jokes at his co-workers' expense that he is as intelligent, if not more intelligent, than they are. Then he is bound to get two divisions of his mates, those who do not like him for his sharp wit but are usually courteous to him, and those who make a real friend of him and may sometimes call him the 'Black devil,' not from derision but from an acknowledgement of his sharp wits." In this setting, the white worker cannot in any way comprehend why the black worker should resent those attitudes, or resent the white assumption that he ought to find it hilarious to be called opprobrious epithets like "Sambo" or "Darkie" or "Snowball." The black response is predictable. "In order," writes a Jamaican cabinet worker, "to work unnoticed in that shop, or get ahead with the men, I would have had to arrest my individualism, work within the confines of the myth they perpetuated about West Indians, and become a black senseless robot, an illiterate migrant from the land of banana and sugar cane."

At the middle-class level the immigrant is subjected, in far more subtle ways, to all of those elaborate disqualification exercises which the English have developed into a fine art. Investigative work on attitudes done by specialists like Christopher Bagley shows how even educated middle-class respondents, albeit liberal on the surface, will evince attitudes to the immigrant ranging from hostility and derision to amused disbelief. That West Indians have "wild parties," are noisy, overly boisterous, excessively demonstrative, and the rest: these are typical middle-class responses which in reality reflect the middle-class puritanical fear of habits which are deemed dangerous because they may infect the English person with a sense of his own emotional hollowness. Education, clearly, is irrelevant to prejudice. Even a mind as cultured as the late Sir Harold Nicholson could confide privately to his diary that he could not tolerate the near presence of a black person. A leading protagonist, Germaine Greer, of the women's liberation movement—where one oppressed minority might have been expected to show some sympathy for another—manages to repeat the crudest of all white stereotypes in a reference to "that most virile of creatures, the buck Negro." There takes place at the same time a process of guilt-transference whereby the middle-class person persuades himself that prejudice is only working-class. The best example of that process is the Alf Garnett television series put together by the TV playwright Johnny Speight. For in making that figure of the archetypal bigot a working-class person his creator gave support and comfort to the middle-class delusive opinion that prejudice was the crime of the working-class "authoritarian personality." That particular legend, interestingly, was exposed for what it is by Speight himself, who has confessed that most of the raw material for the series had in fact been picked up in the upper-class "pubs" of the north London outer suburbia.

In sum, postwar Britain—which in many ways still remains a society of snobs as much as it was when Bulwer-Lytton and Thackeray were writing, although the forms and badges of the disease have somewhat changed—has added the figure of the racial snob to the collection. He appears in a multitude of forms. At times, he is the outright "nigger hater" and, if working-class, glad to have someone whom he can despise as being on a lower social rung than himself. At times, he is the snob indirect, hiding beneath the air of cool politeness with which so many English persons keep the undesirable at arm's length. At times, again, he is the anti-American snob, angry at the fact that so many blacks have taken over the Afro-American ideology and life-style. Or he is the clerical snob, whose missionary mentality makes him believe that blacks are a special case who need peculiar pastoral care. Or, finally, there is the politically radical snob, who feels that he must make a superhuman effort to prove to himself and others that he is not prejudiced; a type nicely summed up in the stern rebuke that the Socialist Labour League at one time unleashed against what it called the "racialist paternalism" of the Communist party, citing as proof the party's exhortation that "every British worker, trade unionist, democrat and socialist should go out of his way to develop personal friendship with the coloured people he meets at work, in canteens, pubs and clubs and help them to understand real class solidarity and democracy."

Among the immigrant groups the price exacted by this is, of course, the loss of the old affection that they possessed, in a very real way, for things English. The West Indian novelist, George Lamming, described in his early novel, *The Emigrants* (1954), the great expectations that the West Indians brought with them at the beginning. To read, merely a decade or so later, books like *Disappointed Guests* by Tajfel and Dawson (1965) or D. Hinds's *Journey to an Illusion* (1966), is to be made aware of the betrayal of those expectations. Even so, those accounts were couched in terms of sad regret only, more of pained rebuke than of angry remonstrance. The tone of the militant groups of the 1970s in their news sheets and pamphlets is even more symptomatic, for now it is one of a bitter and sometimes hate-filled Anglophobia. It is a literature that frequently invokes the ancient Jewish analogy of the Diaspora, for its authors clearly feel that they have come up out of the colonial Egyptian bondage only to be lost in the wilderness of the English industrial cities. The final nail has thus been driven into the coffin of the belief, shared for so long both by the English and their subject-peoples, that England was immune to the disease of racialism.

"The most certain test by which we judge whether a country is really free," wrote Lord Acton, "is the amount of security enjoyed by minorities." It is certainly too early to say that Britain has failed that test. There are no civil or religious disabilities suffered by the new minorities. They participate fully and without hindrance in the political life of the nation. Their numerous organizations, both cultural and political, conduct their business freely. At the wider socio-cultural level, again, the charge, frequently repeated in the more extremist literature, that the minorities suffer from discriminatory patterns comparable to the ghetto regime of the North American cities or the apartheid system of South Africa is palpably false; what patterns do exist are as yet only imperfect approximations to those models. The state power is not—not yet at least—firmly and irrevocably committed to a war of attrition against the minorities, although neither is it dedicated, on the other hand, to policies wholly directed to the positive advancement of the minority cause. It is, in sum, premature to speak of a coming racial conflagration, let alone look forward to it with the morbid enthusiasm of a book like Ronald Segal's *The Race War*.

What has taken place, rather, is a growing erosion of traditional English liberalism in the face of a configuration of forces that has changed Britain from a great empire into a small industrial society bereft at once of its old affluence and its old power. The material expressions of that erosion are ominous enough: institutionalized discrimination, that is to say, in the areas of housing, employment, education, and the rest. But what is perhaps even more ominous is the growth of thought patterns that increasingly help to rationalize those material phenomena. There has taken place a psychological process of abstract color-consciousness, so that the average Englishman comes to see himself more and more as a white person and the Caribbean-Asiatic person comes to see himself not as a guest in a welcoming host society but as a black man in a white society. Correspondingly, the mass media help to create a set of pejorative images or modalities of the black person, with the usual caricatured characteriza-

[321]

tion and the attribution of primary guilt; so, the "yellow press" presents those images unashamedly, especially when opportunity presents them with a field day, as with the Trinidadian murder trial of Michael Malik in 1973, while even the liberal, quality press accepts the stereotype of the immigrant as the symbol of the "problem," albeit under the guise of a superficial concern for "tolerance." There is even a sort of linguistic discrimination at work in the form of a new lexicon of crypto-racism that makes its appearance; thus, to take an example only, whereas the word "expatriate," as used by the English, has a reassuring public-school ring about it, suggesting sacrificial, self-imposed exile from the homeland for noble purpose, the word "immigrant" has come to imply the notion of the person who has deserted his own country for another, driven by parasitical instinct. Prejudice, indeed, expresses itself in forms which, on the face of it, seem unrelated to the feeling. So, again to take examples only, the publication of books like those of Michael Edwardes and James Morris on the saga of the British Empire and the vast popularity of television shows like the *Forsyte Saga* serial can be seen as exercises in mass nostalgia, with the national populace retreating into a romantic remembrance of things past in order to escape an increasingly unbearable present. It is even possible to argue that the entry into the European Common Market has its own racial overtones, constituting a search for new white friends at the same time as successive race-relations pieces of statutory legislation have eroded the principle of freedom of movement of persons that was the guiding principle of the old Commonwealth *familia*. Along with all this, finally, there goes a distinct note of racial apprehension, as can be seen in the successive reports over the years of the House of Commons Select Committee on Race Relations. The constant refrain of those reports is that "we" must do something for "them" or "they" will begin to help themselves, which could lead to violent and rebellious activities harmful to the democratic processes of the national life: racial fear is thus disguised as moral concern. For many Englishmen, clearly enough, possibly even for the majority of them, the imperial dream has become the postimperial nightmare.

All of this, in the final resort, imposes upon any serious observer the fundamental need to produce a theoretical structure that answers at once to its novelty and its complexity. For if, as Professor John Rex has put it, the problem of racism should challenge the consciences of sociologists in something like the same way the problem of nuclear warfare challenges the consciences of physicists, then the British sociologist faces an enormous challenge. If, in addition, he is a socialist, it becomes even more imperative. In that task, there are certain leading principles and considerations he will have to keep in mind.

(1) He must start, as it were, from scratch. The theoretical paucity both of British sociology and of British socialist theory confers upon him a grave handicap. The problem of developing a Marxist theory of ethnic subnationalities within a pluralist society has been a long-standing task of the German, Russian, Polish, and Austrian socialist and communist schools; it is only now, with the recent growth of the Celtic nationalist movements that the British movement faces that problem. In a similar fashion, both the Continental and the British movements, with their Euro-Caucasian orientation, have never had to construct a Marxist theory of race and color. They have absorbed, in fact, without questioning them, the European liberal assumptions about white global trusteeship. In the 1940s a radical publisher like Warburg was prepared to publish Trotskyist exposures of Stalinism but angrily refused to publish *Capitalism and Slavery* by the Trinidadian scholar Eric Williams because it challenged the thesis that slavery abolition had been the result of English humanitarianism. A socialist race-relations theory must therefore begin with a demythologizing process, purging itself of the myths about the black experience which European scholarship, both of the left and the right, have naively accepted.

[323]

(2)   Research must start from the basic Marxist premise that racism, like all other phenomena, is structurally related to the class stratification of modern industrial bourgeois society. The black immigrant groups do not constitute, in Toynbee's sense, simply an external proletariat nor, as some European scholars have argued, a disorganized lumpenproletariat. They constitute, rather, an integral part of the working class situated within the production framework of capitalism and the victims not simply of racial discrimination but—in housing, employment, and education—of the generalized discrimination exercised against the working class as a whole. The race/class dichotomy is, from this viewpoint, relatively anomalous, since the race factor is enmeshed irrevocably with the main structural class factors of the society. The race situation is thus to be seen not, as Warner has argued, as an incipient phase of caste-relationships, but, as Cox has argued, as a class situation disguised and distorted as a racially deterministic phenomenon. This is true at once historically and contemporaneously. Historically, because racism, in its most brutalizing form, arises simultaneously with the emergence, in the sixteenth century, of the commercial bourgeoisie as it transferred its class-stratified forms to the dependent plantation-economy of the American slave-district; by comparison, racism, wherever it was found in the ancient and medieval worlds, was a comparatively benign phenomenon. Contemporaneously, because the black, as he enters the capitalist labor force, suffers from the same alienating process as his white counterpart. It follows from this that the subjection of the black worker, like the subjection of the white woman, in modern Western society, can only be solved by the radical structural transformation of that society in socialist terms. As the Manchester 1945 Pan-African Congress put it, the worker in the black skin can only be free as the worker in the white skin is free.

(3)   Having said that, the Marxist dialectic is in itself insufficient to explain the totality of the black-white point-counterpoint, not because, as some misguided black theoreti-

cians have sought to argue, Marx himself was racist but because, of necessity, he generalized from the nineteenth-century European industrial experience. The assumption, then, of orthodox Marxism—which is the assumption of the modern communist parties—that oppression everywhere, both black and white, is quantitatively the same, fails to recognize the radical qualitative difference that exists between class-natured oppression and race-natured oppression. The white proletarian suffers from a one-dimensional assault upon his humanity; the black proletarian suffers from a two-dimensional assault. Racism leaves behind it a deep psychic wound, an atrocious insult, far more difficult to erase, more terribly profound to forget: a truth that no reader of the accounts written by its more articulate Caribbean victims—Garvey, Césaire, Fanon—can afford to ignore. The various ideologies of the black liberation movement that have grown out of that experience—the Garveyite "return to Africa," the Fanonesque rhetoric of black therapeutic violence, Césaire's rejection of European "civilization" as a racist cesspool—can only be understood in terms of that experience. They may be uncongenial to Marxist rationalistic sociology. But they represent a black apocalyptic vision rooted in the cultural and emotional castration of the black person perpetrated by five centuries of European exploitative colonialism.

(4) The Marxist trajectory of the development of social classes is therefore interfered with at crucial points by the race factor. For, logically, the growth of the white bourgeoisie should have been followed by the growth of a black bourgeoisie. But clearly that has not taken place. Even in the American case, what has been termed a "black bourgeoisie," after Frazier's study, is not a class in the Marxist sense, but rather a loose hodgepodge of occupations, individual success stories, a white-collar stratum, in brief, possessed certainly of its own distinctive life-styles and consumption standards. But it is not a real social class with real interests related to the means of production in American capitalism; it has no foothold in the corporate power structure of American business;

and it is confined in the main to the extreme fringe of both industry and the professions. In Britain, that is even more so the case. The overwhelming mass of Asians and Caribbeans are working class. The tiny group of "prominent" blacks are concentrated in the arts and sports, traditionally a more open occupational stratum. Even the new groups of the Kenyan and Ugandan businessmen belong to the world of petty-bourgeois entrepreneurship. None of this constitutes a class successfully entering the British capitalist strongholds of wealth and power. And when a novel like John Gloag's *Rising Suns* attempts to portray such an entry, depicting a West Indian stowaway who becomes a ruthless business tycoon using his English aristocratic connections and his contacts with the immigrant demimonde for his own aggrandizement, it does not constitute a story about the black productive capitalist but about individual black parasitism only. The point has been well made by a West Indian brick-layer taking the "liberal" London press to task: "Where are the coloured newspaper editors and journalists, accountants, stock exchange personnel, officers in the Army and Navy (there are some in the fair-minded Royal Air Force), solicitors, property magnates, managing directors? Where are the coloured bank clerks, police officers, bus inspectors, lady almoners, head teachers, etc.? Why are all the coloured nurses and doctors in the National Health Service, while private clinics and homes are manned by pure whites? And where are the ghettoes of the Great White Stockbroker Belt?" The primacy of the race factor can alone explain this.

(5) Yet at this point a curious convergence of views takes place. The Marxist dialectic assumes, implicitly, the growth of a black capitalist class that will become, for economic reasons, the ally of the white capitalist class, and, of course, a similar alliance between the black and white proletariats. The "black-power" dialectic, to the degree that it argues for a "black capitalism," assumes likewise the emergence of the same black bourgeoisie, but with a different role: that of acting as the skilled spearhead of the black revolution. Both are wrong. The first is wrong because it fatally under-

[326]

estimates the power of racism at once to survive as an independent idea and as a "divide-and-rule" device operated by the white structural elites in order to legitimize their dominant position. The second is wrong because it fails to see that the nonwhite world is itself class-stratified. In all of the new successor-states to the old empires—Ghana and Nigeria, for example, or Trinidad and Jamaica—new ruling black-mulatto elites have inherited the power position of the old colonial master-class, able to exploit the subject masses more efficiently, to make the turn of the screw even more harsh because, psychologically, they understand the masses better.

(6) What emerges out of this in terms of a theoretical statement of the issue? Cutting through the academic mumbo jumbo with which the issue has been so much surrounded, it seems possible to posit the thesis that the race versus class debate is in many ways sterile. The leading North American-Western European societies are characterized by a horizontal class division and a vertical ethnic division. The divisions tend to coincide, insofar as most minority racial groups are at the same time economically poor. It is, then, impossible to accept the doctrine of mutual exclusivity, which assumes that the divisions can be analyzed as separate compartments. It is equally impossible to accept the doctrine of functional priority, which assumes that one division, either way, is simply a subordinate expression of the other. Both divisions feed each other, intermix with each other, thrive with a veritable tropical fecundity on each other. Nor is there, regrettably, much evidence that the resolution of the one problem will lead logically to the resolution of the other. A society like Soviet Russia may have solved the problem of class oppression, but from the little evidence available, black students in Russian universities meet a racial hostility similar to what they meet in French or British universities. A society like Jamaica may have eliminated the worst excesses of "white supremacy," but the problem of gross social and economic inequality remains as intractable as ever. In societies like Britain, where appreciable socialist equality does not exist and where racialism takes the form not of the

West Indian comparatively benign "shade" prejudice but of the cruder American black-white dichotomy, race and ethnic relations cannot be separated out from the structural-institutional character of the society as a whole. A satisfactory sociology of "race relations," all this is to say, must be seen holistically as enmeshed in and related to the totality of the socio-economic-political structure in which it is located. It is in this sense that both Marxist sociology and the American Talcott Parsons type of sociology, despite their differing normative values, have one thing in common. They both recognize that totality. It is in this sense, by the same token, that the very term itself "race relations" obfuscates the real issue, since it assumes the independent existence of a phenomenon—the recognition, usually pejorative, of social differences based on physical criteria—unrelated to the other constituent properties of the social whole.

(7) Further theoretical presuppositions flow from all this. In particular, all of those theories, mostly rooted in white Western academic sociology, that have sought to disguise racism and racialism under other rubrics must be fully exposed by any researcher interested genuinely in the liberation of the Asian-Caribbean-African minority segments. There is, most noticeably, the thesis of "ethnic nationalism" or "majority nationalism" associated with the writings of Professor Michael Banton. This argues, essentially, that what the immigrant suffers from is not racialism but the notoriously frigid attitude of the English to the "archetypal stranger," keeping him at arm's length, selectively excluding him because he transgresses in his cultural habits so many of the social-behavior taboos which the English cherish as a self-defensive mechanism in order to protect their privacy. Yet this thesis, on examination, collapses on at least three grounds. First, that habit of cultural insularity has been much eroded in recent years under the democratizing pressures of the "permissive society." Secondly, the immigrant, and especially the West Indian, is not the cultural alien that the thesis presupposes, for he shares as an Anglicized colonial person many of the cultural norms held so sacred by the

English. Third, and most important, the thesis fails to explain why so many other immigrants far less Anglicized have in fact been willingly assimilated into the majority mainstream in recent years: the Jewish refugee, the German prisoner of war, the demobilized Polish soldier, the Italian immigrant worker, the Hungarian exile. Zubrzycki's study of the Polish group, to take only a single example, shows how initially its members were traduced by the British press as a race of Casanovas menacing the integrity of British womanhood, only to be absorbed in the long run, usually through marriage with English girls, into the mainstream culture. The failure of the colored groups, by comparison, to be similarly absorbed by a "melting-pot" process strongly suggests that it is racial and not merely cultural antipathy that stands in their way. And all this becomes more intriguing when it is remembered that the assumption that the English are an ethnically homogeneous people will not bear serious scrutiny. On the contrary, they have long constituted an ethnically diffused progeny of various interethnic mixings, probably starting with the mésalliance of the motley crowd of Caesar's Roman legions with the native Englishwomen; a process summed up in Defoe's satiric verse on the "True-Born Englishman":

> Fate jumbled them together, God knows how;
> Whate'er they were, they're true-born English now.

(8) If this line of reasoning is correct, it follows that the assimilationist-integrationist ideal is irrelevant to the real problem. It is irrelevant for two reasons. First, because it is in the long run impractical: there is no evidence to suggest that the British public, even including its more progressive elements, will ever accept, or at least accept in any reasonably foreseeable future, the absorption of the black-brown-yellow minorities as candidates for full entry into the national club. The Marshallian doctrine of an all-inclusive citizenship—which is the prime assumption of the 1969 report of the Institute of Race Relations, Colour and Citizenship—is an impossible dream if only because it requires, in order

to be real, a biological-sexual mixing which Marshall himself never had to consider and which the British people as a whole would certainly reject as constituting ethnic contamination. For the real test of any integrationist ideal is acceptance of interracial marriage; which is why any study of race, to be at all meaningful, must be a study of sex. It is suggestive that the *Colour and Citizenship* volume discreetly avoids any analysis of that aspect of the matter. Yet that an obsessive anxiety about sexual mixing exists in the national psyche is beyond doubt. Its political expression is the "keep Britain white" slogan of the neo-Nazi National Front organization; and although its electoral appeal is still minor it would be foolhardy to simply dismiss that movement as yet another lunatic fringe of the political spectrum. This is what one English writer has called, appropriately, the presence of the Ku-Klux-Klan factor.

(9) The assimilationist-integrationist ideal is irrelevant, in the second place, because, even if practical, it is undesirable. For it assumes as its final end a sort of gray standardization, accelerated by the centralizing tendencies of the modern industrial society, within which all participating groups are expected to relinquish their own unique cultural particularity. That has been the history of all minorities in the American democracy, whether one looks at the emasculation of what has been left of the original Indian tribal cultures or the loss of the old Jewish Yiddish culture documented finely in Irving Howe's *World of Our Fathers.* All of the great civilizations of history, by contrast, have been rich, polyglot mixtures—Greco-Roman, Hellenistic, Byzantine—weaving each particular strand of the general web into a total conglomerate combining variety with unity. That sort of cultural pluralism, by any account, must be deemed to be more aesthetically pleasing than cultural integration. Even if, let it be reiterated, the English native majority were willing to accept the integrationist ideal. The socially possible is not always the ethically desirable.

(10) Speaking, then, in utopian terms, the ideal surely must be a pluralistic, socialist society in which, the economic

basis of racism having been eliminated, each ethnic group is permitted to retain its own special identity, but an identity of which the prime determinant will not be skin color but culture, religion, and language, thus perceiving the minority person not in phenotypical terms but as, variously, a Muslim or a Welsh speaker or a Jamaican Pentecostalist or an Algerian Jew or a Creole-speaking St. Lucian Catholic or a Barbadian Baptist. This means, in essence, a return to ethnicity. It envisages not so much the elimination of ethnic competition as rather its containment within the framework of the particular national polity and its nondestructive and creative expression through the delicate interplay of political compromise, constitutional arrangements, language policy, educational criteria, and the rest. It gets away from the sterile conformist bias of the old assimilationist theme, as well as from the somewhat different theme of earlier writers like Zangwill, in the American case, who envisaged the emergence of an American "new man" created whole out of the American New World crucible. It is worth noting that this is the direction in which American minorities themselves seem to be moving. The older ethnic groups of European origin—Italians, Slavs, Greeks, Poles—have begun to emulate the pattern of the non-Caucasian ethnics—Chinese, Japanese Nisei, Mexican-Americans, Puerto Ricans—in asserting their ethnic distinctiveness; and the popularity, for all of its meretricious quality, of Alex Haley's book *Roots* indicates that all this strikes a responsive chord in Americans anxious to rediscover their ancestral beginnings and thereby their identity. It is also worth noting that books like Dilip Hiro's *Black British, White British* and John Brown's *The Un-Melting Pot* have begun to argue along similar lines in the British case.

(11) The theoretical implications of this position are obvious. Modern technology has made all men members of one world. In such a world, the world itself is ultimately the only viable economic unit. In such a world, too, there is clearly no place for the classical sovereign nation-state, for the only real response to global economic power, as it now rests in the hands of global capitalist forces, is global political power.

It follows, correspondingly, that the nationalist spirit must express itself increasingly along cultural lines and less along the old political and economic lines. Ethnic sentiment is a real thing, and not to be lightly dismissed. But if it continues to express itself in the growth of new political state powers —as is happening both in Africa and the Caribbean in their postindependent period—it can only have the result of accentuating political fragmentation in the form, especially in the Caribbean, of tiny mini-states which, by themselves, cannot hope to resist successfully the blandishments of the new global economic power in the shape of the large multinational corporations. However attractive the temptation might seem, no small group of people can secede from the world as a whole, in the manner of Chesterton's anti-Fabian fantasy-tale *The Napoleon of Notting Hill*. The more appropriate road ahead is that the feeling that sets off one such group of people from another should express itself in the broad cultural areas of art, literature, language, religion, family life, and the rest, rather than in political and economic areas where the future lies, surely, with international planning, preferably along socialist lines.

(12) Again speaking theoretically, it is of some interest to note that the pluralist argument has been restated by recent American analysts of the general race-relations and ethnic-relations debate. It is present in Kallen's concept of an American "federation of nationalities," as well as in Berkson's "community" theory in which each ethnic group should be allowed to create its own communal life and, while participating in the general life of the nation, should thus preserve its own cultural heritage indefinitely; only with the proviso that minority practices that gravely violate the moral norms of the national life as a whole, such as Mormon polygamy, must necessarily be given up. Those interpretations thus get away from the difficulties involved in the more traditionalist thesis of a general assimilationist process identified with the older school of the Chicago theoreticians like Park and his colleagues.

[332]

(13)   Yet a warning note is in order. All of those theories assume, in the American liberal fashion, the continuation of an ongoing national social system at once able and willing to accommodate its minority cultures, either in an assimilationist or a pluralist manner. They assume, that is to say, the continuing economic viability of the American capitalist order. For there is a direct relationship between majority-minority relationships and the condition of the general social order; so that it is no accident that the increasingly illiberal immigration policy of postwar Britain has gone hand in hand with British capitalism in a contractionist phase while, by contrast, the increasingly liberal immigration policy of the United States since, say, 1965, has gone hand in hand with American capitalism as a business society in an expansionist phase. Failure to appreciate that relationship between socioeconomic structure and majority-minority relationships leads to a dangerous optimism. It neglects the very real possibility of regression to less liberal policies, most notably, of course, systematic ethnic destruction, as with Hitler's "final solution" for the Jews, mass expulsion, as with the deportation of Ugandan and Kenyan Asians, and gradual cancellation of continued immigration, as in Britain itself. An ethnically pluralist society is, indeed, the desirable end. But it cannot be discussed in abstract theoretical terms, as does much of the contemporary academic literature in both England and America, as if its possibilities existed in a vacuum.

(14)   Coming back to the particular English case, it is evident that the success of that ideal end depends, as much as anything else, upon the readiness of the native majority to accept its implications. No one is entitled to optimism on that score. It means a relinquishment of fiercely held stereotypes. In that field alone there is a grim lesson secreted in the fact that it has taken the civil-war situation in Ulster finally to disabuse the English of their stage image of the Irish as romantic, lovable, irresponsible revolutionaries. There is an equally grim lesson in the fact that West Indians are frequently called the "black Irish." The analogy is sometimes

made, when speaking of racial toleration, with the growth, earlier on, of religious toleration. "In the British case," one observer has written, "the solution to the Northern Ireland problem is not for the Protestants to stop being Protestants, but rather for the two religious groups to reach a new *modus vivendi* based on increased equality. The solution to the 'coloured problem' on the other hand is not the curtailment of immigration but for white Britons to stop viewing themselves as whites and others as 'coloureds.' " The difficulty with that analogy is, quite simply, that it took over 150 years for Locke's idea of religious toleration to become fact for Jew and Catholic in England itself; and in the changed conditions of modern life no disadvantaged minority group, as the American civil-rights movement has shown, is any longer willing to wait for such a glacial pace of change over such a lengthy time period. And that, too, is increasingly the mood of the new radical elements in the British minority groups as they have been impregnated by the ideology of the American movement.

(15) What, then, is the prospect for the immediate future? The immediate, urgent task, on the evidence, is that the various minority groups must move forward to forge a united front, combining class consciousness and ethnic consciousness, as the only valid strategy for creating a new society at once radically socialist and genuinely ethnically pluralist. God, as the saying goes, only helps those who help themselves. Such a movement must (a) for the moment at least forget the white working classes as an ally, if only because the various reports of the Runnymede Trust Industrial Unit, hardly a revolutionary body, have irrefutably documented the dismal failure of the trade-union movement to identify with the minority struggles in the labor-relations field; and (b) must expose the white liberal middle-class preoccupation with "community relations" for what it is: a social charity exercise founded on the condescending maxim, as one West Indian has bitterly put it, that "they" are the surgeons and "we" are the patients. It must, at the same time, (c) expose the myth of the symbolic breakthrough. One swallow does not make a summer; a small group of black artists or Asian entrepreneurs

does not make a revolution. The most tragic minority person, indeed, is the one who succeeds in the white world, for he lacks cultural roots in either the world of the black-brown masses with which he refuses to identify or the white world which only accepts him on sufferance. It is in that sense that, as the American black sociologist Lerone Bennett has aptly put it, for blacks in America there is only one thing worse than failing in America, and that is succeeding in America. An entire doctoral dissertation could be written on the series of minority-group "successes" in Britain who testify to the terrible accuracy of that observation: Dr. David Pitt in politics, Vidia Naipaul in literature, Barry Reckord in television, Dr. Roy Marshall in education, the late Edric Connor in the theater. They exist in a no man's land; trapped—to reshape Sermiento's famous phrase—between English barbarism and black civilization. They expect to find El Dorado. Instead they find Hell.

(16) Such a movement, in turn, must turn its back on the entire apparatus of white-sponsored "race relations" research and activities. The appropriate text here, again, is the *Colour and Citizenship* volume of 1969. Its authors accept uncritically the assumptions of the earlier Myrdalian *American Dilemma*. Those assumptions, by any standard, have been belied by the subsequent American experience. It is not a noble white response to the American creed, but the angry militancy of the black movement that has brought about the comparatively limited reforms in the American situation. The Myrdalian thesis, indeed, hopelessly exaggerates the capacity of a ruling class to grant equality to a depressed nonwhite minority from whose repression it in fact reaps at once economic profit and psychological reward; at the same time, it exaggerates the power of mere moral conscience to reshape behavior and structure when everything else—power, authority, superiority feelings, prejudice—conspires to rationalize both behavior and structure. The English gloss on all that it is to assume that an enlightened liberal-reform advocacy group of the national Establishment will pass legislation sufficiently liberal to calm down the situation. Its final prescription of cure, that is to

say, rests with the remedial action of the Fabian *état admin-istratif*, staffed by the liberal echelons, with the colored minorities playing a relatively passive role as welfare-state recipients. It is not, then, objective research. It is, rather, policy-oriented research, designed to coopt the leaderships of the immigrant groups into the "community relations" structure and thus effectively neutralize them. It is thoroughly elitist in tone. It conclusively demonstrates the bankruptcy of the English liberal imagination on two counts: (a) it fails to appreciate the truth that the minorities might be capable of building up their own autonomous cultures as against the liberal assimilationist doctrine, and (b) it fails to understand that the same minorities might be capable of engineering their own salvation by their own independent political and industrial action. The *Colour and Citizenship* analysis, in brief, is based upon the old Fabian strategy of permeating the ruling class. It was a strategy summed up in a sentence used by the late churchman J. H. Oldham, whose book of the 1920s, *Christianity and the Race Problem*, was a pioneering effort in the field: his assertion that whenever the need arose for the church to do anything it was not necessary to call a public meeting or even write a letter to the *Times*, but "find the source of power and have lunch with it at the Athenaeum."

(17) That is the view from the top. A militant minority mass movement, on the contrary, must take the view from the bottom. It must base itself on the report of the victims themselves. It must move away, at least for the time being, from the old collaborationist policy of the 1960s which led to the collapse of bodies like the Campaign for the Abolition of Racial Discrimination (CARD). It must engage itself in the fight at every level: the factory floor, the classroom, the search for housing. In that fight, at once economic and ethnic in character, it will have to be careful to avoid at least two pitfalls. The first is a merely rhetorical antiwhite posture, so sterile and self-defeating as it is. For the struggle is primarily against capitalist society; in Malcolm X's admonition, you must not hate "whitey," you must hate the white system. The second is the intraethnic problem. The mutual antipathy

between black and Indian is a well-known phenomenon that, if truth be told, predates European colonialism. But colonialism, even so, has used the antipathy in the classic colonial condition as a "divide-and-rule" mechanism, both in East Africa and the Caribbean. There now exists a real danger that with the new influx of Kenyan and Ugandan Asians the British will replicate an East African colonial situation in which the Asians are utilized as a favored buffer group between black and white, thus introducing a secondary divisive element frustrating the growth of a black-brown coalition. Any student of the North American ghetto will know how those divisive lines, between black American and black West Indian, between blacks and Puerto Ricans, even between mainland neo-Ricans and island Puerto Ricans, work to sabotage the growth of a united front against the granite structures of white racism. The danger is even more immediate in Britain, if only because the British variant of racism presents itself in pseudo-benevolent terms, pretending to help the immigrant when in reality it works to emasculate him. That strategy can only be fought successfully if both minority groups (a) develop a mutual and sympathetic understanding of the contribution that each has made, in their pre-European Asian and African communal societies, to world civilization as a whole, and (b) recognize the brutal truth that, living now in their Egyptian exile, they both suffer from the same oppression, they both are tarred by the same brush.

There is one final point to make about all this. It is palpably clear that the latest chapter in the history of English radical thought will be written by the new minorities of the society. The debate on the class-race issue will be resolved, ultimately, by the new intelligentsia of the second and third generations of the "black British." The whole new complex of the relationships between nationalism, socialism, and ethnicity will figure as a leading task of theory in that exercise. It will draw on the pioneer work done by Tagore, Gandhi, DuBois, Williams, Césaire, Fanon, Garvey, C. L. R. James,

Senghor, and others. Its menu, of necessity, will include the themes of Negritude, black power, Africanism, the crisis of the Third World intellectual, the relationships between Western capitalism and the non-Western world, the strategy of revolution, the relationships between peasant and urban worker, the problems of Third World socialism, and much else.

It will be, this is to say, a debate of truly international dimensions. The pamphlet and periodical literature put out in recent years by the British-based black-brown organizations make that eminently clear. What has happened, in fact, is that the old triangular trade of slavery has been matched by a new triangular ideological trade involving England, Africa, and the Americas. The U.S. black ideologies infiltrate the British groups. Blacks, both in England and the Americas, begin to rediscover their tremendous African heritage. The Caribbean homeland–British Diaspora axis generates a cross-fertilizing movement of ideas between the British groups (who more and more see themselves as groups of the exile) and the new black Risorgimento in Jamaica, Trinidad, and Guyana. The generic idea of Africa, indeed, seen at once as a new continent possessed of a new regenerative social force and as a utopia contrastive with the decadence of Europe and North America, begins to play a role similar to the idea of America in the seventeenth and eighteenth centuries. For a small group of writers, university teachers, and political militants, the idea takes the form of the older Garveyite dream of a physical return to Africa, however temporarily. For larger groups it takes the form of a psychological return, helping to supplant the old colonial "white bias," what the eighteenth-century Jamaican planter-historian Edward Long termed "the pride of amended blood," with a new, proud black identity.

The themes of this new debate will be at once old and new. Old, in the sense that, to be fruitful, they will have to be rooted in the character of Marxist philosophy and sociology. New, because the effective decolonization since World War II of the great Asian and African continents requires that Marxism, which claims to be the heir of the whole culture of man's past, cannot reduce that culture to narrow Western

[338]

terms. It must recognize the essential plurality of models that arises out of that transformation of the ancient non-Western worlds; just as, indeed, after Columbus the European mind was forced to come to terms with civilizations hitherto unknown. The leading concept of alienation, so crucial to the Marxist understanding of the relationship between man and society, will need to be restated in terms of the colonial experience, essentially racist in character; it could be done no more effectively than by reviving the problems stated by Shakespeare in his last play, in which the figure of the rebellious Antillean slave is set against the figures of the European colonizer and the European philsopher who rationalizes the colonial exploitative system. The problem of identity, again, so closely related to the problem of alienation, will have to be reexamined both in its class and its racial aspects, if only because the search for identity, particularly for the nonwhite immigrant living in the white world, involves at once the location of the individual with respect to the personified past of forebears and the social destiny of progeny. There is, again, the need for a new historiography, seeing the whole phenomenon of slavery, for example, from the viewpoint of a radical Caribbean-African sociology, and thus exposing the most recent school of slavery historians, such as Brion Davis, who treat the theme almost as if slavery had been invented in order to provide Western civilization with a large stage on which to conduct a grand and anguished appraisal of its moral principles. The leading note of that historiography will be the insistence, as the Martiniquan poet-politician Aimé Césaire put it in his moving letter of 1956 to Maurice Thorez, that the radical European doctrines must be put at the service of the colored peoples, not the colored peoples at the service of those doctrines. For the colonial peoples, as Césaire put it, have been the victims of a veritable Copernican revolution in which all European leadership, from extreme right to extreme left, has taken on the habit of doing things for us, of arranging matters for us, of thinking for us, in brief of denying to us that right of initiative which is the ultimate right of personality.

There is, furthermore, an important corollary to this movement. It is a cardinal article of faith in the official and semi-official British "race-relations" literature that immigration is a domestic matter. That is a delusive absurdity. Not only because, as already noted, the idea-structures known generally as Negritude and black power are global in character. But because, even more, immigrants into Britain constitute only one segment of an exploited transnational labor army recruited by the transnational business corporations and the public sectors of the advanced industrial economies, performing the degrading, menial jobs spurned by the native labor aristocracies of those economies. There is thus a common bond that unites the Algerian worker in France, the southern Italian worker in West Germany, the Indonesian worker in Holland, the Puerto Rican migrant in the States, the Caribbean and Asiatic workers in Britain. Capitalism everywhere requires a cheap labor reserve-army: the more efficient firms as a means of absorbing the costs of their highly paid, organized native employees, the less efficient firms as a means of operating profitably in a competitive market. It has thus created a new kind of international human being, unskilled, underpaid, and mobile, to fit into its new levels of technical composition. The inherent contradictions of capitalism, at the same time, generate in that new human being an embryonic international class consciousness. The new capitalist international cooperative structures arising out of, for example, the European Common Market will thus facilitate, as the transnational mobility of immigrant labor becomes an even more necessary concomitant of those structures, a new international working-class consciousness.

The wheel of English radical thought thus comes full circle. The historic encounter of the Western and non-Western peoples unleashed by European travel and expansionism after the Columbus voyages, plus the growth of the slave trade and slavery, revitalized English political and social thought, making the eighteenth century the most cosmopolitan of all in that field. But that world view gave way, with the victory of the Victorian bourgeois order, to a narrow, ethnocentric "little

England" prejudice. Only a handful of marginal movements strived to maintain the earlier tradition: the sort of regency patrician populism of Bulwer-Lytton, the Christian Socialists, the Victorian freethinkers, and the groups influenced by the Paris Commune. The emergence, today, of new aggressive imperialistic forms of monopoly-capitalism, the growing disparities between the wealth of the "developed" economies and the poverty of the "underdeveloped" economies, the forced movements of immigrant populations from the colonial areas to the metropoles which is only a part of the pillage of the Third World, promises finally to revive the cosmopolitan character of the Enlightenment. In a sense unanticipated by Canning, the New World will now be brought in to redress the balance of the old.

[Bibliography]

Author's Note: I have not overlaid these essays with the usual apparatus of scholarly notes in the academic manner. I have decided, rather, to append a short bibliography, chapter by chapter, of titles which readers may find useful if they want to follow up the subject matter. It is not meant to be in any way an exhaustive bibliography; and many of the books mentioned in the text are not included.

Chapter 1

Clarkson, Thomas. *The History of the Rise, Progress, and Accomplishment of the Abolition of the African Slave-Trade by the British Parliament*. London, 1968.

Curtin, Philip D. *The Slave Trade: A Census*. Madison, 1969.

Gratus, Jack. *The Great White Lie*. New York, 1973.

Hecht, J. J. *Continental and Colonial Servants in Eighteenth-Century England*. Northampton, Mass., 1954.

Klingberg, F. J. *The Anti-Slavery Movement in England*. New Haven, 1926.

Ragatz, Lowell Joseph. *A Guide for the Study of British Caribbean History, 1763-1834, Including the Abolition and Emancipation Movements*. Washington, D.C., 1932.

Sypher, Wylie. *Guinea's Captive Kings*. Chapel Hill, 1942.

Walvin, James. *The Black Presence. A Documentary History of the Negro in England, 1555-1860*. London, 1971.

Williams, Eric. *Capitalism and Slavery*. Chapel Hill, 1944.

Chapter 2

Bulwer-Lytton, Edward. *England and the English*. London, 1833.

Halévy, Elie. *A History of the English People in 1815*. London, 1938.

Hamburger, Joseph. *Intellectuals in Politics: John Stuart Mill and the Philosophic Radicals.* New Haven, 1965.

Kent, C. B. Roylance. *The English Radicals, An Historical Sketch.* London, 1899.

Lytton, Earl of. *The Life of Edward Bulwer, First Lord Lytton.* 2 vols. London, 1913.

Sadleir, Michael. *Bulwer: A Panorama. Edward and Rosina, 1803-1836.* London, 1931.

Chapter 3

Carroll, David, ed. *George Eliot: The Critical Heritage.* London, 1971.

Haight, Gordon G. *George Eliot: A Biography.* London, 1968.

Newman, Francis W. *Phases of Faith.* London, 1858.

Pattison, Mark. *Memoirs.* London, 1885.

Robertson, John M. *A Short History of Freethought.* London, 1899.

Sparrow, John, *Mark Pattison and the Idea of a University.* Cambridge, England, 1967.

Willey, Basil. *Nineteenth-Century Studies: Coleridge to Matthew Arnold.* New York, 1949.

Chapter 4

Christensen, Torben. *Origin and History of Christian Socialism, 1848-54.* Copenhagen, 1962.

Hammond, J. L. and Barbara. *The Age of the Chartists, 1832-1854.* London, 1930.

McCabe, Joseph. *The Social Record of Christianity.* London, 1935.

Martin, Hugh, ed. *Christian Social Reformers of the Nineteenth Century.* London, 1927.

Raven, Charles E. *Christian Socialism, 1848-1854.* London, 1920.

Reckitt, Maurice C. *From Maurice to Temple: A Century of the Christian Social Movement in the Church of England.* London, 1946.

Thorp, Margaret Farrand. *Charles Kingsley, 1819-1875.* Princeton, 1937.

Tulloch, John. *Movements of Religious Thought in Britain during the Nineteenth Century.* New York, 1885.

Chapter 5

Bruhat, J., Dautry, J., and Tersen, E. *La Commune de 1871.* Paris, 1960.

Communist Party of Great Britain. *Marxism Today.* Commemorative articles on the Commune. London, March, April, May, June, 1971.

Edwards, Stewart. *The Paris Commune 1871.* London, 1971.

Horne, Alistair. *The Fall of Paris.* London, 1965.

International Institute for Social History. *Paris Commune. of 1871.* Commemorative articles on the Commune. Amsterdam, 1971.

Lissagaray, Prosper. *History of the Commune of 1871.* Reprinted. New York, 1967.

Chapter 6

Cole, G. D. H. *Fabian Socialism.* London, 1943.

The Second International. History of Socialist Thought. Vol. 3. London, 1956.

Lynd, Helen M. *England in the Eighteen-Eighties.* New York, 1945.

McBriar, A. M. *Fabian Socialism and English Politics, 1884-1918.* Cambridge, England, 1962.

MacKenzie, Norman and Jeanne. *The Fabians.* New York, 1977.

Pelling, H. M. *The Origins of the Labour Party.* London, 1954.

Poirier, P. P. *The Advent of the Labour Party.* London, 1958.

Webb, Beatrice. *My Apprenticeship.* London, 1938.

————. *Our Partnership.* London, 1948.

Chapter 7

Ashley, Maurice. *Churchill as Historian.* New York, 1969.

Churchill, Winston S. *History of the English-Speaking Peoples.* New York, 1971.

Gilbert, M., ed. *Churchill.* New York, 1967.

Stansky, Peter, ed. *Churchill: A Profile.* New York, 1973.

Taylor, A. J. P., and others. *Churchill Revised: A Critical Assessment.* New York, 1969.

Chapter 8

Abbott, Simon, ed. *The Prevention of Racial Discrimination in Britain.* London, 1971.

Daniel, W. W. *Racial Discrimination in England.* Harmondsworth, 1968.

Foot, Paul. *Immigration and Race in British Politics.* Harmondsworth, 1965.

Hiro, Dilip. *Black British, White British*. London, 1971.

Kiernan, V. G. *The Lords of Human Kind: European Attitudes to the Outside World in the Imperial Age*. London, 1969.

Rose, E. J. B., and others. *Colour and Citizenship: A Report on British Race Relations*. London, 1969.

Utley, T. E. *Enoch Powell. The Man and his Thinking*. London, 1968.

Wright, Peter L. *The Coloured Worker in British Industry*. London, 1968.